ENGLISH POLEMICS AT THE SPANISH COURT

ENGLISH POLEMICS AT THE SPANISH COURT

Joseph Creswell's
Letter to the Ambassador from England

The English and Spanish Texts of 1606

edited by

ALBERT J. LOOMIE, S.J.

FORDHAM UNIVERSITY PRESS
New York
1993

Library of Congress Cataloging-in-Publication Data

Cresswell, Joseph, 1556–1623.
  [Letter written to the ambassador from England. Spanish & English]
  English polemics at the Spanish court : Joseph Creswell's Letter to the
ambassador from England, the English and Spanish texts of 1606 / [edited
by] Albert J. Loomie.
      p.   cm.
  Includes bibliographical references and index.
  ISBN 0–8232–1446–X : $25.00
    1. Persecution—England—History—17th century.   2. Catholics—
England—History—17th century.   3. Religious tolerance—England—
History—17th century.   4. Great Britain—Foreign relations—1603–
1625.   5. Spain—Foreign relations—1516–1700.   6. Religious
tolerance—Church of England—History—17th century.   7. Religious
tolerance—Catholic Church—History—17th century.   8. England—
Church history—17th century.   9. Church of England—Doctrines—
History—17th century.   10. Catholic Church—Doctrines—History—17th
century.   I. Loomie, Albert J. (Albert Joseph), 1922– .   II. Cornwallis,
Charles, Sir, d. 1629.   III. Title.
BX1492.C68   1993
272'.7—dc20   93–22673
                                                                            CIP

Printed in the United States of America

Contents

Acknowledgments

In preparing this book many debts have been incurred. I am particularly grateful to the Director of the Biblioteca Nacional in Madrid, Juan Pablo Fusi Aizpurua, for his generous permission to reprint the original Spanish text of the *Carta escrita al Embaxador de Inglaterra*. I also wish to express my appreciation to the British Library Board for its kind permission to publish a transcription of the original English manuscript of that letter from the Cotton Manuscripts. I also am under deep obligation to Dr. Colin G. C. Tite, who has freely shared the results of his lengthy research into the early foundation of the library of Sir Robert Cotton and has assisted my study of its Spanish manuscripts. The staff of the Archivo General de Simancas and its Director, Asunción de la Plaza, have been extremely helpful in my search for diplomatic documents concerning the embassy of Sir Charles Cornwallis at the court of Philip III. Significantly valuable has been the ready assistance of the personnel of the Manuscript Room of the British Library and of the Readers Room at the Public Record Office at Chancery Lane. Mr. Antony Allison and Dr. David Rogers have continued to assist me over various queries about English Catholic printed books. The original plans for this book were strongly encouraged by George Fletcher, currently the Astor Curator at the Pierpont Morgan Library, when he was Director of the Fordham University Press. The Research Council of Fordham University has provided special grants to assist my investigations in London, Madrid, and Simancas. I am also grateful to David C. Smith, who as my research assistant assisted my transcription of the English manuscripts of Joseph Creswell. The mistakes that have remained are my own.

Fordham University   A.J.L.

List of Illustrations

Carta escrita al Embaxador. The title page of Creswell's Spanish translation of his Letter to Sir Charles Cornwallis, printed in 1606 for circulation at the court of Philip III. Formerly in the Biblioteca Real. [From the Biblioteca Nacional in Madrid]

Sir Charles Cornwallis ca. 1610. Portrait by an unknown artist, formerly in the possession of Cornwallis's daughter Anne. He carries his white staff of office as treasurer of the household of Prince Henry. [From the National Portrait Gallery in London]

Las Leyes nuevamente hechas en el Parlamento. The original Spanish translation of the statutes of parliament of 1606 against which Charles Cornwallis protested to the Council of State. James Wadesworth was the translator; the handwriting of the marginal comments is that of Nicholas Oursley. [From the Archivo General de Simancas, Sección de Estado]

Illustrations follow page xi.

Abbreviations

B.L.: British Library
Cal.S.P.: *Calendars of State Papers*
  Dom. Domestic series
  Venet. Venetian series
E: Archivo General de Simancas, Sección de
    Estado (cited by legajo number)
P.R.O. S.P.: Public Record Office (State Papers
    manuscript series)
STC: *A Short-Title Catalogue of Books . . . 1475–*
    1640, ed. A. W. Pollard and G. R.
    Redgrave (reprint 1946)
Winwood Memorials: Winwood (Sir Ralph). *Memorials of affairs of*
    state in the reigns of Q. Elizabeth and K.
    James I . . . , 3 vols., ed. E. Sawyer, 1725

Biblical Books Cited in the Letter

Ac	Acts of the Apostles	Ki	Kings
Co	Corinthians	Lk	Luke
Dn	Daniel	Mi	Micah
Dt	Deuteronomy	Mk	Mark
Ep	Ephesians	Mt	Matthew
Gn	Genesis	Pr	Proverbs
Heb	Hebrews	Ps	Psalms
Is	Isaiah	Qo	Qoheleth [Ecclesiastes]
Jb	Job	Sg	Song of Songs [Canticle]
Jm	James	Tm	Timothy
Jn	John		

962 Las leyes nueuamente hechas en el Parlaméto de Inglaterra este año de M. DC. VI.
contra los Catolicos Ingleses, que llaman
Recusantes, traduzidas de su original im-
presso en Ingles.

1 QVALQVIERA Persona que no recibiere su hereti-
ca comunion, si quiera vna vez en cada vn año, pagara en
pena por el primer año que lo dexare de hazer
ochenta escudos de a diez reales: por el segundo
año ciento y ochenta: y por el tercero dozientos y quarenta: y lo
mismo en adelante, todos los años dozientos y quarenta. De los
quales la mitad sera adjudicada al Rey, y el resto al denuncia-
dor.

Esta es vna falsedad maliciosa porq esta ley no toca a qualquiera persona, sino a los q han sido conuencidos por tas leyes y se han confor-mado con ellas.

2 Todos los Mayordomos, o Priostes de las yglesias, y todos los Al
caldes de los lugares, que llaman Constables en Inglaterra, seran obligados a denunciar todos los Catolicos, que dentro de sus distritos re-
cusaren de acudir a las yglesias de los Hereges, dando los nombres
dellos, y de sus hijos, y criados, y de los que viuieren en sus casas.
Los oficiales que en esto se descuidaren seran multados en quarenta
escudos, y los que lo hizieren con diligencia y cuydado seran premia-
dos en ochenta escudos por cada vez; los quales se han de sacar de los
bienes del Recusante denunciado.

2 Esto se acostumbrava en el tiempo de la Reyna defunta.

3 La pena pequeña obliga q no presenten.

3 Todos los Catolicos assi denunciados (los quales despues de tal
denunciacion se han de tener por Recusantes, y conuencidos) pagaran en pena de tal delito ochenta escudos por cada mes, o de tres partes de sus bienes las dos, al arbitrio y voluntad del Rey: y si hizieren
falta en tal paga, adjudicarse han luego todos sus bienes muebles, y
raizes al fisco del Rey.

4 Esto se ha hecho en el favor delos de menor calidad q son la mayor parte y al rebez contra aquellos q son de mayor posibilidad porq se halla q mantenian los Tea-tinos y otros clerigos q diciosos q quisieran albo-rotar el Reyno, como se ha visto en muchos ex-emplos.

4 Qualquier Catolico, por tal conuencido, ha de mantenerse de sola
la tercera parte de sus reditos, o hazienda, y no le sera licito, ni a el, ni
a otro qualquier Catolico, arrendar, o recebir las rentas de las otras
dos partes de sus heredades, o bienes.

5 A qualquier Obispo Heretico en su diocesi, o qualesquier de los
Conseruadores de la paz en los partidos adonde presiden, les sera licito de tomar, à qualquier Catolico que sea de edad de deziocho años
arriba, vn juramento nueuo en la forma que despues se dirà: y lo mismo a qualquier hombre no conocido q passare por el camino: el qual
siendo requerido si es Catolico, o no, debaxo de juramento, o lo con-
fessare claramente, o no lo negare.

5 Esto no es contra qual-quier Catolico como es aqui falsam. traducido, sino solo contra los condenados por las leyes: y si fuera assi tal es el juramento q el Archipresbytero q esta alla ordenado por el papa los ha aconsejado de tomarle.

6 Eximense desta ley todas las personas de Titulo, pero las tales tãbien estaran sujetas à los del Consejo de Estado; demanera que si en
nombre de seis dellos fueren requeridos, estaran obligados por esta
misma ley a que hagan no solo este juramento nueuo; mas tambien o-
tro vsado en tiempo de la Reyna Ysabel (conuiene a saber que el Rey

A es

Las Leyes nuevamente hechas en el Parlamento. The original Spanish
translation of the statutes of parliament of 1606 against which
Charles Cornwallis protested to the Council of State. James
Wadesworth was the translator; the handwriting of the marginal
comments is that of Nicholas Oursley. [From the Archivo General
de Simancas, Sección de Estado]

CARTA
ESCRITA AL EM-
BAXADOR DE INGLATE-
rra, refidéte en la Corte de la Mageſtad
Catolica, en que ſe deshazen las calumnias, inuentadas para dar color à la ini-
qua y artificioſa perſecucion, que padecen, los que en aquel Reyno profeſſan
nueſtra ſanta Fê, y la obediencia
deuida à la Ygleſia
Romana.

Traduzida en lengua Caſtellana.

Beati eſtis cùm maledixerint vobis homi-
nes, & perſecuti vos fuerint, & dixerint
omne malum aduerſum vos mentien-
tes, propter me, &c.
Sic enim perſecuti ſunt Prophetas qui fue-
runt ante vos. Matthæi 5.

Carta escrita al Embaxador. The title page of Creswell's Spanish
translation of his *Letter* to Sir Charles Cornwallis, printed in 1606
for circulation at the court of Philip III. Formerly in the Biblioteca
Real. [From the Biblioteca Nacional in Madrid]

Sir Charles Cornwallis ca. 1610. Portrait by an unknown artist, formerly in the possession of Cornwallis's daughter Anne. He carries his white staff of office as treasurer of the household of Prince Henry. [From the National Portrait Gallery in London]

Introduction

In the autumn of 1606, Joseph Creswell, an English Jesuit living
in Madrid, published in Castilian *A Letter Written to the Ambassador from England (Carta escrita al Embaxador)*. Its title page announced that it was a translation from an English version of the
same name, but over the centuries since then that text has been
presumed lost. This book presents for the first time the *Carta* and
the *Letter* together for the convenience of modern readers. The
English text is from a surviving copy in manuscript to be found
in the British Library; the Spanish is from a unique printed copy
in the collection of the Biblioteca Nacional in Madrid. Creswell,
widely known by his contemporaries on the continent for several
works of controversy in Latin and Spanish,[1] can be seen here for
the first time as a voice in the lively intellectual defense of the
English Catholic community during the first decade of the sev-
enteenth century. Resorting to the then familiar literary form of
writing a letter to a public personage, in this instance Sir Charles
Cornwallis, the English ambassador to the court of Philip III,
Creswell wrote this polemic to explain to a wider audience in the
palace the need to support his Catholic compatriots at home as
loyal and peaceful subjects of James I. His English book was indeed addressed to the ambassador, but in Spanish it became an
appeal to an influential circle in Madrid. His first audience may
have been unique, but such diplomatic and apologetical aims are
also found in other English Catholic writings that argued for
change in the official repressive policies of Elizabeth and James.[2]

When reading this short book for the first time, a modern
reader will find that Creswell differs somewhat from his contemporaries in his selection of arguments from history and Scripture
and even in his emotional appeal. If one were to ask what is the
relation of the *Carta* to other contemporary Spanish treatises on
this topic, it appears that Creswell shared the views of political

1

theorists such as Justus Lipsius and his fellow Jesuit Pedro de Ribadeneira, who was at that time living in Madrid. Each had published books about the ideal Catholic prince, who should in certain circumstances concede personal toleration to dissenting Protestants in order to achieve peace and stability within the state.[3] Creswell's readers were already familiar with the major events of the Elizabethan religious settlement through the earlier publication in Castile and Portugal of Ribadeneira's *Ecclesiastical History of the English Schism*, in which the Spanish Jesuit had argued for a similar private toleration of the English Catholic minority instead of the burden of Elizabeth's penal laws. For the English readers of his *Letter*, Creswell would be in the school, of which Robert Persons was already a leading thinker, which argued for the alleviation of any penal laws because of the dangerous unrest that the repression of the conscience could provoke. There was soon to appear in 1607 Persons's *Treatise Tending to Mitigation Towardes Catholicke-Subiectes in England*, which proposed "that it is not impossible for Subiectes of different Religions (especially Catholickes and Protestantes) to live together in dutifull obedience" to King James. This was part of his continuing debate with the Protestant divine Thomas Morton, Anglican dean of Gloucester, who had recently challenged the loyalty of English Catholics in print. Creswell's treatise was addressed primarily to the English resident ambassador and his circle of friends in Madrid.[4]

To help understand the particular historical context in which Creswell's dual treatise was written, this introduction begins with two chronological sections. In the first, the ambassador and the Jesuit are introduced, with some of the highlights of their careers, and a review of the court of Philip III, where they became friends during the ceremonies for the ratification of the peace between England and Spain in 1605. The second section deals with the unexpected turn of events over the next two years in the aftermath of the Gunpowder Plot, when the new legislation prompted publications by the English exiles in Madrid, including Creswell. The later relations between the Jesuit and the ambassador continued to be cordial, and a likely year when the *Letter* was presented to Cornwallis is suggested.

The rest of the introduction concerns the texts of this edition. In a third section some questions concerning why and when the copy entered the library of Sir Robert Cotton are explored. Sometime before the Cotton manuscripts became part of the collections of the new British Museum, the title page of the manuscript identifying Creswell was lost. This appears to be a more likely explanation of why his work has remained until now among the numerous anonymous works of the Cotton manuscripts. A fourth section reviews the background of the rare Spanish copy of the *Letter* now in the Biblioteca Nacional. In the last section the norms for editing the two texts are presented.

I. SIR CHARLES CORNWALLIS AND JOSEPH CRESWELL, S.J., VALLADOLID 1605

The ratification of the treaty of peace between England and Spain was an occasion of memorable splendor befitting this overdue event. The earl of Nottingham, ambassador extraordinary for King James, headed an unusually large retinue of courtiers, friends, and liveried escorts totaling more than six hundred persons to witness the events in the north Castilian city of Valladolid. After nearly two decades of costly warfare on sea and land, the ceremony of the king of Spain's oath of ratification was being followed with keen interest among contemporaries in both capitals.[5] At the solemn moment the earl had a place of honor at the left of the king's throne, and close by sat the first resident English ambassador to the Spanish court in thirty-seven years, Sir Charles Cornwallis. His selection had been a surprise to some observers since he lacked previous experience of the traditions of this foreign court; indeed, it was likely that he had not left England at any time before his recent voyage to La Coruña, followed by a difficult journey by muleback and coach into the capital.

Prior to Queen Elizabeth's death two years earlier, Cornwallis had slight expectations of securing high preferment such as the rank of an ambassador. Born in Norfolk ca. 1551, Charles was the second son of a landed family with traditions of service at the royal court, in the House of Commons, and in local offices. His father, Sir Thomas Cornwallis, had been prominent during the short reign of Mary Tudor, with appointments to her privy council as well as to the offices of treasurer of Calais and comptroller of the royal household. However, as a person of influence in the queen's inner circle with a steadfast Catholic outlook, he had little chance of continuing in office at Whitehall after Mary's death. Consequently, during Elizabeth's long reign Charles grew up in relative obscurity on his family's estates.[6] He did not appear to have a substantial income, for there were three sisters who had to be assured of sufficient sums for their dowries; there was also a feckless older brother, William, who over the years, even with a selection as M.P. in 1597, had been notorious for his extravagance in the taverns and at the card tables of London. Despite the overt Catholicism of his father and an uncle, also named William, who was ordained a priest overseas, Charles declared his loyalty to the established church upon graduating from Cambridge in 1569. Earlier, when Charles had matriculated at Trinity Hall in 1566, Henry Howard, the duke of Norfolk's younger brother, had there begun his lectureship in rhetoric and civil law. Since his father had shown strong personal loyalty to the duke over the years, Charles's studies at Trinity Hall proved to be a providential advantage over the long term.[7] Three decades afterward, when Henry Howard's political fortunes improved immensely through his role in the unchallenged accession of King James, Charles's prospects suddenly brightened. Henry Howard, as earl of Northampton and privy councillor, became his influential patron over the next eleven years until his death in 1614. In May 1603 knighthood was belatedly conferred upon Charles, and when elections were held for the first parliament in the following spring, as Northampton's client, he was returned as knight of the shire for Norfolk.

Since early in 1604 Northampton had shown interest in the commercial issues to be resolved in a treaty of peace with Spain. As one of the commissioners empowered to meet with the representatives of Philip III and the archdukes of the Spanish Low Countries, he was eager to increase the level of English trade after the war. He argued for a treaty article that would ensure England's access to the Spanish Caribbean ports, but failed to secure it. Philip's commissioners had been instructed to pursue secretly the relief of English Catholics from the Elizabethan penal code, but were also frustrated in achieving it.[8] In the end, the treaty turned out to be an acceptable compromise for the commercial needs of both sides, and it was expected that a settlement of the numerous claims of the English merchants, formerly trading in the peninsula, was to be a primary task for any future English

4

ambassador to Spain. For Northampton's purposes, Cornwallis appeared a suitable nomination since he thoroughly understood his patron's views on Spain and held no commitment to England's previous war strategy. He could also be counted on to speak for the rights of his fellow Protestants residing there and, above all, loyally defend the policies of King James against all critics.[9]

From the outset the letters of Cornwallis showed his determination to live up to Northampton's high expectations, but they began to hint at some annoying procedures over which he had no control. It appears that the Spanish council of state rarely dealt with him on major problems but more often instructed Philip's ambassador in London, don Pedro de Zúñiga, to approach the privy council or King James, so that Cornwallis frequently found out about their dealings some time after they had taken place. Furthermore, Zúñiga and his predecessors, the count of Villa Mediana and the duke of Frias, had found friends at the English court since they were entrusted with funds for gifts or pensions, a portion of which reached both Northampton and Salisbury. Cornwallis had no comparable resources or instructions to ensure the goodwill of their counterparts at the court of Philip III; in fact he found his salary of £4 a day barely adequate for his household.[10]

A frequent item in his early letters was the delay in securing action after the legal petition of a merchant had been submitted, or the disruptions in the routine of the crown officials which arose from their obligation to travel with the royal household in a progress from the city. He was irked particularly by the invidious comments that circulated in the court against the new friendship between a Protestant England and a Catholic Spain. He complained in a letter to the lord chancellor, Thomas Egerton, of hearing dire predictions of "the perill that may arrise in Christendome by the continuance of the king our masters confederation and conjunction" with Philip, since James's "profession of a contrarie relligion and his many allies of that sort" would influence Spain away from its traditional Catholic role.[11] He was often provoked by the public statements of English and Irish Catholics in Valladolid, or elsewhere, about the persecution of Catholics under James's governance. He was particularly sensitive to the widespread local attention given to the sudden conversions of English visitors to Spain, such as that of Pickering Wotton, shortly before his death in Valladolid, as he was the son of a privy councillor and the nephew of the English ambassador to Venice. It was the accumulation of these irritating experiences, none grave in itself, which is the background to the tone of isolation his correspondence betrayed. He remained an "outsider" to most of the Castilian court during his first year in office, so that the unexpected role of the Jesuit Joseph Creswell, as an informative "insider" to help him, becomes understandable.

When the two first became friends in the summer of 1605, Cornwallis had left London barely three months earlier, whereas the Jesuit had been living outside of England for a quarter of a century and in Spain since 1592. Although Creswell was only about six years younger than Cornwallis, the differences in their outlook and background were considerable. Creswell had left London at the age of twenty-four in 1580, after serving as one of the escorts of Edmund Campion and Robert Persons when they first reached London that spring.[12] He had studied for three years at the English College in Rome with the gallant intention, as his *Letter* to Cornwallis said, "to be sent thither during the persecution [no. 17]." After entering the Jesuit order, he became an assistant to Robert Persons, who had returned to Rome as prefect, or superior, of the English mission of the Society. Early in 1588 the father general of the Jesuits selected Creswell to travel north to Flanders with another English Jesuit, William Holt, to join the entourage of the prince of Parma, then under orders to gather a large force of veterans for a military thrust into England. Before the armada was to sail, Parma had requested that some English priests be close at hand to accompany his officers. The father general had written to the head of the corps of chaplains in the army of Flanders that Creswell and Holt had reached Parma "with orders to pass over into England to gather fruit in the vineyard of the lord, having authority and instructions for any occasion."[13] After the news of the failure of the armada reached Rome, Creswell was asked to return there to assume the post of rector of the English College as his friend Robert Persons was about to depart for Spain. There Persons secured Philip II's approval to establish a new college for English students to supplement those already in place in Douai and Rome.

This new college of St. Alban's in Valladolid later provoked an angry proclamation by the Elizabethan privy council in October

1591, which excited as much worry overseas as at home. Afraid of the anxieties this public condemnation might arouse among officials in Rome and the Catholics in exile, Creswell wrote his first book of contemporary polemics. In this Latin essay there is a train of thought which would have fuller development later in the *Letter* to Cornwallis. There is the assurance to his readers that the queen, misled by her advisers, was placating Protestant extremists by treating Catholics harshly. There was a reliance on early ecclesiastical writers for illustrative examples of other persecutions which had failed, for he warned that coercion strengthened convictions rather than changed them. He prophesied that once peace between England and Spain was accomplished, the better treatment of Catholics would soon dissipate the fear of any Spanish-inspired sedition. This first book was a good sampling of what Dr. Peter Holmes has aptly called a "Catholic critique of Elizabethan England."[14] Shortly after this rebuttal of the proclamation began to circulate, along with other books by more famous writers, in Spanish territories, Creswell was called by Robert Persons to Spain to assist him in gaining support for another college to be started in Seville.

Over the following years Creswell became acquainted with several councillors of state at the Castilian court as he sought support for English students studying in Valladolid, Seville, and the Low Countries. He also became a regular correspondent of various church officials for whom he prepared newsletters about England and the treatment of Catholics. Skilled in drafting memoranda in Castilian, Italian, and Latin, he sent reports to Madrid, Brussels, and Rome and to Philip II's advisers as he saw fit. Before Robert Persons returned to Rome in the spring of 1596, he appointed Creswell superior of the English Jesuits working in different parts of the Iberian peninsula, in addition to his other duties. In that summer the naval war moved closer to the shores of Andalucía with Essex's damaging raid on the harbor of Cádiz, which prompted Philip to order the preparation of a new armada to attack England. Seizing this occasion, Creswell in September 1596 wrote to Philip to remind him that, when he had been a chaplain attached to Parma's retinue eight years earlier, "his highness ordered me to write a proclamation which was then printed in English to declare your majesty's pious purpose." Philip agreed that a new proclamation would be useful, but Creswell did not have it ready when the large squadron of ships departed. However, after failing to sail safely through unexpected summer storms, this armada was forced to return to its northern Spanish bases without any results. In the following summer of 1597, when Philip ordered the fleet to sail again, Creswell's proclamation was in print, ready for use if there was a landing of Spanish forces on English soil. His principal message was that these forces came to bring help to oppressed Catholics and that, once order was restored, "a parliament" and those "who would have legitimate authority will be able to . . . declare the most suitable successor for the preservation of the Catholic religion." Who this "successor" might be was not declared in print, although Creswell had the vain hope that the Infanta Isabel might be willing to assume the title. The real nuance of this broadside was his evident conviction that a military intervention was the providential opportunity to liberate his co-religionists in England.[15] The proclamation was never used, since violent storms rendered the Biscayan seas impassable again, and the ships returned to port without even engaging the British patrols.

When young Philip III came to the throne in late 1598, the strategy of the naval war turned toward Ireland, so that Creswell was not to have the prospect of a military invasion of England again. However, the mistreatment of the English Catholics was kept before the Spanish public through the efforts of one of his friends, a court chaplain named Diego de Yepes, who had become interested in the printed narratives about them which were circulating below the Pyrenees. Shortly before he was appointed by Philip to be bishop of Tarazona in Aragon, Yepes prepared with Creswell's help a detailed, six-part anthology which came to nine hundred pages when published in 1599.[16] However, Philip's circle of advisers had no plans for military or diplomatic activities against England at this time. His council was preoccupied with the costly stalemate of the offensive in the Dutch war as well as the disastrous domestic crisis of the large epidemic in Castile. Moreover, the Spanish coasts were being increasingly endangered by hostile raids from Dutch, English, and even Moroccan ships. The relief of the English Catholics was of a low priority in the midst of such calamities at home. Creswell met Guy Fawkes and his earliest associates and witnessed their failure to rouse interest in their radical plans among the councillors of the king in 1602.[17]

When Elizabeth died in the spring of 1603 and the peaceful entry of James I occurred, with his proclamation of a cease-fire with Spain soon after, Creswell realized that Spanish military forces no longer had a role in his future expectations for changing the lot of the English Catholics.

Early in 1604 he traveled to Seville, after he had received word that the local magistrates had begun to reconsider their vital annual grant of six hundred *escudos* to the English college of St. Gregory, probably because of the economic depression in Andalucía. In his eloquent printed petition on behalf of the students, he reminded the civic authorities that "having seen that our Lord has made his will clear by the outcome that he does not intend to effect a change for the better in England by force of arms but rather that he will work a cure by the ministry of the word," it was the time to see that, from now on, "a spiritual war" was to be waged with that kingdom, for which St. Gregory would serve as a strong bastion.[18] In this instance his appeal, joined with other influential voices, proved effective, and the grant was continued. He then returned to Valladolid where the ceremonies for the ratification of the peace treaty gave him a welcome opportunity to meet Nottingham and Cornwallis for the first time.

The earl had been immensely pleased with the hospitality provided by King Philip and with the deference paid to him by the court's leadership. He also was gracious and friendly to Creswell at his residence during occasional visits, which prompted the Jesuit to prepare a celebration in his behalf at the college of St. Alban's. The students were urged to prepare poetry and speeches in his honor at a reception in their hall, which was to be hung with special emblems and banners. A similar elaborate ceremony had been recorded in print in 1592 after a visit by Philip II.[19] However, just after everything was in place, Nottingham sent his regrets for not appearing as he was about to depart shortly. The emblems, with their symbolic pledges of loyalty to both king and country as well as their religion, were taken down. However, in the atmosphere of a celebration of peace, Creswell decided to write to Robert Cecil, the earl of Salisbury, a personal letter to be carried back by Nottingham. Praising Cecil's strong role in achieving the treaty with Spain, which was still only a "peace with straungers," Creswell urged the powerful councillor of King James to turn with a similar leadership to giving Englishmen "at home . . . peace amongest them selves." A fresh chance was at hand to practice restraint toward all those who had "peaceable mindes with out forcinge them to more daungerous intrinsecal warre with God and their owne consciences." Coercion to support another church must cease since "those that yield to the oppression, and seeme to conforme themselves, are never the nearer to the purpose pretended, but further off" as they only conform "with interior hart burninge, repugnance and mislike."[20] Creswell was well known to Cecil from earlier reports of his spies below the Pyrenees during the war. He did not reply and for over a year withheld comment on the appearances of the Jesuit's name in Cornwallis's letters to London.

A week after he had written to Cecil, Creswell drafted a longer letter to King James celebrating the peace between the two nations, and with this he planned to send some of the emblems which the students had painted for the reception of Nottingham. Aware that this bold step should not be taken without the knowledge of Philip's council, he sent the letter and the emblems to it for approval. In the absence of Philip on another tour of Castile because of the outbreak of the plague in Valladolid, the council's response was delayed for over two months. In the meantime, Creswell made more frequent visits to the English ambassador, who was also waiting impatiently for the return of court officials. Cornwallis seemed pleased with these impromptu briefings, for early in September he wrote to Cecil that the Jesuit was talking about "the harts and dispositions of the greatest" of the courtiers and then willing to "carry back to his friends . . . any thing that I desire they should give belief unto." His useful advice had convinced him that Creswell remained "loyal to the king and his country," but that he was keeping alert about "his desire to propagate his religion."[21] While it is unlikely that the Jesuit was hoping to lead the ambassador on the path to Rome, it is reasonable to presume that there were conversations about the ideas that he had commended to Cecil and was hoping to expound in another way to King James. Creswell knew that earlier Philip had instructed his ambassadors in London to introduce the question of the Catholics in the treaty settlement. The Jesuit had also been told that both Philip and Lerma had raised the question privately with Nottingham before his departure. He was undoubtedly impatient to hear of the council's views about his letter to the king of England.

Dated from St. Alban's College in late June, his three-page draft began with suitable phrases of deference and devotion from a loyal subject and then celebrated the arrival of peace. This was a new occasion for all King James's subjects to render to "Caesar that which is his" and to God that which is owed by one's faith. He recalled that many "notable persons of our nation" had visited the college recently, and they were now able to assure James of the loyalty of its students despite their difference in religion. His major point was that the previous reasons for severity were no longer in place in England, for the king should know that forcing his subjects to conceal their distaste at being obliged to go to "temples" in which they did not worship in fact had led to violence within them. He held up the wiser policy of the king of France as proof that a king with subjects of different religions could rule them in peace. Saluting Henry IV as a "moderate and disinterested king—*blando y indifferente rey*," he begged James to follow a similar policy to spare his subjects suffering or even bloodshed.[22] When the council finally considered this proposed letter, its collective judgment was, not unexpectedly, against it. At least four of the seven present had in past years considerable experience of other debates about the English Catholic question and were familiar with the English court's religious policies. Juan de Idiáquez and the count of Chinchon had been in Philip II's inner circle, then called the *junta de noche*. A third, the count of Olivares, had been Philip II's ambassador in Rome during the planning of the first Armada in 1588. The fourth, the constable of Castile, had been in London the year before, for the ratification of the peace treaty recently celebrated, and had spoken with King James and most of his privy council.

While all commended Creswell for first seeking advice, they were against sending any emblems to King James, who would be more likely to ridicule them. The letter they considered unsuitable since the occasion for it was long past. They were more concerned about the reports circulating at court about the frequent visits of Cornwallis and Creswell than anything else. Idiáquez, as the most experienced councillor, spoke for all in writing that more caution must be practiced: "Since it is known that Creswell has entered into some very serious talks with the ambassador of

Great Britain, it will be best to advise him that, just as it was wise to inform us about this letter beforehand, so it will be good to do the same with anything else that is going to happen before he becomes involved in talks with the ambassador, so that he can be instructed what he ought to do."[23] As King Philip agreed with this warning, the ambitious gesture of writing to King James was never made. However, the talks with the ambassador were not broken off; instead Creswell seems to have related occasionally to the council what was involved during the following weeks.

Unexpectedly, a new reason why this dialogue could not continue arose in the autumn of 1605, when Creswell was summoned by his father general to Rome "about the good government of the English mission and these seminaries." There were many problems to discuss, so that the Jesuit quickly left the court in November; it was uncertain when, or if, he would return. When Creswell had gone, Cornwallis sent after him a thoughtful note saying that despite "the discords between us" in religion, he was confident in Creswell's "duty and loyalty to my king and countrye." He hoped that he would find "all the happiness that a man of your sorte upon this earthe can desyre"; he thanked him for the "greate good you did here to your poor countrymen" and asked to be considered "your very assured loving friend."[24] They were, of course, to meet later in the following year in different circumstances.

II. WHY THE SPANISH LETTER WAS PUBLISHED: MADRID 1606–1608

While Creswell was on the road to Rome, the sensational reports of the Gunpowder Plot reached the court of Philip. At once, as an official gesture of congratulation, Lerma went with a delegation of high officers to visit Cornwallis to express satisfaction at "the most happie discovery of this horrible treason." Cornwallis was also moved that several courtiers expressed dismay "that so monstrous a wickednesse should be harbored within the breast of anie of their relligion." Over the following weeks details identifying the conspirators, their arrests, and subsequent trials circulated in the city, fed by newsletters and correspondence from London. However, most important business was delayed during the rest of the spring of 1606 after the decision of Philip to move his court back to Madrid. Again there were time-consuming delays for the ambassador since court officials were preoccupied with relocating in the old capital and he had to follow their example by finally placing his household in a large house "towards the Prado" with a garden and view west toward the city. Even then he found time to send some letters to Creswell after he had reached Rome. When Cecil learned of this he ordered Walter Hawkesworth, the embassy secretary, to tell him "not to hold correspondencie" with the Jesuit any further. This Cornwallis promised to observe, but he regretted the loss of his conversations with Creswell since "no dore of the kings, dukes [Lerma] or secretaries [Andres de Prada] is shut against him." Salisbury did not give a reason, but apparently he did not wish it known in London that James's ambassador in Madrid had kept in close touch with an English Jesuit after the recent trial and execution of Henry Garnet, their superior. A few months earlier in a letter to Thomas Edmondes, the ambassador in Brussels, which enclosed a copy of the proclamation for the arrest of three Jesuits, he denounced the "impious order" and its likely links to "this develish conspiracie." He considered them "principall comforters to instruct the consciences of some of these wicked traytors."[25] Creswell did not learn of his friend's "sequestration," as he later called it, until he finally returned to Spain in August.

Meanwhile the second session of the English parliament, which had probed into the plot and passed new penal statutes against Catholics, had ended. Basically this new legislation of 1606 had tried to search out evaders of the Elizabethan code,[26] known to contemporaries as "Church Papists." This meant Catholics who occasionally appeared at the service of the established church to avoid the fines. Henceforth convicted recusants had to communicate in the church once a year under penalty of a fine. Furthermore, a wealthier recusant, who might consider a fine as a sort of unwelcome tax, now faced the possible penalty of having two-thirds of his lands seized at the discretion of the crown until he conformed.[27] There was a wide range of new disabilities imposed upon recusants, for example, the inability to practice as lawyers or physicians, to hold commissions in the army or navy, or to act as executors of wills. Furthermore, those who failed to be married with Anglican rites were penalized by loss of personal rights to each other's property, and each of their children had to be baptized by the Anglican rites under threat of a severe fine. By far the most widely debated enactment was that which presented a new Oath of Allegiance, whose wording denied a contemporary Catholic doctrine that the pope could declare the deposition of a monarch under certain conditions. This oath could be tendered to anyone convicted, or even suspected, of recusancy. Apparently because this oath did not become law in England until the end of June 1606, there had been less attention paid to it by the English exiles in Madrid. Creswell mentioned it only in passing in his *Letter,* and he did not enter into the long, heated controversy that surrounded it for close to two decades.[28]

By the end of June 1606 Pedro de Zúñiga, ambassador in London of Philip III, had secured a copy of these statutes and sent a translation of them to the Spanish council, which arranged a review of these developments by the middle of August at the Escorial. Although disturbed by the news of additional statutes against Catholics, they were relieved to find out that Zúñiga had been privately informed that James and some of his councillors had not been in full accord with parliament and that the laws would not be rigorously enforced.[29] The Spaniard's informants reminded him that, since his accession, James had been moderate about the penal code. There had also been a notable falling off in the collection of recusancy fines during 1604 and 1605, a loss of revenue which could not have occurred without the king's connivance.[30] Since this report was not contradicted by earlier despatches about his private meetings with the friends of the countess of Suffolk, where a plan for secret payments by the king of Spain for the recusancy fines was discussed, it was accepted as James's current attitude. Philip and Lerma were determined that peace between the two kingdoms should be maintained, and accordingly Zúñiga was instructed to express regret about the laws but to avoid any rupture over the Catholic issue.[31]

However, few outside of the councillors at the Escorial knew how well Philip had been briefed by his ambassador about James's real intentions over the new statutes, including even the English ambassador in Madrid. In the capital disquieting stories about a new persecution and rigorous enforcement of the penal code became an accepted fact. Always sensitive to hostile comments about James's governing of England, Cornwallis became exasperated about the alarming conduct of many English exiles in the city. He reported that there were "a more than ordinarie congregation of caterpillars . . . who accused us of makeinge of late most bloody cruele laws against Catholiques of all sorts." By early October he discovered that there was already in circulation among high officials at court a printed Spanish translation of the "lawes against popish recusants," which at first he thought, mistakenly, was printed by the Jesuits. Once he had gotten hold of a copy of the eight-page tract, he wrote two strong protests to the council of state which warned of a serious crisis on the horizon. In his first memorial, he charged that this sort of printed matter was "intended to produce abhorence and hostility in the people of Spain against the king of England and his parliament." Since he still held his office as an elected M.P., he seemed piqued at this image of a bloodthirsty assembly. He urged the council to move swiftly, as in fact the English privy council had done recently at his request over some English books about the cruelties of the Spanish inquisition. Here in Madrid, he noted, false statements against a friendly monarch were freely circulating in print without a license.[32]

In his second letter to the Spanish council, he demanded the punishment of the English refugees responsible for the recent publication about the new statutes. As evidence he submitted an annotated copy of *Las Leyes nuevamente hechas* . . . , or "The Laws recently passed in the English Parliament in the year 1606 against the Catholics whom they call Recusants. Translated from the original printing into English." On its margins he had left comments where the translations were incorrect or where provocative words such as "heretical" were inserted. Faults were pointed out in exaggerating the fines, and in some places the English king had been slandered.[33] Andres de Prada, the secretary of the council, soon tracked down the writer of the unsigned and unlicensed tract, who proved to be James Wadesworth, the former chaplain of the embassy. Although Cornwallis was not told about the author, Prada decided to request that Wadesworth submit a response to the complaint of the English diplomat in order to guide the council about the state of the question before a decision was reached.

In his three-page "Comments upon the marginal glosses of the ambassador," Wadesworth excused his various changes by saying that "heretical" was meant only to warn the Spanish reader that this church was not "Catholic." In other instances he insisted the addition was of minimal significance, and finally he offered to lend his copy of the original English statutes to the ambassador so that a difference in words could be judged by others. He thought a translation of "all the laws" would let the readers know how much better off they were as subjects of King Philip.[34] Wadesworth defended his printing of this work by noting that "only a few" copies were printed and then given out "to the lords of the council of state and those of the Inquisition and other high officials." He did not observe that this elite readership was the very group that Cornwallis wanted to impress most of all. He concluded with the comment that perhaps the ambassador was "confused" about the Spanish translation and that he believed the handwriting of the glosses showed they were "more by Nicholas Oursley than by him."[35]

However, the anger of the ambassador could not be pushed aside as lightly as Wadesworth might have hoped. The council of state was well aware that more than a single publication's authorship was at stake since reports of disrespect to the name of King James, or even of parliament, could create considerable difficulties for Philip's embassy in London and lead to a rupture. By the time these reports were received it was November, and Joseph Creswell, whom Cornwallis and Wadesworth had not seen in a year, was finally back at the court in Madrid. Much had happened to him since then, and a brief résumé will assist the understanding of the next step taken by the council.

News of the Gunpowder Plot and its aftermath had caused more concern in the papal curia than at the court of Philip III since little of the information available to the Spanish council was passed on to the duke of Escalona, the ambassador in Rome. Convinced of the likelihood of a more severe persecution of the English Catholics, Cardinal Borghese, the secretary of state, advised the nuncios in Madrid and Paris to urge Philip III and Henry IV to have their ambassadors in England plead for restraint. Because of his frequent correspondence in the past with the cardinal, when Creswell left Rome in the middle of May 1606 he carried letters of recommendation both to the nuncio, Giovanni Garzia Millino, the archbishop of Rhodes, and to the president of the council of Castile, Juan de Zúñiga, the count of Miranda. They were asked to listen to the Jesuit in trying to assist the plight of the Catholics of England.[36] Unfortunately, when he reached

Guadalajara on the road to Madrid late in August, Creswell became so seriously ill of fever that proceeding farther westward to the court was out of the question for many weeks. For a time he was under the care of the physicians from the palace of the duke and duchess of Infantado at Guadalajara, after which he was moved to rest for a long convalescence at Jesus del Monte, the country house of the Jesuit college in Alcalá de Henares.[37] Here he learned of the growing furor that Cornwallis had excited over the comments of the English exiles in the capital about England and, particularly, their circulation of a tendentious translation of the new penal laws. However, his first concern during his slow recovery was to write to the papal nuncio in Madrid.

It was probably late in September when he had recovered sufficiently to send the nuncio a paper to assist him in his current dealings with Lerma, which he entitled "on the way in which the English Catholics could best be helped."[38] The discourse was a series of reflections on what he believed to be the underlying reasons for King James's continuing uncertainty about the loyalty of the Catholics in his kingdom. Leaving aside the provocation of the Gunpowder Plot, Creswell suggested that the king would never let the Catholics live in peace until some deep-rooted theological, financial, and political questions, which were disturbing him, were addressed. The king, he noted, was an educated and zealous Protestant who abhorred certain current Catholic teachings. These would have to be discussed as soon as possible, and he believed the time was ripe to have someone write a vigorous Catholic apologia which might bring him to reflect on his objections and even call a conference where such issues could be debated. Where, or how, such an assembly would be convened was not stated, but perhaps he had in mind that James had relished the role of theologian during the meetings at Hampton Court two years earlier. Next, concerning the financial profit which the penal laws gained for the English treasury, Creswell had little to say but he did not consider this a strong consideration in James's treatment of his recusant subjects. Unaware that private discussions on this subject were going on with Pedro de Zúñiga in London, Creswell observed that matching sums could be arranged from foreign Catholic princes once the pope personally appealed to them for their assistance.

It was the political scene which Creswell considered to be of highest significance in James's views of the Catholics in his three kingdoms. He believed that the king was not yet convinced that his throne could be secure without coercion or some threat of severity against all Catholics. The king, he pointed out, was credulous of all rumors circulating about their loyalty and remained suspicious of the rulers of Spain and France and their likely influence over his own Catholic subjects. James could not see as yet, he concluded, that clemency toward Catholics could be a boon for his new dynasty, for he did not consider that his Puritan critics were a danger to his throne. This private memorandum to the nuncio was consistent with some of the ideas in his letter to Cecil, and even in the draft letter to King James, but he would write a much fuller explanation of them in his *Letter* to Cornwallis, which he now began to compose "whiles I recover my health by peece meale as I could [no. 92]."

He did not wish to take up the controversial translation of the laws, which preoccupied the English ambassador, but to dwell on the situation at present in England to "give your Lordship light and information" so that, "by your office" of diplomat, he would later have the opportunity to mention this point of view to the king or his councillors, "as perhappes his magesty by other waies may not come to know them so plainely [no. 62]." Separated from the ambassador by his illness, distance, and diplomatic restrictions, he used the *Letter* as a medium to explain many of the issues he had first explored in conversations before his departure for Rome. However, once it was finished, he began a Spanish translation of it, which he decided to put into print. Two considerations must have influenced his decision to print his apologia for distribution at the court at this time. First of all, he had been advised in September of the preceding year by the council of state that all topics of substance in his conversations with the diplomat had best be first referred to it in advance. A second consideration was at work in the way he disassociated his text from all the tensions created by the strident tone of the printed pages of *Las Leyes*. This was to be a moderate message about the Catholics for many of the same readership.

Cornwallis heard that the *Carta escrita al Embaxador* was in circulation by late November 1606 after a friend had read it and told him some of its typical ideas. He wrote to London a brief summary of this development:

Creswell having bene long sicke and after his recoverie . . . now stirres abroade . . . and . . . goes lightly up the staires of the councellors of state to smoothe over the much mallice and little truth they have showed in that worke of theirs . . . I am informed by one (that both did see and read it) that he hath written a Letter to me commendinge my former carriage in this court [no. 1], wishing the countenance of my temperance [no. 62] and insynuating scandal and peril that followeth vyolence [nos. 36, 39]. He showed it himself to one of good sort as a thing he was well pleased in but hitherto he hath not adventured to send it.

He also gave other details to Robert Cecil in another letter to London, in which he said that he had heard about the Jesuit's "booke . . . wherein he endeavoreth to cleere himselfe [no. 5] and his colleagues of the treasons layd to theire charge [nos. 52, 53] and to prove that this late powder treason (howsoever undertaken by the intemperate heades and hands of certaine ingnorant young people) yet was plotted and devised by some counsellors in England for the overthrowe of the Catholique Religion in England [nos. 57, 58, 59]."[39]

While curious about Creswell's book, the ambassador now pressed for action about *Las Leyes*, which he felt was still doing damage to the reputation of King James within the court. Therefore, in December 1606 the same four councillors of state, who were already familiar with Creswell's attempt to write to the English king a year ago, and had been kept informed by Zúñiga's letters about the situation in London, took up the ambassador's case. They realized that it was important to end the affair as soon as possible and soothe the feelings of Cornwallis as well. Idiáquez summed up their dislike of the indiscreet printing of *Las Leyes* in crisp language:

I would have been more pleased with two things. First, that this had not been printed and, secondly, that so many copies had not been passed about. Even if this was prompted by deep zeal, a warning still must be sent around through Father Creswell, who keeps his hand on this sort of thing, that before such a thing is put into print, the secretary of state must be informed as has been the custom, and the command awaited according to your majesty's pleasure. Although no public example will be made out of the printer, still an order has to be issued, . . . to the effect that unless there is a memorandum about the facts of a lawsuit or some legal arguments, nothing should be printed for another to read without having a licence for it.[40]

Then, taking up the written response of Wadesworth to the "glosses" of Cornwallis, Idiáquez advised that "the ambassador must not learn about this, for it should have been written with more restraint, and so it will be good to tell Creswell about this as well." While he felt that the mistakes denounced by the ambassador were not serious, or a slander against parliament or the king, still, to placate him, another translation of the laws should be commissioned in which "the meaning would be given precisely." For this he suggested another English exile staying in Madrid named Sir Andrew Wise, who was the titular prior of the knights of St. John in England, "without letting him know what has been happening." This seemed to have ended the crisis, for shortly after the new year Cornwallis reported to London that he was "very secretly advertised" that the "laws against recusants" were now to be "trulie translated out of English."[41] Probably his friend Andrew Wise had told him.

Because of two unexpected clashes between Creswell and the ambassador, the presentation of a copy of his *Letter* was postponed for over a year. While the court of Philip was involved during the spring of 1607 in grave charges of corruption against a close friend of the still powerful duke of Lerma, the English residents of Madrid began to debate the merits of an official narrative of the trial and execution of Henry Garnet, the English Jesuit accused of counseling the Gunpowder Plot conspirators. Creswell found parts of it offensive. When he met one of Cornwallis's secretaries at the residence of Andres de Prada, he warned him that this book "should not want an answere," for he "had wrytten concerning some matters in it" and even if Cornwallis was still "sequestered" from a Jesuit, "yet out of his love and respecte" to him he would send him "the first coppie."[42] This might have been the right moment to give him the *Letter*, except for the fact that over the following weeks Garnet's case began to be widely known in the streets of Madrid by *coplas*, or street ballads, and broadsides which always pictured the deceased Jesuit as a martyr. There was a fascination among the people about a "miraculous tincture of a strawe with the bloud of one Garnet" found near the scaffold at Tyburn. For Cornwallis this crude cult of a "traitor" and the reawakening of the obnoxious image of an English persecution were perhaps even more disquieting then the printing of *Las Leyes* the previous autumn. He denounced this notoriety of Garnet as a clever machination of some English refugees against the good name of King James, "whome they in their divinitye hold it lawfull to slaunder." Once more, over a period of weeks, he tried the patience of Andres de Prada, secretary of the council, with requests for an order to suppress the "scandalous" images of bloodshed in England. This, he charged, was a violation of the treaty. As the agitation for an end to stories of the "supposed martyrdome and fabulous myracles" of a close friend of Creswell continued, it was hardly an opportune moment to present his *Letter* to Cornwallis.[43]

Not only had this unexpected turn of events cast a shadow upon the Anglo–Spanish amity that both James and Philip were trying to preserve, but it had also begun to render more difficult Cornwallis's private conversations with Lerma about a marriage alliance between Prince Henry and the Infanta Ana, the eldest daughter of Philip III. Although neither side was thinking of an immediate alliance, the preliminary talks were of importance as a basis for the future diplomatic ties that could occur if these were successful. Reports of persecution in England made the meetings of Lerma with the ambassador more difficult and even embarrassing.[44] In an effort to end the controversy, Cornwallis had assured the Spanish council of state on one occasion that should the marriage with the Infanta take place, "in tyme she maie be the meanes that the lawes now in force against those of her religion maie either be mitigated in the letter or softened in the execution. . . ."[45]

Although this assurance by the ambassador occurred in a private meeting, in a short time Creswell was told about it by one of those present. He apparently considered this statement to be an inadequate protection for the English Catholics and, as Cornwallis later reported to London, sent a message "by a man of myne owne" that during these talks of a "conjunction by allyance with England" it was more proper to extend to the Catholics of England "a kind of toleration" that had been recently announced in Ireland.[46] A mitigation of the enforcement of the penal laws, such as had in effect been quietly introduced with James's approval in the Pale, was in Creswell's view essential; otherwise the ambassador would "labour in vayne." He added that the Spanish court "so much abhored" the present treatment of the recusants that "they would sooner bestowe their daughter upon a sone of the Turke or the King of Morocco." Flustered by the Jesuit's awareness of his private dealings with Lerma, Cornwallis sent a message back that he was as little desirous for a marriage with the Infanta as Creswell was "to get a benefyce in England."[47] Despite this spark of friction, a mutual deference continued to be the keynote of their exchanges; the ambassador acknowledged that he still held a "very good opinion" of him, particularly as he thought him to be "the openest person for secretes that this court affordeth."[48]

Sometime in 1608 Creswell finally presented the English copy of the *Letter* to Cornwallis. A convincing proof that this was the year is found in a deliberate change which he made in his text where it mentioned his long-term friendship with Robert Persons as his superior. In paragraph no. 17 of the original Spanish version of 1606, he had written that "in the twenty five years that I am his subject," the only favor that he had asked of him was to be sent back to England. In the English copy of 1608 he increased the time span to read "in more then seaven and twenty yeares" that he had known his superior. Since the *Carta* was completed at Jesus del Monte by the end of October 1606, this English copy must have been finished in Madrid about two years later. There is no further meeting of interest between the two that is recorded in their correspondence prior to Cornwallis's departure from Madrid in the summer of 1609. Apparently among his chests of papers which he brought back to London was the *Letter* from his former Jesuit friend. Zúñiga, who had been privately informed by King James, related to the Spanish council that Cornwallis had much praise for the friendly service of Lerma and the court on behalf of the Englishmen living in Spain. On his own behalf, James assured Zúñiga that Philip would always find in him "a most sincere and devoted brother." Shortly afterward a new Spanish ambassador, Alonso de Velasco, was asked by Philip to present Cornwallis with 2,000 *escudos*, about £500, as a parting gift for his service at Madrid.[49]

III. THE ENGLISH TEXT OF THE *Letter* IN THE BRITISH LIBRARY

The only known copy of the original English version of Creswell's *Letter* to Cornwallis is to be found today in the British Library's Cotton manuscripts. Unfortunately, some years after Sir Robert Cotton's death in 1631, the written identification of this manuscript was lost, so that its author was not named in the full catalogue prepared at the British Museum in 1802. Nevertheless, clues remain in another volume of this collection which point out that during the early years of the Cottonian Library the contents and authorship of the manuscript were known to the librarians. Precisely how and when this interesting treatise became part of Sir Robert's papers were not recorded, but there were certain periods of time when he and the former ambassador were closely associated. These years, in which a gift of the *Letter* to him becomes more plausible, are to be reviewed. However, to understand this evidence better, it will be helpful to see the unique arrangements of the Cottonian Library upon which recent scholarship has shed considerable light.[50] In addition to this, there survive notes written by Sir Robert about his personal loans of the Spanish papers to a few chosen friends. Although cryptic in style, his phrases still offer unique hints about how he first organized his Spanish papers during the reign of King James.

It is only to be expected that during these years the final arrangement of Cotton's manuscripts and books was far from complete. His Spanish papers were a very small part of his wide-ranging holdings in history and antiquities, which would eventually reach a total of more than nine hundred and fifty bound volumes. During his lifetime the full contents of many of his still unbound books escaped satisfactory identification. At the request of influential courtiers or members of parliament, he was known to have used his Spanish papers on various occasions in search for important precedents, such as the instructions he gave to the earl of Northampton about England's precedence over the kingdom of Castile during the discussions for the treaty of 1604. He also drew upon his documents for a brief history of earlier marriage negotiations between the two kingdoms for the House of Commons in 1624. He used his expertise in local charters to assert his rights in litigation against his neighbors to protect his own estates.[51] The fact that his papers were used, rather than simply stored in various covers, inevitably implies that, in internal arrangement or even chronological sorting, changes were regularly being made.

He was careful to maintain the private character of his library, to which only a few trusted friends were normally admitted.

These original manuscripts were a source of pride, but since political and diplomatic secrets were contained in many of his papers, he was reluctant to allow admission to a casual reader. For example, during the short-lived parliament of early 1614, when the speaker of the House of Commons wrote to ask his permission for some M.P.'s to enter to look for documents that would help in their current debate over impositions, Cotton gave his approval. However, as he was absent from London convalescing from illness, he urged caution in selecting those who might appear: "For I have been entrusted with most of the main passages of the state and to suffer these secrets to pass in vulgar may cause much blame to me and little service to the House."[52]

Early in the 1620s a more secure place for all his varied treasures was constructed in his new residence near the Thames river close to the palace at Whitehall and the houses of parliament. Here a room was specially designed which resembled a short corridor holding several cabinets along the walls on each side with open shelves for the rows of manuscript volumes.[53] As a record of the place of each volume, Cotton and his assistants began in the late 1620s to compile a catalogue of his entire library. This lengthy inventory had a unique Latin–English format listing each volume in terms of its place in this chamber by the *latus*, or side, of the room, the number of the *scrinium*, or cabinet, and the *classis*, or shelf. From the inventory's evidence it appears that the Spanish papers at first were not shelved as a group pertaining to the same area, and the contents of most volumes were not clearly stated, largely because of the wide variety of documents within them. For example, a large unbound book concerning mainly the relations of England and Spain during the reign of King James was here identified by three separate manuscripts within it but failed to note that the majority of its contents concerned the recent treaty of 1604.[54] In this initial stage, when Cotton used the word "book" or "volume," he had in mind a bundle of documents collected within a parchment cover tied with a string, to which he could later add other pieces of a similar character. The limitations of such a random descriptive style of identification were obvious, so that a table of contents was needed, but not always available, to guide his readers.

Unfortunately, just as this first catalogue was in progress, Cotton's library was sealed by an official order of the privy council since, during the second session of the 1628–1629 parliament, it became suspicious of his collection.[55] This closure continued past Sir Robert's death, so that a last opportunity to supervise what Dr. Colin Tite has aptly called the "*Scrinia*" catalogue was denied to the great collector and student of English manuscripts. Later, at the request of Sir Thomas Cotton, his son and heir, the library was reopened and fresh efforts were made to complete the collection's organization. During the decade before the civil war, it was decided to place all the Spanish papers, now in thirteen volumes, on one shelf lettered "C" in a cabinet (*scrinium*) on the top of which a small bronze bust of the emperor Vespasian had been placed. Furthermore, a new catalogue to supplement the one first attempted in the lifetime of Sir Robert was needed to clarify the new location of the volumes. This second important inventory has been appropriately called by Dr. Tite the "*Emperor*" catalogue.[56] In this decade the now familiar but unique identification of all items in the Cottonian Library by the name of the Emperor, the letter of the shelf, and the number of the volume on it was first used. This arrangement was observed during the difficult years of the civil war and interregnum, so that by the end of the century, when the grandson of the founder, Sir John Cotton, commissioned Thomas Smith, an Oxford scholar with considerable experience in consulting the great collection, to provide a new comprehensive guide for it, the Emperor designations continued as before.[57]

Aside from his pioneering effort to write a catalogue in which most of his Spanish holdings were somehow included, Sir Robert planned to sort the contents of selected volumes, which pertained to certain countries, into what was in effect an historical chronicle. Traces of this careful resorting of documents concerning France or Scotland, for example, can also be seen in some of those pertaining to Spain. To fill in important gaps in his files, he was prepared to read in the crown's official records and order transcriptions of significant supplementary letters to complete his information. Sir Thomas Wilson, at that time keeper of the records in the Tower of London, recalled that Cotton "perused and transcribed att dyvers times" many important letters in his custody.[58] While Cotton did not have the opportunity to complete a full documentary chronicle within the thirteen volumes of his collection in Vespasian C, he succeeded in annotating a least a five-volume sequence. This can now be identified as starting in Volume XII (documents from the mid-thirteenth to the fifteenth centuries) and continuing in Volumes I to IV (documents of the early sixteenth century). Although the later librarians, when numbering the volumes, had clearly not been faithful to observe Cotton's original chronicle, a reader may still discover a sequence of original charters, autograph letters, or his own seventeenth-century copies, placed in their correct order of dating. For further guidance many items have Cotton's brief note at the top of the first page of a document with a hand-printed title such as "*Hispania*," "*Castilia*," or "*Aragon*."

Further clues about Cotton's preferred arrangement for his Spanish papers may be seen in his list of the early loans made at the request of some important individuals before he moved to his new house at Westminster. Eager to read in volumes of his papers were Salisbury, Northampton, Ralph Winwood as secretary of state, Daniel Dune, a judge of the High Court of Admiralty, and even the count of Gondomar. These people either came in person or sent their secretaries to borrow papers for a time. In these cases Cotton recorded the volume with an informal title which was not to be used later in either of the first catalogues, yet they remain of value to show the first groupings of manuscripts. Here is found "My book of Spayne before the union bond [*i.e.* bound] in whit[e] and string. Foll," near to which was a second one called "my first book of Burgundy and Spayne in foll. White." In similar white parchment covers, these papers had been divided up according to their dating of before or after 1497, when the marriage of the infanta of Castile with a prince of Burgundy was agreed upon. At another request he loaned "Spayne the volume from *primo* [*anno*] Elizabeth," which was not the same as "a book of Spayne from 1568 to 1578." Inevitably the majority of his Spanish file of papers pertained to the sixteenth century and the relations of the Tudor dynasty with Charles V and Philip II. The only seventeenth-century title which he recorded was "My papers of Spayne since the Kings coming unbond in cover as many as would make a great book."[59] It is reasonable to ask whether the English *Letter* might have been placed here alongside other papers concerning contemporary Spain.

The friendly association of Cornwallis with Cotton after his return from Spain in 1609 is easily established. Opportunities to meet were abundant since as M.P.'s they were at the final session of the first Stuart parliament. Shortly afterward Cornwallis received a major court appointment, similar to that which his father had held in the reign of Queen Mary, as treasurer of the household of Prince Henry. Among the prince's inner circle, Cotton was a welcome figure too. Furthermore, each of them remained clients of Northampton and had more occasions to discuss contemporary diplomatic developments.[60] It is plausible to suggest that at this time Cotton became interested in the *Letter* since both he and Northampton would be curious to see the Jesuit's recent treatise, which had already been described in part in the ambassador's correspondence to London earlier. The *Letter* touched upon the controversial theme of James's policy toward English Catholics and even the Gunpowder Plot, about which Northampton especially would be alert to read further.[61] Sometime after this it is known that Cotton secured from the state papers a transcript of Creswell's letter to Robert Cecil, which had been written after the ratification of the treaty in 1605; it is edited here in the Appendix.

The date when Cornwallis presented the *Letter* to Cotton cannot be established, but there is a tantalizing hint in his cordial invitation to Cotton to dine with him in 1611. There is clear evidence of an exchange of documents following their meal:

> S^r, Yf yow shalbe pleased to doe me the favor to take a court dinner with me to morrow at St. Jams I shalbe very glad of yor company & wyll take yt kyndly. Those records yow told me of or some bryef of them, yf yow wyll also bryng wth yow, yow shall fynde that I wyll not retorne yow empty handed but wyll geve yow an exchange that perhaps wyll not dyscontent yow. And so in great hast I leave yow. Thys present Saturday 1611. Yo^r very assured lovyng frend Charles Cornwaleys[62]

This hurried note, with its nuance of other private convivial meetings, does show their shared satisfaction with important documents and that a gift from Cornwallis to the notable library occurred. Upon Prince Henry's death in November 1612, when Cornwallis lost his court appointment, there were fewer meetings since he was absent from London for most of 1613 as a member of the privy council's committee to meet the leaders of the Irish parliament in Dublin. After the death of Northampton in 1614,

Cornwallis and Cotton were seen to be frequent visitors at the residence of the Spanish ambassador, Diego Sarmiento de Acuña, later the count of Gondomar. The Spaniard, who was delighted with Cotton's interest in Spanish documents, provided him with significant items to copy from his personal library.

King James, who was well aware of their congenial conversations, briefed Cotton to become his intermediary in a new series of discussions about a marriage of Prince Charles with the Infanta Maria. Cornwallis, who had firsthand experience of the earlier talks in Madrid, was also on hand to speak about the matter. When their foray into informal diplomacy was halted abruptly by the protests of an anti-Spanish clique at court, the association of the two with Gondomar fell under suspicion. Accused for a time of passing secrets of state to the diplomat, both had to retire from court politics for the present. The Venetian ambassador heard a rumor that Sarmiento had been sending to Madrid "copies of all the papers of the ambassador Cornwallis,"[63] but there was in fact no basis for this sort of betrayal by either of them. However, what can now be inferred is that Cotton had a span of about six years, from 1610 to late 1615, to learn of the former ambassador's activities in Spain and receive papers of value from him including the *Letter* of Creswell.

That the *Letter* was already among Cotton's Spanish papers by the time the first catalogue was being written at the new residence at Westminster can be seen in some of the librarian's notes of the 1620s. In the cabinet under the bust of Julius Caesar, on a shelf marked "F" in the sixth volume, was a collection of documents mainly pertaining to Mary Queen of Scots. Cotton had shown considerable interest in her captivity in writing additional chapters for an edition of William Camden's *Annales* which appeared in 1615. In this volume in Julius F is a two-page anthology by an unidentified reader concerning recent Catholic polemicists which has three excerpts from Creswell's *Letter*. These concern his comments (nos. 45, 46, 47) that certain plots had been discovered in the reign of Elizabeth so as to frighten her against Catholics. Then the same reader copied out some later sentences from another paragraph (no. 57), where he charged that some of the attendants of the Queen of Scots had been said to have asked for a reward after betraying her.[64] At the top of the first folio of these quotations, one of the librarians, knowing the source, had added "*ex defensione Creswellij ad C. Cornwallis,*" or "from Creswell's defense to C. Cornwallis." This suggests that the *Letter*, which was placed among the Spanish papers in Vespasian C XIII, was then familiar to the staff and being consulted by Cotton's readers, probably because it still had its title page.[65] In any case, what was printed in the full *Catalogue* of the Cotton Library in 1802 was the following anomaly. For Julius F VI the excerpts of the *Letter* were aptly described as "A paper of depositions in vindication of the Roman Catholics etc. said to be by Creswell and [*sic*] C. Cornwallis," while the original in Vespasian C XIII became only "a long polemical discussion of some English Catholic (probably a Jesuit) concerning the reformation in England, from Jesus del Monte, a convent in Spain."[66] It is now possible to set the record straight with Cotton's original identification.

IV. The *Carta escrita al Embaxador de Inglaterra* in the Biblioteca Nacional, Madrid

According to the evidence already seen, this unique printed copy of Creswell's translation into Castilian of the *Letter* appeared in the autumn of 1606. It was probably printed in Madrid, although the printer has not been identified. On its title page and fol. 2, it has the seals of the Biblioteca Real, which indicate that it was previously part of the private collection of the Spanish monarchy in the Palacio Real del Oriente. There is no notation in its pages or on its cover of any other collector. It may be recalled that in 1734 there was a disastrous fire in the Alcázar, the old palace in which the previous rulers had once housed a part of their famous collections of art, manuscripts, and books. The library of the current palace, completed in 1764, as part of the official court of Spain, owes many of its important acquisitions to the keen interest of Charles III (1759–1788) and more particularly Charles IV (1788–1808). The early history of this copy of the *Carta* is virtually impossible to trace. What is certain is that after Queen Isabel II (1833–1868) founded the royal public library in 1836, which later became the Biblioteca Nacional, the *Carta* was one of the numerous manuscripts and rare books bequeathed to the Spanish people by the monarchy during the nineteenth century.[67]

The book was printed on forty-seven folios numbered on *recto* only, or ninety-four pages in total. Creswell kept the same ninety-two numbered sections as in his original English text. This book is bound in a light-colored, well-preserved parchment cover, more typical of the early eighteenth century. It has two thin straight lines in gold ink drawn along the four borders of the front and back,[68] with its shortened title "*Carta al Embaxador de Inglaterra*" lettered in black ink by hand on the spine (signatura 3-6463).

V. The Edition of the Two Texts

Creswell made small additions and omissions occasionally to his Spanish translation. The omissions have been indicated in the footnotes to the *Letter*. His Spanish additions have been translated by the editor and inserted near where they occurred in this English text with a symbol (★★★) for the reader. The original page size of the *Carta* was small: 5½″ wide by 7⅞″ long (14 × 20 cm).

The English manuscript (Vespasian C XIII, fols. 342^r–371^v) is fifty-eight folios in a clear, uniform early seventeenth-century secretarial hand, which is not Creswell's own handwriting. There are occasional erasures and a few minor additions of a word apparently by Creswell himself. The paper is thin, white, and unwatermarked, but there are chain lines visible in it. Its quality is comparable to that in use at the Spanish court at this time. The folios are uniform in size, approximately 8¼″ wide by 12″ long (21 × 30 cm). The copyist wrote thirty-three lines per page in about a 6″ width (15 cm), using fifteen signatures of four folios each. Originally they were numbered consecutively, but a later clipping by an early binder has left only a few of the signature numbers visible: for example, "2" on fol. 344^r, "10" on fol. 360^r, "12" on fol. 364^r. After the cover page was lost, the first folio has become slightly soiled. Some early readers of this copy have left a trefoil, or cloverleaf design, in the margins of fols. 355^r, 355^v, 357^r, near Sections 34, 35, and 38 which concern the role of religion in strengthening a subject's due obedience to his prince. These signs of interest by early readers can also be seen in other contemporary papers relative to the library of Sir Robert Cotton.[69]

The original spelling has been preserved as far as possible, except where clarity would suggest: "j" for "i" in "joye," not "ioye"; "F" for "ff"; "v" for "u" in "love." Contractions have been expanded.

The folios of the present Vespasian C XIII pagination have been placed in square brackets. Within both the Spanish and English texts, there are Latin quotations which are translated and identified in the footnotes. Creswell's Latin biblical references have been translated where appropriate in the words of the Douai-Rheims version of the New Testament, which was first published in 1582 and 1600. Although the Douai college version of the Old Testament did not appear until 1609/1610, it has been used in order to be consistent and to retain its typical contemporary English vocabulary.

NOTES

1. Bibliographical details of Creswell's Spanish books are in A. F. Allison and D. M. Rogers, *The Contemporary Printed Literature of the English Counter-Reformation Between 1558 and 1640. I. Works in Languages Other Than English* (Aldershot: Scolar Press, 1989), pp. 40–43 (hereafter Allison and Rogers).

2. Some notable examples include Thomas Clancy, *Papist Pamphleteers: The Allen–Persons Party and the Political Thought of the Counter-Reformation in England 1572–1615* (Chicago: Loyola University Press, 1964); Arnold Pritchard, *Catholic Loyalism in Elizabethan England* (Chapel Hill: University of North Carolina Press, 1979); Peter Holmes, *Resistance and Compromise: The Political Thought of the English Catholics* (Cambridge: Cambridge University Press, 1982); J. P. Sommerville, *Politics and Ideology in England* (London: Longmans, 1986).

3. *Historia ecclesiastica del scisma del Reyno de Inglaterra* . . . (Madrid, 1588), with a *Segunda Parte de la historia del scisma* . . . (Alcalá, 1593). Ribadeneira relied upon information provided by Nicholas Sander and Robert Persons. Its numerous printings are identified in Allison and Rogers (see note 1), pp. 138–39. The significant role of Ribadeneira at the Spanish court is shown in Robert Bireley, *The Counter-Reformation Prince: Anti-Macchiavellianism or Catholic State Craft in Early Modern Europe* (Chapel Hill: University of North Carolina Press, 1990), pp. 111–35.

4. The specific issues, with the authors, dates, and titles of the contemporary debates during which Creswell wrote, are described in Peter Milward, *Religious Controversies of the Jacobean Age: A Survey of the Printed Sources* (London: Scolar Press, 1978), pp. 1–71.

5. John Stoye, *English Travellers Abroad, 1604–1667*, rev. ed. (New Haven: Yale University Press, 1989), pp. 233–44, has a full account of the ceremonies; Maurice Lee, *James I and Henry IV: An Essay in English*

Foreign Policy, 1603–10 (Urbana: University of Illinois Press, 1970), pp. 17–40, explains the treaty's significance to Europe.

6. David Loades, *The Reign of Mary Tudor* (London: Benn, 1979), pp. 70, 85, 102, 104, 108, 264; S. T. Bindoff, ed. *The House of Commons, 1509–58,* 3 vols. (London: Secker & Warburg, 1982), I. 708–709; D. MacCulloch ed., "The *Vita Mariae Angliae Reginae* of Robert Wingfield of Brantham," *Camden Miscellany XXVIII,* Camden Fourth Series 29 (London: Royal Historical Society, 1984), pp. 255–56, 296n32.

7. For his father's Catholicism, see P. McGrath and J. Rowe, "The Recusancy of Sir Thomas Cornwallis," *Proceedings of the Suffolk Institute of Archeology,* 28 (1961), 246–56; G. Anstruther, *The Seminary Priests.* I. *The Elizabethans, 1558–1603* (Ware: St. Edmund's College, 1968), pp. 88–90; D. MacCulloch, "Catholic and Puritan in Elizabethan Suffolk," *Archiv für Reformationsgeschichte,* 72 (1981), 247–61; for the Cornwallis estates, see A. Simpson, *The Wealth of the Gentry, 1540–1660* (Chicago: The University of Chicago Press, 1961), pp. 142–78; for Charles's attendance at Cambridge, see J. Venn and S. A. Venn, *Alumni Cantabrigenses,* 4 vols. (Cambridge: Cambridge University Press, 1922–1927), I, 399 and *Dictionary of National Biography.*

8. A. J. Loomie, *Spain and the Jacobean Catholics.* I. *1603–1612* (London: Catholic Record Society, 1973), pp. 26–63.

9. Linda L. Peck, *Northampton: Patronage and Policy at the Court of James I* (London: Allen & Unwin, 1982), pp. 104–106, 173–74, 196–97, 205–10; new details are in L. L. Peck, " 'For a King not to be bountiful were a fault': Perspectives on Court Patronage in Early Stuart England," *Journal of British Studies,* 25 (1986), 39–43.

10. The major events during his embassy at Madrid are found in the biography of his secretary; see Martin Havran, *Carolina Courtier: The Life of Lord Cottington* (Columbia: University of South Carolina Press, 1973), pp. 6–24; P.R.O. S.P. 94/12, fol. 163, "Instructions for Cornwallis being sent into Spain, 1605."

11. Henry E. Huntington Library, Ellesmere MSS. vol. 7, fol. 419, Cornwallis to Egerton, Valladolid, 24 Aug. 1605; the king's unusual absences are explained in P. Williams, "Lerma, Old Castile, and the Travels of Philip III of Spain," *History,* 73 (1988), 379–97.

12. A. J. Loomie, *The Spanish Elizabethans: The English Exiles at the Court of Philip II* (New York: Fordham University Press, 1963; repr. New York: Greenwood, 1983), pp. 182–229; A. Allison, "The Later Life and Writings of Joseph Creswell, S.J., 1556–1623," *Recusant History,* 15 (1979), 79–144.

13. Leo Hicks, ed., *Letters and Memorials of Father Robert Persons. S.J.* (London: Catholic Record Society, 1942), pp. 313–14, Persons to sec-

retary of duke of Parma, 24 Feb. 1588; pp. 361–63, "Special Instructions" for Holt and Creswell; Francisco de Borja de Medina, "Jesuitas en la armada contra Inglaterra (1588); Notes para un centenario," *Archivum Romanum Societatis Jesu*, 58 (1989), 3–42 and 29*n*96.

14. Paul L. Hughes and James F. Larkin, *Tudor Royal Proclamations.* III. *The Later Tudors, 1558–1603* (New Haven: Yale University Press, 1969), pp. 86–93; Joannes Pernius, *Exemplar literarum missarum e Germania ad D. Guilielmum Cecilium* (Antwerp, 1592) (Allison and Rogers [note 1], no. 275; Holmes, *Resistance* and *Compromise* (note 2), pp. 136–46.

15. E 838/137, Creswell to Philip II, 12 Sept. 1596; his Spanish proclamation is translated in A. Loomie, "Philip II's Armada Proclamation of 1597," *Recusant History*, 12 (1974), 216–25. In the edge of his Spanish version he added: "for many reasons its seems best not to indicate the right of the Lady Infanta until the Catholic party is superior." For the lack of reliance on the Catholics among Philip's councillors, see A. Loomie, "The Armadas and the Catholics of England," *The Catholic Historical Review*, 59 (1973), 385–403.

16. Diego de Yepes, *Historia Particular de la Persecucion de Inglaterra* (Madrid, 1599) (Allison and Rogers [note 1], no. 284). David Rogers, in his introduction to the reprint (London: Gregg, 1971), has identified several authors whose books were included.

17. A. J. Loomie, "Philip III and the Stuart Succession in England, 1600–1603," *Revue Belge de Philologie et d'Histoire*, 43 (1965), 492–514, and *Guy Fawkes in Spain: The 'Spanish Treason' in Spanish Documents, Bulletin of the Institute of Historical Research,* Special Supplement no. 9 (1971); Jenny Wormald, "Gunpowder, Treason, and Scots," *Journal of British Studies*, 24 (1985), 141–68.

18. *Informacion a la ciudad de Sevilla por parte del Colegio Ingles de la misma ciudad* (Seville, 1604); see Allison and Rogers (note 1), no. 279.

19. R. Persons, *A Relation of the King of Spaines receiuing in Valliodolid and in the Inglish College of the same towne* . . . (1592). Thomas James prepared a Spanish translation of this (Allison and Rogers [note 1], no. 899), which was reprinted in Yepes, *Historia Particular,* to reach a wider audience at court (see note 16).

20. See Appendix for complete text of Creswell's letter to Cecil, 20 June 1605.

21. B.L. Cotton MSS., Vespasian C IX, fol. 102, Cornwallis to Cecil, 8 Sept. 1605.

22. E 2512, fol. 47, Creswell's draft, "Carta al Rey de Inglaterra," 24 June 1605. See the *Letter,* no. 71, for his praise of Henry IV again.

23. E 2512, fol. 48, *consulta*, 17 Sept. 1605.

24. Archive of the Society of Jesus, Rome, Castilla, Epistolae Patris

Generalis, vol. 7, fol. 149ᵛ, Acquaviva to the P. Provincial of Castile, 22 Aug. 1605. B.L. Harleian MSS. 1875, fols. 292ᵛ–293ᵛ, Cornwallis to Creswell, 23 Dec. 1605.

25. P.R.O. S.P. 94/12, fol. 128ʳ, Cornwallis to Cecil, Valladolid, 26 Nov. 1605. B. L. Cotton MSS., Vespasian C IX, fol. 408ᵛ, Cornwallis to Cecil n.d. (May? 1606); B. L. Stowe MSS. 168, fol. 301ʳ, Cecil to Edwards, 22 Jan. 1606. This proclamation was for "the apprehension and discoverie of John Gerrard, Henry Garnet and Oswald Tesimond," 15 Jan. 1606. See J. Larkin and P. Hughes, *Stuart Royal Proclamations. I. 1603–24* (Oxford: Oxford University Press 1973), pp. 131–34.

26. The contemporary term "recusant" described those who refused (Latin: *recusare*) to attend the official services with the Book of Common Prayer. Legally, either "Popish" or other Protestant non-conformists were included, but usually the Catholics were meant. Martin Havran, *The Catholics in Caroline England* (Stanford: Stanford University Press, 1962), pp. 1–17, has a convenient summary of the Elizabethan and early Stuart penal codes; Wallace Notestein, *The House of Commons, 1604–1610* (New Haven: Yale University Press, 1971), pp. 145–60, has excerpts of the debates in parliament preceding the statutes of 1606. John Miller, *Popery and Politics in England, 1660–1688* (Cambridge: Cambridge University Press, 1973), pp. 51–66, identifies the later legislation. A review of the entire code of the sixteenth to eighteenth centuries in England, Scotland, and Ireland is found under "Penal Laws," *The New Catholic Encyclopedia*, vol. XI, pp. 62–68.

27. See J. Anthony Williams, "Sources for Recusant History (1559–1771) in English Official Archives," *Recusant History*, 16, No. 4, (1983), 367–82, for litigation over confiscated recusant estates in the Exchequer and Treasury Rolls.

28. Milward, *Religious Controversies* (note 4), pp. 89–119, describes the different stages of the debate on the oath in England. A. F. Allison has recently established that Creswell did not write, as formerly believed, the 1610 attack on King James's penal policies in Spanish, *Vando y Leyes de rey Jacobo de Inglaterra* (see Allison and Rogers [note 1 above], p. 42), or its English original, *A Proclamation . . . with a briefe and moderate answer,* also 1610; see A. F. Allison, "Did Creswell Write the Answer to the Proclamation of 1610?" *Recusant History*, 17, No. 4 (1985), 348–57.

29. E 2512, fol. 121, *consulta*, 12 Aug. 1606, on letters of Zúñiga of 22 June and 18 July 1606.

30. For the returns from recusancy fines, see John La Rocca, "James I and His Catholic Subjects, 1606–1612: Some Financial Implications," *Recusant History*, 18 (1987), 251–62, and " 'Who Can't Pray with Me Can't Love Me': Toleration and the Early Jacobean Recusancy Policy," *Journal of British Studies*, 23 (1984), 22–36, for a possible mitigation in

official policy. Both archbishops of Canterbury, Bancroft and Abbot, complained of James's negligence in enforcement of the penal statutes; see Kenneth Fincham, *Prelate as Pastor: The Episcopate of James I* (Oxford: Oxford University Press, 1990), pp. 46, 60, 61, 303.

31. E 2571, fol. 180, Philip to Zúñiga, Escorial, 3 Sept. 1606; earlier letters concerning Spanish payments are in Loomie, *Spain and the Jacobean Catholics* (note 8), pp. 55–58, 81–82, 87–88.

32. B.L. Cotton MSS., Vespasian C IX, fol. 411ʳ, Cornwallis to Cecil, 3 June 1606 and fol. 586ʳ, Cornwallis to Cecil, 16 Nov. 1606, E 2512, fol. 130, Cornwallis to Spanish Council of State, B. L. Cotton MSS., Vespasian C V, fols. 55ʳ–56ᵛ, copies.

33. B. L. Cotton MSS. Vespasian C V, fols. 59ᵛ–60ᵛ, Second petition to Spanish council. He enclosed E 2512, fol. 129, *Las Leyes nuevamente hechas en el Parlamento de Inglaterra este año de MDCVI contra los Catolicos Ingleses que llaman Recusantes traduzidas de su original impreso en Ingles*, 8 pp. (Allison and Rogers [note 1], no. 1342.2). The English book to which the title referred was *Ano Regni Iacobi regis Angl . . . 3°, Scotiae 39° at the second Session of Parliament* (London, 1606) STC 9502. This Spanish version was an abridgement of twenty-eight articles of chapter IV and of nineteen in chapter V.

34. E 2512, fol. 128, "Apuntamientos sobre las glosas marginales del Embaxador." In a *consulta* of 23 December 1606 Juan de Idiáquez of the council of state called this "el papel que Jacobo Wadesfort (que es el ministro que se conbirtio) dio al Secretario Andres de Prada respondiendo a las anotaciones del Embaxador." (In *Guy Fawkes in Spain*, I erred in ascribing this to Creswell.) James Wadesworth I (ca. 1572–1623) had disputations with the Jesuits at St. Alban's College in Valladolid in the autumn of 1605 and then left to stay in Salamanca where he professed Catholicism. Cornwallis thought he left his post as chaplain "perhaps through discontent of a shrewd wife, a burthen of children and a benefice unequal to his desires" (*Winwood Memorials*, II, pp. 109, 131; James Wadesworth II, *The English Spanish Pilgrime* [London, 1630], pp. 1–4). He then received denization as a Spanish subject and a royal pension while he assisted Creswell until 1610. After serving as an inspector of English ships in Andalucía for the Inquisition, in 1612 he was appointed consul of English merchants in Seville. See A. Loomie, "Thomas James, the English Consul of Andalucia," *Recusant History*, 11 (1972), 174–75; *Dictionary of National Biography*.

35. Nicholas Oursley was born in Bristol in 1557 and brought to Spain in 1565 (P.R.O. S.P. 94/2, fol. 86). He became a merchant's factor and then an agent for Walsingham and Burghley during the war. He served as a secretary for Cornwallis from 1605 until the summer of 1608 when he was dismissed "for his bad behaviour and condition" (*Winwood Memorials*, II, p. 464; III, p. 37).

36. Archivio Segreto di Vaticano, Rome, Fondo Borghese, Serie Ia, vol. 308bis, fols. 46, 76, letters of 16 May 1606 from Scipione Caffarelli, Cardinal Borghese.

37. It is likely that the friendship of Creswell with the duke of Infantado came through his long association with Jane Dormer, the dowager duchess of Feria. Her son, the second duke of Feria, was married to doña Isabel Mendoza y Enríquez, the daughter of the duke of Infantado. In the catalogue of the Jesuit Province of Toledo, this country house, "*Residentia Jesus Montani*," had a staff of three Jesuits at this time.

38. "Disquisitio de modo quo maxime juvari possint Catholici in Anglia," holograph draft of Creswell endorsed "Nuncio 1606," Archive of St. Alban's College, Valladolid, Manuscripts, Series II, legajo 2, fols. 18–19.

39. B.L. Cotton MSS., Vespasian C IX, fols. 617^r–617^v, copies, Cornwallis to Privy Council and to Robert Cecil, n.d. (Nov.? 1606).

40. E 2512, fol. 131, *consulta*, 23 Dec. 1606.

41. B.L. Cotton MSS. C IX, fol. 662^r, Cornwallis to Cecil, 6 Feb. 1607 (see also *Winwood Memorials* II, pp. 155, 441). Although Wise's new translation does not appear to have been printed, the English council was disturbed by the printing of *Las Leyes*. Boderie, French ambassador in London, related that Cecil had an angry interview with Zúñiga over printing of books that make the penal laws odious. He replied that he was unaware of any such publication (*Ambassades de Monsieur de la Boderie en Angleterre . . .* , 5 vols. [Paris, 1750], II, p. 277, letter of 21 Feb. 1607).

42. B.L. Cotton MSS., Vespasian C X, fol. 42^r, Cornwallis to Northampton, 5 April 1607. This book was *A True and Perfect Relation of the Proceedings . . . of the late most barbarous traitors . . .* (London, 1606), STC 11619.

43. B.L. Additional MSS. 39853, fols. 83^v–84^r, Cornwallis to Spanish Council of State, 26 May 1607; B.L. Cotton MSS, Vespasian C X, fols. 152^v–154^r, 163^r, Cornwallis to Cecil, 29 Aug. 1607.

44. Cornwallis later reported on his talks with Lerma in 1607–1608 in his "Relation of the Carriage of the Marriages that should have been made between the Prince of England and the Infanta Mayor," printed in *Somer's Tracts*, ed. Walter Scott, 13 vols. (London, 1809–1815), II, 492–501. He also sent two "discourses" to the privy council in London in support of the alliance (B.L. Cotton MSS. Vespasian C X, fols. 180^v–188; P.R.O. S.P. 94/4, fol. 265).

45. B.L. Cotton MSS., Vespasian C X, fol. 579^r, Cornwallis to Privy Council, n.d. (May? 1608).

46. In April 1607 the privy council ordered Sir Arthur Chichester, lord deputy of Ireland, to end rigorous enforcement of the penal laws

against Irish Catholics (Colm Lennon, *The Lords of Dublin in the Age of the Reformation* [Dublin: Irish Academic Press, 1989], pp. 182–83, 317). Subsequently there was widespread non-conformity in the Pale for over a decade.

47. *Winwood Memorials* II, pp. 344–45, Cornwallis to Privy Council, 7 Oct. 1607. Creswell occasionally sent messages by the embassy's secretary, Francis Cottington.

48. B. L. Cotton MSS., Vespasian C X, fols. 265^r–271^r and 282^v–286^r, Cornwallis to Cecil, 10 and 18 Jan. 1608.

49. Creswell enrolled in the English College in Rome on 5 Nov. 1580, when Fr. Persons was its rector. In the *Carta*, no. 17 (written in Oct. 1606), he originally referred to himself "en veinte cinco anos que soy su subiecto," which implied his role of subject for the twenty-five years. E 2587, fol. 46, Zúñiga to Philip, Highgate, 23 Nov. 1609; and fol. 93, Velasco to Philip, London, 14 June 1610.

50. The surviving inventories of the earliest decades of the library are explained in Colin G. C. Tite, "The Early Catalogues of the Cottonian Library," *The British Library Quarterly*, 6 (1980), 144–57. The career of Cotton as antiquarian and collector is newly documented in Kevin Sharpe, *Sir Robert Cotton, 1586–1631: History and Politics in Early Modern England* (Oxford: Oxford University Press, 1979).

51. James Howell, ed., *Cottoni Posthuma* (London, 1651), "The Remonstrance of the Troubles," pp. 93–107; Roger Manning, "Antiquarianism and the Seigneurial Reaction: Sir Robert and Sir Thomas Cotton and Their Tenants," *Historical Research*, 63 (1990), 277–88.

52. Maija Jansson, ed., *Proceedings in Parliament, 1614*, Memoirs, American Philosophical Society, vol. 172 (Philadelphia, 1988), pp. 306–307.

53. A long, narrow room, 38 feet in length and 6 feet across, with a window at each end and the cabinets against the walls.

54. B.L. Additional MSS. 36789, fol. 174^v: "Latus Sinistrum, Scrinium 2, classis 5ta [Left side, second cabinet, fifth shelf]: *Item* another lesser bundle, being a punctual relacion of all the superior councells and tribunals, which ordinarily reside in the court of Spaine, as also the Chanceries and Audiences and the Tribunall of the Inquisition there, with all the tribunals depending thereon. *Item* the state of the Low Countries provinces which obey the king of Spaine, when they were possessed by the Infanta and the Archduke Albert. *Lastly* a large note of the distribution of the monies which Philip the second allowed the English Catholiks as they are called, residing in the provinces in the yeare 1570."

55. It contained a treatise describing how a monarch might achieve absolute power. For new details about the closure, see Tite, "Early Catalogues" (note 50) p. 147 and note 24.

56. B.L. Additional MSS. 36682 A and B. The final plan of this library with fourteen cabinets, each topped by a bust of the Twelve Caesars, Cleopatra, and Faustina, is described in Sharpe, *Sir Robert Cotton* (note 46), pp. 71–73.

57. See the important introduction by Colin G. C. Tite, ed., *A Catalogue of Manuscripts in the Cottonian Library, 1696, by Thomas Smith* (repr., Cambridge: Brewer, 1984), with an explanation of the later arrangements of the manuscripts before their arrival in the British Library in 1753 (pp. 1–15) and a translation of Smith's Latin biography of Cotton (pp. 25–58).

58. P.R.O. S.P. 45/20, fol. 133. I am indebted to Dr. Tite for this citation.

59. B.L. Harleian MSS. 6018, "A List of such books as I have this April (1621) lent out of my study," fols. 154^v, 155^v, 160^v, 174^v. With the exception of Gondomar, all the borrowers were deceased before late 1617. Salisbury used his secretary, "Mr. (Thomas) Wilson," and Gondomar used his English secretary, "Mr. (Henry) Fowler."

60. Peck, *Northampton* (note 9), pp. 104–105, 111–12, 191–92, 196–97; Sharpe, *Sir Robert Cotton* (note 46), pp. 120, 134, 157.

6. Northampton had been one of the commissioners presiding at the trials of Guy Fawkes and Henry Garnet, s.j. His lengthy speech at Garnet's trial was printed in *True and Perfect Relation of the Proceedings against . . . Garnet a Iesuite* (London, 1606). A Latin translation by Cotton's close friend William Camden was published the next year.

62. B.L. Harleian MSS. 7002, fol. 189^r. The writing of the date might read "1612." I am grateful to Dr. Tite for this citation.

63. For Cotton's diplomatic role see E 2594, fol. 3, Sarmiento to Lerma, London, 2 July 1615 (English translation in S. R. Gardiner, ed., *The Narrative of the Spanish Marriage . . .*, Camden Society, First Series, vol. 101 [1869], pp. 295–98). For Cornwallis see *Cal.S.P. Venet. 1615–17*, p. 95, Barbarigo to Doge, 31 Dec. 1615. See the List of Manuscripts below for the earliest descriptions of the four volumes of Cornwallis's papers from Spain, which became part of Cotton's Library.

64. B.L. Cotton MSS. Julius F VI, fols. 51^r–51^v. This early volume contains the signature of Sir Robert Cotton and a full table of contents, where vol. 466^r has "f.51 Creswell to Sr Charles Cornwallis."

65. B.L. Additional MSS. 36789 (the earlier "*Scrinia*" catalogue), fols. 133^r–133^v; the volume was called "A great booke conteyning many things of different subjects but greater part concerneth the Q. of Scots . . . ," followed by selected typical items. In the later inventory, B. L. Additional MSS 36682 (the "*Emperor*"), fols. 37^r–40^v, the full table of contents (as above, note 64) was copied out again.

66. Joseph Planta, ed., *A Catalogue of the Manuscripts in the Cottonian Library Deposited in the British Museum* (London, 1802), p. 468.

67. The Count of Las Navas, ed., *Catalogo de la Real Biblioteca*, 7 vols. (Madrid, 1910–1930), I, "Introduction," pp. i–cclxxi, discusses the earlier libraries of the Spanish crown. The article "Real Casa y Patrimonio de la Corona de España, "section IV, pp. 1035–37, in *Enciclopedia Universal Illustrada*, 70 vols. with supplements (Madrid: Espasa-Calpe), vol. 49 (1923), explains the link between the Biblioteca Real's collections and those of the Biblioteca Nacional in Madrid.

68. Creswell's *Historia de la Vida y Martirio que padecio . . . Henrique Valapolo* (Allison and Rogers [note 1], no. 276) in the Biblioteca Nacional (signatura R 26658), has an identical binding and the same seals of the Biblioteca Real as the Carta. This can be compared with the different binding of the copy formerly in the Colegio Imperial of the Jesuits (signatura R 31061).

69. Tite, "The Early Catalogues" (note 50), pp. 153n8, 155n45. The signs appear in Harleian 6018, Additional 35213, Additional 36682.

A Letter Written to the Ambassador from England

[342^r]   Right Honorable my very good Lord

1. Having observed your Lordships moderate proceedings at
your first cumming into theise cuntryes, I must needes confesse
the opinion that then I conceyved of their judgement and prudence, which had made choice of a person of such discretion, as
not withstanding he disagreed from us in religion yet was able
with his good cariage and curtesye, to set forward the correspondence alreadye begonne between princes of different professions,
satisfying in so difficult an occasion the charge and office of an
ambassador, which is to be an angell of peace and not of discord
as some others, who for want of those honorable respectes, which
your Lordship by your education and birth must needes acknol-
ege from your auncestores, and that regarde of conscience and
justice, which we see many tymes in men indued with morall
vertues, though otherwise deceyved in Religion, contrary to the
commandement of the Holy Ghost: *quaerunt iniquitatem in domo
Justi,*[1] and (not to seeme barren intelligences) laye hande upon
every surmize and tale which is tolde them. Yet wanting matter
they forge it themselves, and interpret good and indifferent
thinges to evill purposes, where withall they deceyve and abuse
those that believe them. As every daye maye be seene by their
publike actions, not so well grounded as were to be wished, by
which they come to loose the good opinion and affection (which
others had gayned) with hurt to themselves, and to the publike
state.

2. And whereas I have understoode by dyvers other experiences the sincere and honorable proceeding which your Lordship
doth use (as all ambassadors [342^v] should), and lastly by letters
receyved in Roome out of England from persons of good place,
that your honor had written to the king and counsell there, the
same which here you seemed to acknoledge, and testyfyed my
earnest desyre (manifest to you in divers occasions) to conserve
and set forward the friendship begonne between these two
princes. And how far off I am to doe wrong to any man whosoever, and much lesse to persons of that respect, to the ende that
your Lordship maye be assured and satisfied that you were not
deceyved in the saide good opinion and maye the better justifie

your former information if neede require, (in which, howsoever in other things I may be inferior to all, I professe and procure not to yeild unto any) to give your Lordship satisfaction in such thinges as it seemeth others have unadvisedly beleeved or invented of purpose, to put in doubt your Lordships good report, and the like, which by other waies maye have come to his Magestyes eares, by such as knowe better my affection to himselfe and his, then they which (without cause given on my part) have conceyved a different opinion.

But howsoever others maye be satisfied or offended, I were obliged to your Lordship for this your honorable proceeding. And consequently doe desyre that it maye please you to informe yourselfe of the truth, respecting little the censures and judgements of such as seeke it not, but only that which (true or false) may serve to their purposes, as maye well be seene by divers thinges thrust on without eyther grounds reason or order in Father Garnets late accusation, and some of them touching persons absent and innocent, and yet affirmed and exaggerated. As lawyers use to doe (many tymes for mony) in causes which they knowe to be unjust. And so I marvele the lesse considering who was the spokesman,[2] though I cannot but wonder greatly that the like thinge unprooved and unjustified, and so fouly mistaken as your Lordship shall understand, should be set out in the name of the parlament. And upon them grounded so many violent lawes and so contrary to all orderly dispositions of God and man, that they blemish the authority [343ʳ] of that honorable senate, in old tymes so grave and so worthyly respected at home and abroade, when there concurred (according to the institution and lawes of the same) true and lawfull bishopes, men of learning and conscyence, and noble men so zelous of their own honor, as they suffered not to appeare in that place any accusation or other matter veyled with the shadoe or tainted with the smell of injustice. And much lesse that any man unheard or unknowen should be condemned, only upon suspitions of spies and pickethankes.[3] And in the lower house those persons of the layetye and clergye which by right and custome, were to be present, not rulled out by canvase and particuler negotiation, but chosen by free and lawfull consent of their burroughes, cities and provinces, nor tied to any mans girdle to folowe his humors and dissignements, but with the freedome which that honorable court was wont to performe to every one, that without prejudice he might boldly speke his minde for the benefite of the commonwelth. But such have bene the changes which it hath suffered of tymes and persons, especyally of those who have falen from their ancestores faith, that it is not much that withall they have also changed their manner of proceeding, nor to be marveyled, that they which have broken fidelytye with God, do not mainteine justice with men.

3. Comming to Guadalajara, weary of a longe jorney and so sicke as I coulde not passe any farther, with the charitye of the good Duke and Dutches of Infantado, and the comoditye I found of diligent phisitians by theire appointment, I rested some daies in that city to recover my health where came to my handes a long processe and history[4] of all that had passed with the happie memory of Father Garnet, and another preiste of the Socyety lately martired in England. Which I red with so much comfort and joy that it was a greate cause of shortening my sickness, wondering on the one side at the fatherly providence of almighty God, and through what difficulties, labors and wronges, he caryeth his children to the participation of his glory, and on the other, at the blindness and temerity of those who dare strive [343ᵛ] against him and his truth, which prevayleth alwayes and getteth the upper hand, discovering all contrary inventions and theyre inventor and leaving them besooted and branded with markes of ignomynie, as they deserve.

4. Afterwardes comming to Jesus del Monte I receyved the statutes of this last parlament, in which appeareth the scope where to they be directed and out of what forge come the shakles and snares in which some procure to intangle that good prince, in no wise affecting him nor his children with true love of benevolence but with selfe love seeking to serve their turnes with his name and authority. As they and others served themselves for many yeares of the late Queene Elizabeth, keeping her as it were amazed with divers suspitions, shadoes, and feares where with all they would now also possesse his Magesty present, and bring him to the breach of his worde and promise given both to princes abroade (as from some of themselves I have understoode) and to his subjects at home, and oppresse the persons to whome he hath the greatest obligations that may be in this life, and finally soyle his handes with inocent bloud. For the present he is procuring to himselfe in all the world, and much more with posterity, an opinion and name so contrary to his condition, and so much by himselfe detested, as may appeare by his manner of proceedings in former times, before he fell into their handes which now pretend to governe him and make him partaker of theire passions and devises, which in no wise can come to good.

5. But to come nearer to that which doth concerne myselfe, it may please your Lordship to understand that they have done me notable injurye as may be proved by evidence and witnesses of much more authority then be the contryvers of these laste statutes. And the Atorney (as in many other thinges) spoke at randon[5] in those which he laide to my charge. For (as it is well knowne) I was not the author of that booke in which he grounded his whole accusation gainst me, and as many as have seene anything of mine in latine, and can judge, will be able to testifie that the book is not mine, seeing [344ʳ] men are knowen no lesse by different stiles then by different faces.[6] But what should I saye of this unadvised spokesman? When those of the Parliament itselfe were so far mistaken as shall appeare, or at least the inditers of the statutes not by them controuled and amended.

And it is lesse to be marveyled that such excesse was used against persons of meaner quality when it was extended with so little respect against his Catholike Magesty, and in a manner which not withstanding it had passed (as themselves would make men beleeve) yet in all wisedome they should have dessembled it, and forborne to harpe upon that string and so much the more, as theire supposition was false, and consequently the whole tale out of tune.

6. For your Lordship shall understand that not withstanding persons of authority and learning have judged that in lawe and conscyence his saide majestie and his might pretend right to the Crowne of England, yet I doe assure your Lordship it was a meere untruth, which the Atorney so boldly affirmed at the barre, and is supposed in the second statute[7] of the parliament that Mr. Thomas Winter, or any other, shoulde come to Spaine to move his Majestie to pretend any such right, or I helpe them in any such pretention, or the king to give eare to any such proposition, or shewe any such desire.

7. No: To the contrarye, his Majesty and the Duke of Lerma (whose testimony is to be preferred before a thousand such calumniations founded only in false surmizes) can not have forgot-

ten that in Aranjuez upon Saint Leocadias daye, the nineth of December in the yeare 1599, the king being then newly come to his crowne (to prevent his majesty and preocupate all contrary impression) I tolde him (the Duke being also present) that the Catholikes of England not withstanding they did esteeme and love his majesty as in all reason they ought, yet in no case would have him for theyre king, what title so ever he might pretend to the crowne. For that to neyther parte it could be profitable, to them nor to him, who already had kingdomes enough. And that in all tymes he should receyve more benefit by holding friendship and alliance with England, then if it were his owne and therefore that the Catholikes did only desyre (as to my knowledge they did and no further) that upon the death of Queene Elizabeth all discorde should ende with theire nighbors, and all robbery, piracye, and other [344ᵛ] wronges by which the warres were begonne and contynued should cease, and that God would give them a prince that might governe them as a father with love and justice, and mainteyne the good correspondence which in other tymes was wont to be betweene that kingdome and the rest of Christendome. The which proposition his majesty with his great integritye and zeale of the common good, did highly approve and like of, and the daye after the Duke confirmed the same with very affectuous wordes. And by that which the kinge since hath donne, consenting to the late peace in such manner as he did, it may well be understoode that this alwaies hath benne the intention not only of him and of his councell, but also of the Catholikes of England, of which your Lordship may enforme yourselfe further if you please.

8. Yea, more then this. I doe assure you that I could never discover that the late glorious memory of king Philip the second had any intention to possesse himself of England, or that he pretended any other effect (yea with his army 1588) then to remedye the injuries which his subiectes receyved by English pirates, and by those that nourished the rebellion in Flanders, and molested his Indies, and to help to reduce that kingdome unto the old honorable estate which it enjoyed in the times of our forefathers.[8] And in parte also to satisfie his own conscyence, for that perhappes he might thinke that the clemencye which he had used with some offenders, who afterwardes requited him but badly, hindering the execution of justice apointed by the Queene his wife and the councel against them, and some errors of his officers and the want of care to remedye divers thinges which were in theyre handes, whilest he governed that kingdome,[9] had bene some occasion that the same and the Lady Elizabeth who succeeded, did fall into theire handes who gave her counsell to seperate herselfe and her subjectes from the unity of Gods church and from the old honorable frindships of that crowne, and to enter into league with rebels and base people and beginne thouse bloudye tragedies at home. Which some would have his majesty that now is to continue and finally to set abroach manye other hurtfull novelties not seene nor hearde of before in that cuntrye, and so annoyous to theire nighbors, as might not only oblige one so provoked and injured by them as the kinge catholike had bene, [345ʳ] but any other Christiane prince to procure the remedye. And these have bene and be the true causes (for as much as I can understand) of the good will which the saide king always shewed to the Catholikes of our nation, and of his compassion in their calamityes and of the releefe which as well he, as the king that now is, (the worthy inheritor of his fathers obligations and virtues) hath given and still doth give them of whose royall munificence there are fewe nations under the sunne which, by one waye or other, doth not participate. And of the same causes above saide have proceeded the warres which the said Catholike kinges have had with our cuntrye, wherein we have alwaies bene instruments to procure mercye and lenitye whereof many of our cuntrymen by our meanes have tasted. And not of any desyre that they have had, for as much as I could ever perceyve, to intangle themselves with the government of that kingdome, having their handes so full and so many kingdomes alredy in them and under their care, as may suffice. Nor is it any other such purpose as some have procured to publish, and to make both our prince and people beleeve, having no other grounds for their surmizes but the advertizements of spies and the confessions of prisoners, which (God knowes) be but weake foundations where upon to build so strange and so publike consequences as they doe. Seing the one sort, to please the parties that mainteine them abrode, inlarge themselves many times beyonde the truth. And with tortures they drawe the others to what note they please and make them confesse many tymes for feare of torment, thinges which they never knewe nor thought of.

Besides that some use to publish (as in this last case of the Earles of Arundel, and Essex and many others we have seene) the confessions and other successes of persons imprisoned, before and after their deaths, contrary to truth; aleaging deade witnesses for such thinges as they would have beleeved,★★★ so as whatsoever your Lordship maye have hearde in this from that which is above saide, assure your selfe it is untruth.

9. And according to this, your Lordship shall understand, that the comming of Thomas Winter into Spaine towardes the end of Queen Elizabethes raigne, was only to procure some lawfull and convenient meanes for [345^v] the Catholikes, that when the Queene should dye, in the confusion that then was justly feared, they might not be runne and oppressed with violence of theire adversaries.[13] Which might seem a necessarye providence of those that sent him, for theire owne security and for the safety of many others and benefit of the kingdome and prince which should afterwardes succeede, and where unto any other Christian prince might worthyly give eare. And the others that came after, came only to give accompt of that which had passed in England at the Queenes death, where seeing that his majesty that now

---

★★★The *Carta,* pp. 6^v–7^r, adds:

"As was done with the Earl of Arundel of illustrious memory, by charging him with writing letters to the Duke of Guise and with other matters which were later proven to be false and the inventions[10] of his enemies. And in a similar fashion the Lord Deputy of Ireland, Sir John Perrott, was disgraced after the accusation by a Calvinist minister who, having fled England on account of his crimes was arrested in Ireland, and while he was in prison plotted the death of the same Lord Deputy, and although it is contrary to the law that a person without legal standing would be permitted to give testimony, and even more so one known as the principal enemy of the person accused, despite all this they condemned the Lord Deputy through his testimony, wherein the fabrications[11] of another person were published abroad as true and proven things. And what is even more to this point is that which they did to the Earl of Essex to whom, when imprisoned they sent his Puritan chaplain named Ashton, under pretence of offering him comfort. After the earl's death they forced him to produce a confession, which they said was that of the earl's, filled with imagined and false things, which indeed that poor man admitted in tears to the same earl's various friends who had thus accused him, alleging as his excuse the influence of the people who had forced him to do this with promises of advancement and reward and through threats, if he should not want to do so. The one who related this to me was a person of authority who heard it from Ashton[12] himself. Since this way of acting is held suitable by our adversaries for maintaining their regime, and happens as often as their daily bread, as is known and has been seen in this last case, no credence is to be given to whatever they publish unless it is proven true by other means."

reyneth had entered, not only with good liking but with aplause of the Catholikes, and with the hopes they had conceyved and he given, that they shoulde finde him a meeke just and indifferent prince, as no lesse could be presumed of so goode a mother, and having alredye pledged the faith and promise of a king to intreate them well. With these considerations and of the good correspondence which had bene alwaies betweene these Catholike princes and him, whiles he was king of Scotland, which this king present was inclyned to continue for his parte, with the affection that seemed due to him, for his owne and his mothers respect, and the many good offices which he had receyved (in his owne persone to keepe him from violence in his tender yeares, and in the persone of his saide mother of glorious memory to the end that shee and he might come to succeede in the Crowne of England) both of these Catholike kinges and of the Sea Apostolike, and most of all of the Catholikes of England, for the which it seemed that his magesty in obligation of humanity, setting all other respectes aside though he were a panime and no Christian prince, could in no wise fayle to be thankefull, all men of wisedome and honourable respectes did presume and with greate reason, that God almighty had sufficiently provided as well for the security of the Catholikes as for the quietnes of the whole kingdome, and that therefore there rested no more to be donne for the one nor for the other.

10. Your Lordship may see in what plaine termes I discover unto you this whole matter, for according to the saying of the holy Ghost: *est tempus loquendi et tempus tacendi,*[14] and now it seemeth tyme to speake. And how soever others procede and suspect all mens intentions according to theire owne measuring the world, each one by his owne foote, Catholikes, as well [346ʳ] princes as others that governe and are governed by conscyence, doe not give eare nor consent to any thinge how secret so ever it be, that may not be published in time convenient, with commendation. Whereby it may apeare with how little discretion was foysted into that longe idle speech the worde *Spanish Treason* so offensive to honest mens eares, so contrary to reason and truth, so ill beseeming that honorable audience, that as well the procurers as the spokesmen, for it seemed that he came with his lesson without booke, did discover themselves to be enemies to the peace with Spaine and consequently to theire king and cuntrye.

And so I can not but wonder how the Lordes of the Counsell present did not rebuke and put to silence one that used so bad language, and durst speake with so little respect of the persons he touched in that assembly.

11. But of theire publike speches and actions may be gathered something of that which they practice in secret. And these be the enemies of peace who would intangle the kingdome againe with robberies and warres, and therefore procure to put the king and his counsell into disconfidence with his Catholike subjects, and raise such false aprehentions against his holines and other princes, and in particular against priestes of the seminaries and Jesuites, as though we were not more frindes to the king and kingdome a thousand times then they. As is evident, seing all that wee labor and suffer even to the shedding of our bloud is meerely for charity and for the common good, yea of the persecutors themselves, if they will understand it, and without hope, yea without possibility as all men maye see, of temporall rewards. In which only is founded the shewe of good will and fidelity to his magesty by many of our persecutors that folowe him and faune upon him, filling and fatting themselves with the spoyle and pillage of theyre nighbors, and care not if his magesty breake with all the world so they sucke out the foysen[15] of the land and leave their families increased and advanced, some of them devouring the revenewes of the church, which I wish they enjoyed and a greate deale more so they forced not men to iniquity, and others preying upon the poor Catholikes goodes, now that they can not goe and send abroad [346ᵛ] to mainteine theire prodigality by roving.[16]

12. For these and the like causes (forsooth) it is with them so criminall a matter to be a Catholike, and under this title they raise so manye callumniations against innocent persons and against Christs successor and substitute in the government of our soules as though his holines were their enemye, or would take anything from them and not give them much more, as most willingly he would upon condition they would doe well. But this hath bene in all ages and still will be and is a naturall thing, that as the sheepe love and folowe theire shephard, so the foxes and other ravenous vermine flye from him and abhorre him.

These that be so greate enemies to the pope and persecute so violently the Catholikes, if they would returne to Christes folde in which theyre forfathers most happily lived and died, they shoulde finde theire hatred to his holynes presently changed into love and respect, and theire rapine into innocensye and these suspitions and surmizes where withall now they trouble themselves and disquiet the king, would cease, the subject from whence they come being removed.

13. To which purpose and that themselves maye the better understand how far they goe astraye, I beseech your Lordship to consider how violent and absurd a thing it is, and how evill taken and reprooved by all wise mens judgements at home and abroad, to cover injustice with the change of wordes. They are calling the misteries of theyre ancestors faith *tresons*, the use and administrations of the holy *sacraments* (without which there can be no Christianity, Religion nor Church) *practices against the state*, priestes, *traytors*, Catholikes, *fellons*, *fellony* to receyve them into theire howses, and such other like. And they not only alter the true and proper significations of wordes, wresting them to unnaturall sences, but turne up side downe all the olde lawes and well ordered government of that kingdome and invent so many novelties that serve only for snares where into intrappe the pore subjectes and take from them theyre goodes and their lives, for doing their dutyes to God. And for that it maye appeare how short, unproper and disproportionate meanes these be for the endes which the persecutors pretend, your Lordship is to [347ʳ] understand first, that in all ages and places the bloud of martirs hath bene the seede of the church, for that as Saint Leo saith and before him Tertulian, *Grana singula cadunt et multiplicata nascuntur*[17] and secondly, that this was the follye of the heathen Emperor and of olde persecutores who some of them with violence, and some with crafte, and others (as Valens and Julian the Apostate both together) were persuaded that everye one of them in his time could make an end of the Catholikes. But God almighty brought them to theire endes, as he hath alredye manye of our persecutors in England and all of them are laide up for the daye of judgement, when they shall be restored to suffer in their bodyes, and in the meane tyme in theyre soules they goe paying the penalties due to theire hatred and persecution against Gods church which being purified and renewed by the same persecutions, did alwaies increase and growe more stronge, as all histories and much more her present greatenes and magesty doe make evident to whome soever doth not shut his eyes by voluntary blindnes.

14. Wherefore, we can not loose that confidence by which our forefathers from the beginning have overcome all the enemyes of truth, nor *feare the anger of those who when they have taken from us our temporal life can doe no more* [Lk 12]. It being one of manye other thinges little esteemed by Catholikes who live not by sense but by faith, when in lewe and with losse thereof,[18] wee maye gaine life ever lasting and the crowne of martiredome. And the cause for which we suffer is such, as for it (without losse) we maye loose not only every man his life, but many lives if we had them, being sure that neyther the power of man or of hell itselfe can doe against us more then God doth permit them, who never permitteth but that which (finally) is to turne to our greater benefit and his greater glory.

Besides[19] I would your Lordship and by you others should understand, that this confidence and patyence of those who suffer for true religion is not founded only in discourse or hope of future rewarde and felicitye. But the very persecution and affliction it selfe though it presse and molest the bodye with greefe, yet if it finde the soule disposed as [347ᵛ] it should, it dilateth it and giveth it strength and worketh in it such inward consolation and present joye, as it maketh the exterior losses and paines not only tollerable but joyful also. For they be the matter, foode and nourishment of that divine and supernaturall comforte which (as the Apostle saith) sensuall and carnall men cannot imagine, for that it is above theire understanding and indeede no man understandeth it, more or lesse as the meanes and measure of his suffering deserveth. Which was the reason that the olde persecutors were so astonished to see Christian religion increase with persecution, admiring the constancye of all sortes of Christians, men, women and children, and that they suffered the greatest torments not only with patience but with joye, not knowing this secret that *Gaudium Domini est fortitudo nostra*,[20] as if a man should cast oyle into the fire and marveyle to see it burne the faster, not knowing that it is the fires naturall foode. Finally all that which in this and in other former persecutions hath passed for foretolde by Christ our Saviour to comforte and strengthen his servants and dispose them to live as persons forwarned and redy to suffer all that was to befall them. As for example that they should be troubled and vexed for his sake, not only by strangers and enemies but by theire owne cuntrymen and domesticall frindes, and be betrayed by false brethren and caried before the judgment seates of princes and other majestrates, and as malefactors, slandred, accused and condemned, as himselfe was by Pilate by the procurement of the ungratefull falseharted Jewes and theire scribes, Pharises and heades of the people who tooke upon them to be statesmen and to represent the whole ecclesiasticall and temporall bodye of that wretched and unfortunate commonwealth. By whose avarice and ambition the sonne of God, theire owne Messias, through error and false reasons of state was betrayed and delivered up to the most cruell and infamous death that could be devised. And yet for all this, he bad us be of good cheere and not loose hart but trust in him, seeing all that men can doe against us, is but a blast that quickly over bloweth and frighteth, but hurteth not such as will helpe themselves with [348ʳ] spirituall helpes and not over runne Gods providence with human desyres. For we have an infallible promise that when all is ended, we shall finde our selves not only without harme or losse of one heare of our heads but by our suffering much bettered with vertues upon earth and joyes in heaven. And in the meanetyme *induimur virtute ab alto*[21] and are animated with a thousand examples. *Sufferentiam Job audistis* (saith Saint James) *et finem Domini vidistis.*[22] Wherefore feeling that which we feele and knowing before hand what is to folowe we rejoyce being persecuted and wee take it for the greatest honor, and holde ourselves for most happie when for this cause our adversaries doe slander us and forge false testimonies against us, torment us and put us to death. For all these wronges which we suffer are pledges of our salvation and assurances that God doth love us. And so we praye continually for those that persecute us, as for our greatest benefactors desyring his divine magesty from the bottome of our hartes *ut non statuat illis hoc peccatum.*[23]

15. And to saye something more in particuler to your Lordship in this matter, and certifie you more plainely how vaine theire suspitions are, and how far from the truth and from my disposition and cogitation those thinges be, which the Atorney and his consortes would make the king and others beleeve against me, I will here set downe (to Godes glory) the mercy that I have receyved at his handes many yeares agoe, yea from my childhoode far above my desert where with I have lived, by his goodnes, without doing any man injury or harme, as many others also doe live, who be persecuted and reproached by the same persons. And I will speake only that which is knowen to many and in the presence of him who knoweth all and is not pleased but with truth, and although I would gladly excuse to speake of any thing concerning myselfe, yet here it seemeth necessarie: *et si in hoc fuero insipiens, vos me coegistis.*[24]

16. Your Lordship hath in parte seene how free I live by Gods goodnes and how far from all temporall hopes and desyres. For if I had any such in Spaine, I would not have left it so easyly and with some resistance and offence of those who, as your Lordship knoweth, would have excused my jorney to Roome. Where also, if I had founde any temporall thing to my liking, [348ᵛ] there wanted not persons of much authority desyrous to keepe me there, and his holines himselfe, and the cheefest about him, did use me with such curtesye, as I might have presumed of any favour at his hand.

The same I may saye of England, where I had many friends when I left it, and in particuler the persone who at that time could doe most in that kingdome and others of his rancke (not knowing me to be Catholike) did favor me. And for my estate I had more then I needed, so as, if I had esteemed anything eyther that I had or might have had in England, if longe agoe God almighty had not holpen me with his grace and taught me to treade under foote that which others wrest their conscyences to enjoye, and all that which I could desyre according to the discorses of the children of this world, I would not have left my cuntry with so good possibilityes so many yeares agoe, and without any necessity. For only the desyre to spend my tyme well, finding our English universities not fit for me being a Catholike recusant, and to enjoye more freely my conscyence and the sacraments and other benefites of my religion, and to flye from that which folowed me and others seeke after, was the first occasion of my comming abroade.

And truly, in this I rest with so greate obligation and so thankfull to the late queene deceased and her councelors, who (though indirectly by the generall persecution of Catholikes) did helpe my resolution to come out of England, that if I could with my temporall life delyver them from whence they be, I woulde thinke it well bestowed. Seing that by theire occasion I have enjoyed now more then twenty yeares in God almighties service, and received in his family (with that contentment of minde which your Lordship perhappes may have observed) manye inestimable benefites, the least of which I would not have changed in all this time, with the Crowne of England, so much the comfortes of the minde surpasse the pleasure of the bodye, and the inheritance that doth not ende is to be esteemed above that which passeth with time, which can not be greate, how greate so ever it seeme. And by this your Lordship may inferre how different mens cogitations and desyres be in this world, of each one according to his experience, and to the light and grace which he receyveth from above.

[349ʳ] **17.** Yet, this not withstanding I can not denye one particuler desyre that I have had, and have still, in England and is the only preferment which I have procured in my religion, as is well knowne to the Superior thereof. To whome divers tymes I have made instance to be sent thither during the persecution, and the only particuler favor that I can remember I have asked for my selfe in more then seaven and twenty yeares that I have bene his subject[25] and sixteen of them with protestation that, if he did not sende me in this tyme of necessity, when soever the church should come to have peace in that kingdome (when a persone of so meane talents as mine would not be missed) from that daye forward, I did disclaime that request offering my selfe for the Indies, or for Japan or for any other part of the world where the Christians are in the greatest spirituall necessityes. Which for the present the Catholikes of England in my opinion doe suffer more then any others, and therefore me thinke I should doe some service gratefull to Christ our Savior who bought them with his pretious bloud, if I could with the shedding of mine owne or with any other personall labor or danger, comfort so faithfull and loving servants so beloved by their maister, and so well deserving of his church and of their owne nation and cuntry that it is more esteemed in other partes for them and for their constancy in Christian religion, then for all the rest which hath passed in that kingdome since it was first inhabited by men. So as if I were master of mine owne will and at mine owne disposition, I would (God willing) be with them ere many dayes were past, not withstanding these newe lawes and all the harmes which could befalle me, only to be where I might doe them any little service and cooperate if it were but to the salvation of one only soule, of many which in these troublesome tymes live there in perplexity and danger for want of spirituall comfort.

18. And your Lordship must not thinke that in so doing I should doe any greate and extraordinary thing, nor that this desyre is singuler in me for many others have the same not only in the Socyety but in other Religions, and since these newe lawes much more vehemently then before, according to the grace and supernaturall light that God giveth every one whereby to judge truely of these matters. And not only Englishmen, who have more obligation [349ᵛ] then others to desyre the good of their cuntry, but many strangers also, zealous of the glory of Christ and salvation of soules, have the same desyres. But what doe I speake of religious men? Seing that to as manye as are brought up in the Seminaries, God giveth the same desyres. Yea, from their childhoode they have them and with them come out of England, not with intentions to doe hurt to any and much lesse to their prince or cuntry, for such cogitations can have no place in their innocencye and tender yeares, and to thinke it were eyther malice or ignorance. But they come to be instructed in true doctrine, flying as others have done before them, the unlawfull oathes and vexations which good men suffer in our universityes at home, and to get heroycall vertues which pass theire tyrall in overcomming difficulties.

19. As for example, heroycall faith which maketh us believe Gods wordes and promises though above the reach of our understanding, and is the foundation of all the rest; heroycall hope trusting most in Gods assistence in the greatest difficulties; heroycall charity by which men have hartes to suffer death for their nighbors salvation; heroycall humility by which we subjecte our willes and understandings wholy to God almighty and, for him, not only to those which may justly command us but to our equales and inferiors, as occasion shall require; heroycall longanimity which proceedeth of the same and giveth us comfort and strength to expect Gods visitations and not to be weary how longe so ever he seemeth to differe them, for that he only knoweth tymes and seasons convenient and doth all for the best.

20. Heroycall meekness by which we doe not only pardone but love our enemies, not seeking (as malice doth suggest) to shorten their dayes, but to prolonge them that they may repent, knowing that they live not, nor that God suffereth to live the most wicked man that breatheth upon earth without some good ende, *aut ut corigatur* (as Saint Augustine saith) *aut ut per eum bonus exerceatur.*[26] So, as some of our adversaries in this doe us more then wronge to charge us with conspiracyes against higher powers, which is wholy needles on our part and should be unadvisedly [350ʳ] thought of by us. Seing we have for our defense and protection, him that is lord of life and death, as the prophet saith *aufert spiritum principum*[27] when he pleaseth, and needeth no mans helpe to doe it when he seeth his tyme and doth it infallibly when it is convenient. So that for men to attempt any such thing and to anticipate Gods judgements could not be excused of error and sinne. And this is Catholike doctrine and not that which the children of falsehood and lies dreame and devise and would say upon us.

21. And finally they come to get heroycall fidelity which our Catholikes in England at this daye exercise more then any other people in the world, suffering some of them seasures and loss of their goodes, not only willingly but with joye, a thing so highly commended by the Apostle [Heb 10] in the tyme of the primitive church. And the rest induring banishment, infamy, torments and violent deathes, even to the pulling out of their loyall hartes out of their bodies, rather then they will transgresse the least pointe of many which their Lorde and master left them and their ancestors in trust more than 1600 yeares agoe, *et hoc est semen quod dedit nobis Dominus,*[28] which is not in mans power to hinder in that it growe not and give frute.

22. And to the ende it may so doe and that, with such examples of constancy and fidelity Christ our Saviour and his father may be glorified, as they are now in England in the highest degree that may be imagined upon earth, and many Catholikes in all cuntryes incoraged to doe their dutyes and others that sleepe in errors and sinne be wakened, especyally in our cuntry where we see not only multitudes of harmeless soules dayly converted, but the greatest persecutors, their judges and executioners, open their eyes and come to repentance with edification and joye of the whole church of God, the author and worker of all these wonderfull effectes, it is not to be marveled (though there were no other superior reasons of his everlasting providence with surmount our capacytie) that his divine magesty doe permit for the time that he seeth convenient this and other like persecutions and

58

the undeserved hatred of our adversaries [350ᵛ] against us and the manifold errors in to which they falle by the same. Seing they falle into them by their owne default and in punishment of their other sinnes and that without their fall and obstinacye the former vertues could not be had in so eminent degrees, nor the martirs obteine their crownes without victory, nor get victory without spirituall warres, nor such warres should be, if there were no oppugnation of enemyes, and finally in this kinde of war none doe perish but only the children [Jn 17] of perdition.

23. And so, as to those that now perish in that kingdome for persecuting of Gods saints, it is very probable that, though the cuntry were Catholike, they would have fallen into the same sentence of damnation for their other vices and disorders. And the chosen of God (whome no fraude nor violence can wrest out of his handes [Jn 10]) be saved with far greater glory then other waies they should by his ordinary providence, by which all creatures are governed with unspeakeable wisedome and justice. And as (for example) beastes lesse noble by the same justice and providence are permitted to dye, that the lions life may be conserved, and much more for the temporall sustenance of man, we see how many more and how different creatures be distroyed and consumed, and generally the more base and inferior serve for the conservation and perfection of the more noble. So passeth it in this our case, and with much more ground of reason and justice and more particuler providence, that by losse of the reprobate the chosen are exalted.

24. Wherefore, this truth supposed, the desyre we have the persecution should cease is not so much for the constant Catholikes, which have tasted the supereminent knowledge of the charity of Christ [Ep 3] and the sweetnes of his crosse, in whome (according to the measures of their suffereings) abound celestiall comfortes [2 Co 1], which exceede all the harmes theire adversaries can doe them, as much heaven is above earth. And in which respecte many Catholikes of other cuntryes desyre to beare them company in their tribulations and comfortes and have a holy emulation of the occasyon which they have to endure some what for Christ. I saye our desire that the persecution should ende [351ʳ] is not so much for the quietnes of these resolute champions, who alwaies gaine whether they live or dye and be sure of an eternall rewarde for a short agony, but in respecte of the weaklings which of humane infermity dessemble their faith and yeild to the persecutors importunity, and most of all for the persecutors themselves whose dangerous and miserable estate we pitye with charitable affection and compassion, and in no wise wishe them harme as they imagine. For to many of them as shall persever in their errors, there resteth harme enough, much more then any man may wish them. And of none of them in particuler (how far soever he be out of the waye) we can dispaire, seing the infinite mercy of God called a publican to be an apostle and (as St. Augustine well noteth) did ordeine the death of Saint Stephen to the conversion of Saint Paule. Who, when it was least expected, with only one glance of the magesty of Christ, was changed sodenly from a ravening wolfe to a meeke lambe, and of a persecutor became so greate an apostle and piller of the church, as we knowe, and the like hath happened to others without number in this present and in all other persecutions. Whereby the waye is worthy to be noted for our adversaries admonition, the difference betweene the spirite of Christ and the spirite of error, and how those three bad qualityes which the apostle acknowledged in himself before his conversion, *blasphemus, persecutor et contumeliosus,*[29] be ordinarye companions and for the most parte goe togeather. And we see them in some in such a degree, as is evident, they be not men that write and speake with such exorbitant malice more then humane, but that it is to be atributed to the malignant spirite that speaketh in them [Mt 10], as the spirite of Christ is the direction of his saintes and of their speeches and actions.

25. And if your Lordship please to heare one of them speake and how he answered his adversarye long agoe in the same maner and matter that our priests and martirs answere now in England, you shall see that Christ is the same in his servants (as the apostle saith) *heri et hodie et in secula.*[30] And because the conference is worthy the reading and much to the purpose I will set downe the demandes and answeres as they passed and are written by Saint Gregory Nazianzen.[31]

[351ᵛ] In the persecution of Valens the Arrian Emperor one of his leiftenants by name Modestus, but in his workes barbarous and cruell against the Catholikes, not so much beleeving that he did well, as for to please and flatter the Emperor, as many others doe this daye in England, having called before him Saint Basill, after he had bene tempted by divers others in vaine with greate promises and threatnings, spake unto hime in this manner.

What reason hast thou (Basill) that you darest resist so greate a magesty and alone amongst so manye men persever in thine obstinacye?

To what purpose (saide Sante Basill) tendeth this speeche? And what noveltye is this? For I doe not understand it.

Because (quoth he) thou does not professe the Emperors religion, to which all the rest have consented and subscribed.

I doe it not (saide Saint Basill) because the Emperor whome I serve doth not aproove it, nor would be contented that I his creature, and one having charge to represent his persone, should adore any other but him.

And we (quoth Modestus) that command thee, whome dost thou thinke we are?

In good sooth, nothing (answered Saint Basill) when you command thinges unjust.

But tell me (saide Modestus) dost thou not thinke it much more honorable and of more credite for thee to become one of our parte, and to have us for thy companions, then to resist in this manner?

Where unto Saint Basill: I doe not denye but that you be great men and command in the commonwealth but yet you are in no wise to be compared to God. And I should receyve both comfort and honor to have you for companions, with many others who be under our charge, creatures also of almighty God and in this your equals. And in Christian religion honor is judged more due to integrity of faith then otherwise to any dignity of person.

Modestus insensed with this answere rose up from his judgement seat [352ʳ] and beganne to handle him more sharply saying in anger: What dost thou not feare our authority?

Why, saide Saint Basill, should I feare it? What can you doe? What must I suffer?

What? quoth he, Any one of many thinges that be in my handes to doe unto thee.

What thinges be those, saide Saint Basill, let us know them I praye you?

Confiscation of thy goodes (quoth Modestus) banishment, torments, death.

To which Saint Basill answered, if there be anything else that you can threaten me let me heare it, for these of which you have spoken be not to the purpose.

How so? quoth the other. Because (saith Saint Basill) he is not subject to confiscations that hath no goodes, unless perhappes you have neede of these threede bare clothes and a few bookes which be all my riches. And as for banishment, I knowe not what it is nor make difference of cuntries. Nor this wherein now I live doe I accompt as mine more then any other whither soever you can sende me. Yea, to speake more properly, the whole world is Gods possession, wherein I ame a stranger and a pilgrime for some fewe dayes, passing through it apace as my forefathers have done. And as for your torments, what can they doe when the bodye fayleth? Unlesse you make reckoning of the first stroke, for that only is in your power. And lastly, by death you shall doe me a good turne, sending me sooner to God almighty, to whome I live and whome I serve, and already have gone the greatest part of my jorney to-wardes him and make as much hast as I can to ende the rest with ernest desyre to be with him.

The leiftenant amased with these wordes answered: no man, o Basill, till this daye hath spoken to me in this manner nor with this liberty of speech.

Perhappes, saide Saint Basill, you have not met with any of those that have the like obligation to speake, for other wise, if you had urged them as you doe me, they would have answered you in the same manner. [352ᵛ] For in other thinges we be meeke and humble, put our selves under all mens feete as Christ our maister taught us to doe with his word and example, and we be so far from resisting the Emperor as we resist not the meanest of the people. But where Gods cause is handled and we be pressed to forsake him, then we contemne all the rest and fix our eyes only on him. Your fire, your swordes, your wilde beastes, your rackes, your instruments where with you teare our flesh, doe not feare us but comfort us. Therefore (O Modestus) revile us, threaten us, torment us, doe what thou wilt, use the uttermost of thy power (and the very same I saye to the Emperor), you can not overcome us, nor make us consent to your wicked doctrine though you could threaten us with greater thinges then these.

26. The leiftenant hearing this answere and seing such reso-lution and constancy in the holy man that no force could feare him, he dismissed him not with sharpe wordes, as before, but with curtesye and respect. And making all hast he could to the Emperor, spake unto him in this manner. O Emperor we be overcome. This Basill can neyther be mooved with promises nor yeildeth to threatenings. We must attempt some of the weaker sort and eyther lay handes upon this man with open violence, or let him alone, for with him wordes be to no purpose.

27. The Emperor understanding all that had passed did not a little admire the holy mans sincerity and constancy, and reprehended the leiftenant for having passed so far with him, and uppon this occasion dealt more meekly with the Catholikes. and in the sicknes of his sonne made recourse with all demonstrations of humility and repentance to Saint Basills prayers, and afterwardes upon other occasions caled divers Catholike bishops out of banishment, and (as another Pharao) gave hopes of his amendment when he was touched by God with afflictions.[32] Yet for that he had intangled himselfe over far with the Arrian heresy and given his eare and hart to be possessed and overruled by wicked persons, and that greate men some times apprehend it for reputation to goe still forward not with standinge they be out of the waye, besides that it is a particuler punishment due to some sinners, that God permitteth them (as the prophet saith [Ps 80]) [353ʳ] to goe forwarde in theire owne inventions, the Emperor continuing in the same miserable estate came to a miserable ende. For he was overcome by the Gothes who invaded that part of the empire in his tyme, and by them wounded and persued was burnt alive in a cottage to which he had fled to hide himselfe, passing from temporall tormentes of fire to eternall. Wherein Orosias noteth[33] Gods just judgments that he should temporally perish by their handes, who had perished spiritually by his. For by him the Gothes were first infected with the Arrian heresye, who requiring to be instructed in the faith of Christ, the Emperor sent them false prophets that taught them his owne, that was the Arrian heresy.

28. Another thing also recorded in histories[34] touching this Emperor is worthy to be remembered for our example, and how almighty God useth to justifie his judgements, warning before he strikes, as he did by this Emperor. For he inspired a certeine holy hermite caled Isaac to come out the wildernes, and (as another Daniell [Dn 13]) to meete him in the waye as he passed with his army and finding his comodity spake unto him in this manner. O Emperor restore to the Catholikes their churches which thou hast caused to be shut and God almighty will prosper thy jorney. To which the Emperor made no answere.

Another daye Isaac met him againe and to the same effect that before, saide, O Emperor open the Catholike churchs and God will prosper thee in this battle and thou shalt returne with victory and peace. The Emperor mooved with these wordes now the second tyme, and with the reverend presence of the persone, caled togeather his counsell with purpose to restore the churches. But he was diswaded from doing it as a thinge contrary to his reputation especyally by his leiftenant an Arrian heretique, who rebuked the holy man and commanded him to silence. But he being sent by God, respected not the others comandement but folowed the army and overtooke the Emperor, and laying hand upon his bridle stayed his horse, and spoke unto him againe to the same effect but with more efficacy then before. Where with-all the Emperor being offended commanded him to be cast into a pit there adjoyning so covered with bryers and bushes as he could not probably come out alive. [353ᵛ] But God delivered him miraculously and he making hast overwent the army by a shorter waye and meeting the Emperor againe (who was amazed to see him, for he thought he had bene deade) spoke unto him in these wordes. Thou thoughtest (O Emperor) that I should have died where thou commandest me to be cast but the angels of God tooke me out presently as thou mayest see without hurt. Where-fore heare me and open the churches and thou shalt overcome thine enimies and returne with glory. To which the Emperor made no answere, for that his hart was estranged from God but committed the holy man to the charge of two senators Saturninus and Victor commanding them to keepe him in prison till he re-turned in peace that his insolencye might be punished. Where unto the holy man replied (as Micheas did to Acab [Mi 1]): if thou returne O Emperor in peace then God sent me not to speke unto thee, but thou shalt meete and fight with thine enemies and shall be overcome and put to flight and finally taken and burnt alive. All which happened a little after as hath bene saide and the two senators were converted and not only set the holy man at liberty, but continued in his devotion all the dayes of their lives and by his counsell and meanes did many good deedes in rec-ompense of their former errors. And these be the hidden wayes and workes of God which he only understandeth, for the salvation of such as yeilde to his warninges, and the punishment of others that be wilful and obstinate, alwaies proceeding with justice and mercye according to each mans desert disposing all for our greatest goode.

29. Here (my Lord) we see how only one servant of God almighty gave this warning to the Emperor and his divine magesty with this one admonition held for sufficyently justified his judgements and the punishment that was to folowe. Wherefore I lament seing how many of his servants the same God sendeth to give warning to our cuntry and those that governe it, and that they still bury them in the thornes and brambles of their persecution. I lament also and my hart bleedeth because I feare that the delaye of punishment, and so many meanes as God almighty useth to move them to repentance, be signes that his justice is to be so much more rigorous with [354ʳ] those that harden their hartes, by how much his mercyes have bene greater sending them before hand so many forwarnings to take heede. And therefore I desyre earnestly their amendment and speake so much the more playnely and confidently to your Lordship in this occasion, if happily it might helpe to make you and them enter in dew consyderation of this lamentable and dangerous case in tyme.

30. This story of Isaac I finde recorded by Simeon Metaphrastes, and how in the same cottage in company of the Emperor was also burned the leiftenant that gave him bad counsell. But to returne to Saint Basill and to Modestus the other lieftenant, he (after some time) faling dangerously sicke and now humbled and brought to knowe himselfe by Gods visitation, sent for the holy bishop and saide unto him with many teares: Lo Basill, for thy sake God hath punished me and by thee I must be holpen wherefore praye for me, that I may be delivered from this affliction. And so St. Basill did forgetting former injuries, and by his prayers the sicke man was restored to health which benefit he ever after acknoledged gratefully, far other wise then the Emperor his maester, who in the like manner sent for Saint Basill (as hath bene saide) in the sickness of his sonne and by his prayers he was likewise relieved but lost againe by the ingratitude of his father not acknoledging Gods mercye. For by perswasion of some about him he admitted certeine Arrian bishopes to visite the prince, who relapsed and dyed presently after the heretikes tooke him in hand.

31. Saint Gregory Nazianzen also remembreth[35] another act of the same Saint Basill, how he saved another lieftenants life caled Eusebius, delivering him from an uproare of the people at the very same tyme that the lieftenant had called him to the bar threatened him and was about to give him tormentes, and in this manner Gods servantes revenge injuryes with benefits. Histories are full of these and the like examples and successes, all which, and the different proceeding of the servants of God and the children of this world in all places and occasions, especyally of those that wilfully oppugne the truth, and Gods mercyes to the one and his punishments to the other, may all be applyed to our present case and confirme greately the [354ᵛ] thinges above saide.

32. And not withstanding some of them be so testified and others in themselves so evident, as no man that liveth in the light of the Catholike church can chuse but beleeve them, yet they perhappes at the first reading may seem strange to your Lordship and much more to others further off from this light and deeper in darknes, which (alasse) is another ground of the miseries of our countrye. For that darknes of itselfe without any other cause, doth naturally breede suspitions and feares, and of such as walke in darknes saith the prophet, *trepidaverunt timore ubi non erat timor.*[36] And therefore it is no marveile that they goe alwaies with troubled conscyences and fearfull unquiet hartes and so readye (as we see and alwaies hath bene sene) to admit whatsoever impression or suspition against the children of light. Nor that the one and the other forme so different conceits and judgements of the very selfe same thinges and inferre so different consequences, having so different dispositions and governing themselves by so different principles.

33. From hence it cometh that some not well affected to the Catholike religion have prevayled so much with his Majesty of England, as to admit distrust and evill opinion of those who alwaies have especyally loved him faling (as the proverbe is) into Scilla whilest he flyeth Charibdis. Seing that to remedye their forged suspitions and feares they drive him against his owne inclination and honor and the good of his kingdome, into a laberinth of confusion and cares with perpetuall unquietnes of hart, obliging him to proceede with his subjectes, so differently from the custome of other kings reputed for magnanimous and just as it is pitye to see it. And this (forsooth) because they professe their

66

forefathers faith (for if they folowed noveltyes as others doe, they were inexcusable) the same faith in which all the good kinges that governed well lived and dyed with glory, and by which the first inhabitants of those cuntryes were caled Christians, and reduced from savage and barbarous life and from ignorance of the true God to the light of the gospell, and brought to that civill and orderly government far from all violence and wronges, where withall their successors [355ʳ] have bene kept in order so many ages since with continuall increase of reputation and felicyty. And finally for the same faith for which his magesties owne mother the late Queene Mary of Scotland suffered death,[37] and in rewarde of whose fidelity we may, in all law of reason and equity, thinke that God almighty hath bestowed upon her sonne the crowne, which she chose rather to loose, then that faith which he now suffereth to be persecuted in his subjects under cullor of I wot not what security to himselfe and to his state. Seing it is the surest meanes that is possible in this world (as experience of all ages doth teach) for the conservation and security of kingdomes and kinges, and with which alone his magesty should finde more safety and quietnes of bodye and minde then with all the inventions which (without it or against it) can be found by novelers.[38] For this faith teacheth and introduceth all the vertues by which kingdomes are upholden, and destroyeth the vices by which they are brought to ruine, and with it *ipso facto* (and without any other industry) the subjectes rest bound with the greatest obligations that may be to love, reverence and obeye their princes as Gods substitutes and leiftenants, and to be faithfull unto them as to those that governe them in the place and name of almighty God to whome all love, fidelity and obedience is due.

34. According to this, we see that the kinges and princes which professe this faith and governe by lawes and customs according to the same (as well they as theire subjectes) live with greater quietnes, comfort and security and with dayly increase of mutuall good will, proceeding from those mutuall obligations which this faith putteth upon the princes and upon their subjectes and on both sides are to be kept.

And the reason of the security of good Catholike princes is for that the just prince unto whome his subjectes have resigned and given over their willes to be directed by his, holdeth as it were in prison, in his owne good and universal will, the evill disposed willes and vices of many. And with his just and well ordered will maketh manye live within the boundes of order and justice which other [355ᵛ] wise would not, hindering with his goodnes innumerable evils every daye and houre and causing inumerable good effectes to the people that be under his government. And therefore such a prince (as a fruteful tree perpetually laden with pretious and wholsome frutes and a welspring of life and generall good) is in himselfe most pretious, and for himselfe amiable above measure and worthy more then can be expressed of all honor and respect, and that his subjectes not only spende their goodes for his conservation and security but their lives also when occasion requireth. Whose hartes and good willes he draweth into his power sweetely without violence and yet vehemently as the lode-stone doth the yron, and other thinges attractive drawe their ob-jectes with a certeine secret and naturall force. And that which most importeth, he gayneth and draweth God almighty to favor him, who is king of kinges and lord of lordes and giveth and taketh away, troubleth and quieteth kingdomes at his pleasure, and is ready alwaies with his particuler protection to assist and defend good princes, frindes of justice and peace, and that handle their subjectes as they ought. And in this is especyally founded their security, for that making themselves amiable as is above saide they cannot fayle to be beloved, and who is loved in this manner and for these respectes needeth feare no hurt from those that so doo love him.

35. To the contrary, the king or prince which having (as is before saide) many mens willes resigned into his, doth prevert them to evill endes following errors and vices, whether it be by evill counsell or his owne inclynation, for his pleasure or for his temporall interest, as Jeroboam [3 Ki 12] who by that deceitefull rule which in some places contrary to all reason is caled Reason of State, supposing thereby that he should have had the ten tribes more assured to himselfe and his successors, withdrue them from the true service of almighty God, such a prince as this, holding as it were vertue imprisoned and the good desyres of many chayned and fettered, justice and peace and truth oppressed and the gates open to falsehoode and flattery, and to innumerable disorders which spring up dayly from so contagious rootes in the common-wealth, maketh himselfe a generall evill and like a founteine of poysened water distempereth and infecteth in such manner his people. [356ʳ] As no mans wit can conceyve and much lesse utter by tongue or writing the enormity of his sinne, nor how detestable such a prince becometh (*ex ipsa natura rei*) to God and man, of whose malice and wickednes they also are partakers who give him bad counsell, as the others that counsell the good prince to well doing, doe participate of his goodnes and deserve to be beloved and honored of all. And the justice of God beginneth (infallibly) to prepare rewardes and punishments for the one sort and for the other, from the very hower that they beginne to put in order or disorder themselves and others. And not withstanding it seemeth some times *quod sit sera numinis vindicta*[39] and that the punishment is longe acomming, yet this is no benefit for those that are culpable, for the higher he liftes the scurge the heavier he giveth the blowe, and in conclusion howsoever men deceive themselves with the shadoe of present prosperity, *Gaudium hipocritae ad instar puncti.*[40]

36. But to saye something to those that thinke not of God, nor remember his dreadfull judgement, I wish they would but consider a little with only humane reason and prudence (setting passion aside) into what inconveniences and dangers they may bring their prince, specyally if he be a stranger and newly entred into his goverment, urging his subjectes with violent proceedings to make experience what they are able to doe in their owne defence, and pressing them in such manner with wronges that they make their case desperate, which with enemies is no wisedome to attempt and much lesse with their owne domesticall people and subjectes. And is the very same counsell of those yonge violent counselors to whome God permitted that the King Roboam [3 Ki 12] should give eare when he was resolved to divide from him the greatest part of his kingdome. And neyther forced oathes nor any other exterior protestations of fidelity if mens hartes doe not concurre, are sufficyent to remedy this inconvenience. Yea how much the more dissembled and secret the discontentment is and more hidden within mens brestes, so much the more perilous it becometh and more hard to be cured and is of more dangerous effectes. For that feare without love and injury without hope of justice cause (naturally) affliction and passion in mens mindes, which passions continuing and [356ᵛ] by little and little increasing and changing it selfe into detestation and hatred of those that be authors of the wronges, maketh the injuried goe contynually thinking upon their afflictions and feeling out meanes how to remedye their distresses. And wherein many be thus afflicted and occupied in such melancolike cogitations, it is a dangerous case and almost impossible that (first or last) some of them hit not upon the convenient remedies which others doe not imagine. And here it maye please your Lordship to consider that many thinges may have place in people overcome by wars or con-quered, or forreyners admitted by a prince or state to inhabite within their dominions, which ought not to be used with the naturall borne subjectes, nor with other auncyent inhabitants of any cuntry, not only in molestations for theyr conscyences but in taking from them their arms and other vexations, as any man will judge that doth examine the case with indifferency.

37. This is that which passeth naturally amongst men, and hath bene cause of lamentable successes, for, in fine, men be men, yea, *habet et musca splenum et formicae sua bilis inest*,[41] and the meek-est and most hurtlesse creatures of all may be so chased and urged that they will turne againe for their owne defence. And therefore greate violence★★★ is subject to greate calamities, and in the bal-ance of Gods justice everything hath his might and measure and it must needes be so, and only Catholikes, who have their hopes and riches laide up in eternity and therefore are lesse moved then others with temporall wronges, are they who in all ages and cun-tries have had longanimity in their sufferinges. Wherein they be strengthened with supernaturall grace and with inwarde com-fortes from above and with the consideration of the cause for which they suffer and testimony of good conscyences, and above all the rest the example of Christ our maester who suffered for us in the same manner willingly and without faulte, to give us ex-ample and desyre to suffer in the same manner for him and would not enter into his owne kingdome but by his crosse.

★★★Here the *Carta*, p. 24ᵛ, is different:
"And for this reason Nero, Domitian, Commodus and other tyrannts were shortlived and great calamities usually follow upon monstrous violence. In the scales of divine justice, wherein an admirable proportion is maintained, where each thing is matched by another of proper weight, perforce this has to be so. Christ indeed has given warning that he who takes the sword shall perish with the sword [Mt 26:52] and also there was that from the prophet David that bloodthirsty and treacherous men shall not live out half their days [Ps 54:24]. Only Catholics who esteem "the reproach of Christ greater riches than the treasures of the Egyptians" [Heb 11:26] are the ones who in every time and place have had the patience and endurance, in similar cases."

These comfortes all they want which suffer for other causes. And therefore the Catholikes★★★ only are they which have true patience and suffer [357ʳ] without amaritude or desyre of revenge, knowing that though their suffering be painefull it is not hurtfull, but that they gaine honor and profit with what losse soever they beare for Christ.

And according to this truth, your Lordship shall understand that the late Queene Elizabeth was more beholding to the Catholike priestes and religious men that taught this true doctrine in England for the quietnes which she enjoyed so many yeares in that kingdome, then to others which in her name did many thinges (pretending perhappes to quiet it) in deede most fit and able to revolve it, if they had not bene counterpoysed with those other peaceable principles and with the generall perswasion above saide, that the persecution was hurtfull to none that had constancy and patience to beare it.

38. And for the more proofe of this, your Lordship maye consider if the Lutherans in Germany, or the Guses in Holand,[42] or the Huguenotes in France, or the Calvinistes in Scotland, or the Puritans in England, would have suffered the oppression which the Catholikes have borne so many yeares more then the Turke (holden for the greatest tirant now living) durst ever put upon his most barbarous and brutish subjectes (for he suffereth them to live each one in his religion so that in the rest they pay him his tributes and be obedient) for the greate inconveniences which otherwise would folowe in his kingdomes. And your Lordship can not be ignorant of the seditions, rebellions and warres which the above saide sectaries have raysed as lawfull and supported by others of their owne profession. Where as it is *ex raro contingentibus*[43] that Catholike men, strengthened with the light and comfort and perswasions above saide, procure to redresse with violence wronges done unto them for their religion.

39. For all which reasons his magesty hath lesse cause to feare any harme of the Catholike recusantes against whome all these

---

★★★The *Carta*, pp. 24ᵛ–25ʳ, is different:
"Catholics are consoled in this occasion and so are alone with those who can say with the Apostle "we suffer persecution but are not forsaken" [2 Co 4 v. 9] since they learn that the way out of all troubles is in knowing in an assured and true conviction that there is honor and advantage in losing property, liberty and life on behalf of Jesus Christ and his holy religion."

lawes and penalties be put, then of innumerable others whome they doe not comprehende. Yea, then of any that condescend to denye their beliefe, whether they be Catholikes or of whatsoever profession. [357ᵛ] For such persons findinge their consciences oppressed and afflicted with remorse, and having within them selves a contynuall sting and unquietnes of minde, and without that spirituall comfort which God giveth the Catholike recusants in recompense of their temporall damages (as hath bene saide) are much more disposed then they and more provoked to deliver themselves from that inward torment and bondage of their soules, and may have a thousand occasions and comodities to doe it from which the declared Catholikes are debarred. And of these people so oppressed and discontented all the relmes of England, Scotland and Ireland are full.

40. Wherefore,★★★ as many wisemen as I have met with, informed of the proceedings in those cuntryes and specyally such as have seene or heard of these laste Statutes, wonder to see so many cautions against those with whome they are lesse needeful, and none at all with whome they are much more necessary. And above all the rest, to see such importunity to make men professe and sweare that the temporall prince is heade of the church, which Calvine the author of their secte did so eagerly reprehend[44] and caled it antichristian arrogancy in King Henry the Eight, and such adoe to make men goe to their prayers though they have no devotion to them, and to eate their communion breade perforce though it goe against their stomakes, and such other like. For if already they beleeve the thinges to be good and true which they make them professe, these exteriour protestations to which they urge them so violently be wholy needelesse: and if they beleeve them not or thinke them to be naught, though they sweare and forsweare them ten thousand tymes and goe as often to their churches as they list, it serveth for nothing. Yea, it is quite contrary and hurtefull to the very same ende which the persecutors pretend, and against the rule of good phisitians who never drive into the body that which they desyre to cure, and against the

---

★★★Here the *Carta*, p. 26ʳ, begins:
"For this reason I do not understand upon what sort of prudent judgement are based the restraints against the Catholic Rescusants in keeping them in prison, in arresting them in their houses and in prohibiting them from living in London and approaching near to the court."

custome of all prudent princes that hold it for a great absurdity in government and a dangerous thing in itself to induce the people to flatter and lye, and to force them to take oathes against their inwarde judgement, or by any other waye oblige them to cover and dessemble their greeves without putting remedy to them.

[358ʳ] **41.** And this I saye not only for the Catholikes but much more for the rest, puritans and others which beleeve not the doctrine, nor aprove the proceedings of the protestants to which they make them subscribe and sweare against their consciences.

And for my part, I should a thousand tymes rather trust my selfe (as the king or any man may doe) to those which should refuse (not withstanding it were with an erronious conscyence) to sweare or protest exteriourly that which they holde to be false then to them that for any feare or interest denye their religion, when they are obliged to professe it.

42. And if your Lordship will see that I speake not this without example and reason, omitting that which Carolus Sigonius writeth⁴⁵ of the King Theodoricus and other examples olde and newe of which histories are full, it may please you to remember that noble and prudent action of Constantius the Emperor father to our greate Constantine, who if he were alive might pretend the first voyce in our parlament and no lesse in the privy counsell, as one that governed well and pacyfied that kingdome, and by that which he did in his tyme reproveth the present proceedings of our persecutors, and aproveth for the best and wisest goverment that which immidiately before hath bene saide. For being informed that divers of his servants and officers were become Christians, he gave a generall commandment under greivous punishment that all such persons should departe from his court and service, as the constant Catholikes presently did, leaving behinde them only those that for feare of temporall losse made more bolde with God almighty and with their conscyences then they should. Which done and the Emperor enformed of that which had passed (contrary to all mens expectations) he remooved these from his service and recaled the constant Christians, advanced them and alwaies after used them in places of most confidence about his person and in the goverment, giving this reason that those which were so constant in their religion and so faithfull to their God, would also in like manner be faithfull to their Emperor.[46] Wherein he judged as a prince worthy his [358^v] place, and the contrary is error and much more to thinke that Gods truth can be over borne with mans force. For (as Gamaliel saide) that which is of God will goe forwarde,[47] and for men to undertake to hinder it by their inventions is to folowe the example of the pharises, and as little to the purpose as it were to make bulwarkes of wax against the fire. And sheweth evidently that eyther they knowe not or at least doe not consider, the force of truth nor the nature and obligation of an oath, which is confirmation of a truth acknowledged and beleeved to be so, is the most forcyble bonde that may be amongst men, but to wrest it to the contrary is an injurious and unnaturall thing and wholy unprofitable.

43. And therefore I coulde never finde any other true and reall cause of the oathes, which in Queene Elizabeths tyme men were urged to take that they beleeved and acknoledged and in their conscyence were perswaded that shee (being a woman) shoulde be heade of the church[48] (which oath Saint Paule would never have taken nor aproved that was so far from making weoman spirituall Superiors as he did not permit them to speake in the church), nor I thinke your Lordship nor any man else shall finde any other cause or ground for the same, nor for the like protestations and exterior actes, where unto they force the people in England against their conscyences, but only the envye and malice of the devill, who without any other purpose or profit, deliteth to make men sinne. Seing all these demonstrations be (as I have saide) wholy unprofitable for their purpose that procure them, unlesse they coulde (withall) make men beleeve (which with such as have capacity to judge betweene right and wronge is impossible) that the religion they make them professe and sweare to perforce is good and true. Besides that violence used to force them to a thing so unprofitable, and the many base inventions contryved to raise some colour of justice to so unjust and so unnecessarye violence, discredite the state and blemish much their reputation and of the whole government otherwaies commendable in manye thinges, and openeth waye to the same inconveniences which some woulde prevent by these unconscyonable and dishonorable meanes. [359^r] In confirmation whereof I could bringe examples in divers other kingdomes which make undoutable as much as I have saide.

44. But because your Lordship will (perhappes) aledge to the contrary the late conspiracyes,[49] which we have heard of in England against his magesty that now is, it may be answered that the first was imputed to persones who had taken oathes enough, and went to their churches, eate theyre bread and were well knowen to be no Catholikes. And I woulde to God that all the greefes within that relme were only about religion, and that the protestantes and others also had not their hart burnings more deeply impressed, and more harde to be cured then the Catholikes discontentments, which if it were not so, some of our statesmen might (with lesse perill to the whole) goe forward in the confusion which they have begonne. But I hope that God will have mercye upon our cuntry and open their eyes, or at least his magestys, to moderate theire vehemencye in this behalfe.

45. And as for this last supposition of conspiracye from Flanders, it is here holden for a meere fable, forged by Nuce[50] and those that set him a worke, to empeach the honor of the Spanish embassadore, and the testimonies seeme evident for the innocency of some apprehended and accused by such as are thought to be enemies to the peace. And if his magesty give eare to such persons and shewe himselfe readye to receyve such apprehentions as these, they will rayse him every daye new conspiracies in the ayre. As others did some yeares togeather with Queene Elizabeth, which with a woman was more tollerable but with a king were to shewe lesse respect and opinion then is dewe to his persone. And for the same reason we heare not of the like whisperinges and raysing of tales with other princes, for it would not be well taken. And that which they used with the Queene was playne flattery to curry favor with her, and to gaine opinion of vigilant officers and men (forsooth) carefull of her security[51] and to entertaine the people with noveltyes, and incense both her and them against the Catholikes and as preambles of the parliaments make waye for taxes, subsidies and privy seales, [359ᵛ] which might better have bene procured by other honest and lawfull meanes. Though none more easy where conscyence and the feare of God doth not hinder, for what can be more easy or of lesse cost then to raise suspitions against whome soever? Seing there is no armore against suspitions and they that raise them be never caled to accompt nor punished.

46. Wherefore, to give some shewe of truth to thinges which have it not in themselves, they use so manye of these practices and in some sorte they can do no lesse, proceeding upon such groundes as they doe, for as truth is not upholden but with truthes, so devises can not stand if they be not upholden one with another.

But howsoever they be borne out with aucthority they cease not to be what they are, and to be censured as they deserve, and can not chuse but be misliked of all when they come to lyght. Such as these were those inventions, so ordinarily whiles we had warres with Spaine, to bringe out certeine men of nothing as though they had bene sent or set on by the Catholike king, or others on his behalfe, to kill Queene Elizabeth. As for example Doctor Lopez[52] the Jewe, who at the hower of his death declared to be false that which they imputed to him, and made a protestation like himselfe that he loved the Queene better then Jesus Christ.

47. The same maye be saide of Williams and Yorke,[53] the one a young stripling, the other a boye, falsely accused by a serving man set on to doe it, and all men did see that they were innocent at the tyme of their death. And to omit many other examples, one may suffice for all, of Squire, knowen to be notable cosenor[54] and a shifting companion, who to the ende his confession might be beleeved was brought to the gallowes, and contrary to his expectation though according to his desert, was made aweay quicly and interrupted, when seeing the matter went in earnest, he would have quitte himselfe and declared the truth.[55]

48. These were the practices in those tymes whilest the war lasted, to bring the Spaniards in hatred with the people. And those that be enemies to the peace beginne now againe the like inventions, though not being knowen from whence they come, they cannot worke such effectes [360ʳ] as before, in at least they should not with his magesty.

49. But what do I speake of these particular untruthes sufficyently discovered by others? when some are not ashamed to affirme and publish in forreine cuntries that none are persecuted in England for religion, whilest the very lawes, the arraignementes and condemnations of the martirs, and all theire manner of proceedings for many yeares make manifest the contrary. And not withstanding sometimes seeing the general mislike that men should be put to death for having beades, or *Agnus Dei*s, for being priestes or harboring them, or going to confession or other like actes of religion, it was holden by some as a pointe of state to raise slanders of treason against preistes and other Catholikes. Yet seing they might not only have had their lives but preferment, if they would have gone to the protestantes churches, it is evident that the treasons laide to theire charge were false and thinges meerely feigned. For in no state in the world heynous offenses of treason are so easyly pardoned.

50. I know not whether our adversaries have ever called to memory the persecution of Julian the Apostate, who envying in the martirs the honor of their martirdome, caused false witnesses of treason to be raysed against them and because they should not be thought to suffer for religion gave them torments and put them to death under coulor of other offenses. As we reade in the ecclesiasticall histories,[56] in St. Gregory Nazianzen, St. Chrisostom, and others.

Thus he commanded to proove St. Juventinus and St. Maximus, by all waies possible with promises and threatnings and gave order that if they yeilded to denye Christ, they should be brought out in publike with honor, but if they would not, to put them to death under title of traytors without mentioning theire religion.

He banished the bishopes, preistes and other constant Catholikes and men of exemplar life, tolerating others whose behaviour might discredit their religion.

He protected and favored the Arrians, the Aetians, the Donatistes, and all the sectes that were at that tyme under the name of Christianity, and the Jewes also, and who soever woulde or coulde oppose themselves in any thinge to damage the Catholikes.

[360ᵛ] He made himselfe arbiter of the differences that he had stirred amongst them, to the ende he might understand their affaires and norish discord, as he did by divers waies.

He accused the bishopes and preistes to the people, to put dissidence and dislike betwixt the one and the other, and so infamed[57] and discredited both.

His lawes against the Catholikes were the very same which (with compassion) we see in these our daies renewed against them in England and be so like, as they seeme copied out of his, though perhappes those that suggested them fell not into this reckoning, and much lesse the princes in whose name they were executed. For if they had, it is probable they would have bene more carefull of theire owne reputation with men (though the feare of Gode had bene wanting) then to have suffered themselves to be drawen to this waye, and unawares folowe so ignominious a president.

Julian (for example) put intollerable taxes uppon the Catholikes and confiscated their goodes, excepting only such as would leave their religion and make profession of his.

The recusantes he banished out of his courte and family, debarring them from all the offices of the commonwealth and specyally from being Governers, Magistrates, Capteines or pretorian soldiers, if first they denyed not Christ. Wherefore Jovinianus (who a little after was chosen Emperor in his place) in his owne presence cast awaye his soldiers girdle, which with them was an ensigne of honor as the Garter is now in England.

He deprived the Catholikes of theire schooles forbidding them eyther to teach or learne the liberall scyences, and tooke from them (as much as he could) all possibility to bringe up well their children, in so much as he forbad them the bookes which at that time were taught. Where upon St. Gregory and other learned men composed others more to the purpose and God hath now provided better education for our Catholikes children in seminaries abroad then they could have had in their fathers house, or in their universities at home.

He obliged them by force to goe to his churches and to be present at the [361ʳ] sacrifice he made to his false gods, and such a desyre he had to make men participate in some sorte with his sinne, as he caused to be offered to his idoles the breade, frutes and other victuales that were to be solde in the markets. But the Catholikes understanding it would buye nothinge, susteyning themselves with sodden wheate till the Gentiles did tumult, and the Emperor wearied gave over his importunity.

Finally (to omit other thinges) he tooke occasions of the counsels of our Saviour in the gospel, to make lawes whereby to spoyle, molest and vex the Christians by many waies, denying them the benefite and defense of the common lawes (which were not denyed to the greatest malefactors) and all redresse for the wronges which dayly they receyved of the pagans and of his owne officers, by which meanes he did persecute them.

51. The very same manner of proceeding hath bene used

these many yeares in England (rather by instigation of bad counselors then by inclination of the princes themselves) with the
Catholikes of that cuntry, who have bene no lesse scandalized
with the calumniations and false witnesses contynually raysed
against them, then with the spoyles of their goodes and personall
damages which they have receyved. And yet, not withstanding all
this, for the reasons above saide they have borne all with patience
and lived quietly, as the world hath seene with admiration. But if
they had dealt with the puritans as they have dealt with the Catholikes many yeares, they would have had not only suspitions
wherein to exercise their wittes and suggest to their princes, but
true causes of feare. And because they knowe it well enough,
they have not bene very busye with them.

52. But to come to the conspiracye of the powder which for-
went this late session of the parliament, supposing it as contryved
by Catholikes (though many be not of that opinion) to this I saye
not withstanding it were as hath bene published, yet one swal-
lowe makes no summer. And although the authors of the persecution goe about to extende this fact (as it were originall sinne)
to all mankinde and have inserted into the fourth chapter of the
parliament to the same purpose, a notorious untruth, that it was
done by instigation of Jesuites and seminary priestes (wherein any
man may [361ᵛ] see the marke they shoote at) and in other bitter
and slanderous libles they feigned that his holynes was one of the
complices, speaking against him with so little shame and civility
as it is a wonder to see it. The truth is already knowen and publike in England, that only those six or eight gentlemen were the
dooers, and for theire owne security, they kept in secret from all
others. And therefore it is a notable and unconscyonable injustice
to draw generall consequences out of this particular fact, and to
make such rigurous lawes against all Catholikes because those
fewe were of that religion.

53. And not withstanding all the stirre that our good frindes
the persecutors have made and the noise they have raised, it hath
prooved but little to their purpose, that a priest or two came to
knowe of the matter against their willes and by auricular confession in such a sorte that they coulde not discover it.[58] Seing it is
well knowen they consented not to it, but diswaded it and al-
ledged all the reasons they could against it, which was as much as
they could doe in a cuntry where the magistrates doe not beare

that respect which is due to the sacrament. For in a Catholike cuntry they might and would have done more, where no man would have pressed them to have discovered the persones, nor breake the seale which Christ hath put upon the ghostly fathers mouth, who many tymes heareth things that he would not (as comonly they be all, or the most, which priestes heare in confession) but with obligation *de jure divino* (which no lawes made by men can prejudice) to bury them in perpetuall silence and oblivion, and much more, not to reveal the penitent in any case.

This is the case and cause for which good Father Garnet died, whose innocency discovered at the tyme of his arraignement and execution, did so much the more confound his adversaries, as the rumors which malitiously they had caste abroad against him were evidently convinced to be false and many that before had beleeved them, were mooved with admiration of his modesty, and compassion of his case, and to detestation of the others crafty and unconscyonable manner of proceeding.

54. And in confirmation of this blessed mans innocency your Lordship shall understande that I did see now at my being in Roome letters[59] of his, written with greate affliction and perplexity of minde, in which [362ʳ] he complayned that with occasions of the dayly molestations and exorbitant wronges which the Catholikes did suffer some of them (whome he caled sworde men[60]) were so scandalized and offended, that theire wrath and indignatione increasing with newe injuries might breede inconveniences. And not withstanding that he for his parte, had procured alwaies to induce all men to patience and longanimity, as the other priestes did also as much as they could, and that his wordes as he thought would have some force with such as did give him hearing, yet for as much as the persons injured were many through out the whole realme, and the priestes coulde not be present in every place and occasion to give them good counsell, he thought it not only convenient but necessary to pacyfie mens mindes, and make sure that no Catholike should doe any thinge which might offende the kinge or incense any of his councell to the prejudice of all, that his holynes shoulde sende a generall comandement exorting the Catholikes to expect patyently Gods holy will and disposition, till it might please him to deliver them from theire afflictions and charging them that in no case they should attempt any violent remedie, which prohibition his holynes did hereupon send[61] and some of our adversaries can not be ignorant of it.

55. By which is evident, first how unjustly the holy man suffered, who deserved rewarde of the kinge and state and in no wise punishment, and the greate charge that lieth upon their conscyences which contrived his condemnation and consented to his death. And secondly that neyther his holines nor any Catholike person of authority; no nor any man of forsight and experience, was privy to this conspiracye. And thirdely into how dangerous an estate that kingdome is brought, and how desperate a kinde of government it is to drive men to such extremityes, as they maye thinke (yea with the least appearance of reason that may be) that for want of persones that will heare and remedy theire oppressions, they are freede from the lawe of nations, and by the lawe of nature may *vim vi repellere* and defende one violence with another,[62] which in no case should ever be permitted nor thinges brought to that exigent in any [362ᵛ] commonwealth. And finally for the same reason, it is manifest that they are no lesse blameworthy which with their importunity and continuall vexations, gave cause to the same conspiracy, then those that went about to put it in execution.

56. And truely my Lord when I hearde of it first, the 11th of December past by the poast which brought the newes to Spaine, it seemed to me a thinge so strange and so far from the cogitations of Catholikes that knowing how their adversaries use to proceed, and the false accusations they have produced many times before against divers persons in England, France, Flanders, Germany and elsewhere for hatred of theire religion, not withstanding I had seene the printed proclamation[63] and divers letters both here, and in France, and in Italy as I passed, that made mention of the case, yet I could not beleeve it till I came to Roome and saw it confirmed by divers waies. Yea, I thought that all that provision of powder had bene made by others and the blame afterwardes laide upon the Catholikes. For that it seemed a thing impossible that Catholikes should laye togeather such a quantity of gunpowder and other implements necessary for such a purpose, or make mines in such a publike place having bene so longe aboute it, as was reported in the letters, if some of the counsell had not knowen and dissembled what they were adoing. Neyther seemed it (as I have saide) an enterprise fit for Catholikes, nor a proportionable means for any good ende that they could pretende, nor a project set downe with any providence for the harmes that might come thereby to the actors if it should be discovered, and much more if it should have taken effect to the distruction of so many innocent persons, and other reasons to the like effect which at that time came to my minde.

57. The which reasons, since I have seene the actes of this parliament, assembled only to distroye the Catholikes as is evident, seing in it nothing else of moment is done, but only lawes made against them, and nettes to intangle them, and is the scope where unto [363ʳ] all the project is directed and that all the designement and concepcion thereof (plotted before the conspiracye) yet supposeth it, and was to be grounded in it, or in some other thing of the like quality, and the greate eagernes that the plotters shewe to extende the faulte of those fewe gentlemen (as if it had bene Adames sinne) even to the children unborne, these considerations, I saye, togeather with the reasons above saide and some others which heere I omit, move me to thinke it may be true (which some doe affirme with very substantiall groundes) that not withstanding those gentlemen were the immediate instruments, yet that others were the authores of that conspiracye. *Viz.*, the same persons which had by their substitutes suborned the yeare before to stir up the Catholikes in Herefordshyre to take armes,[64] and thereby to have occasion to perswade the king to continue the persecution. And that knowing one of those gentlemen to be a man of greate courage (and although in his religion a Catholike yet not so patient to suffer injuries as men shoulde be that live where they be offered with authority) laide him a baite and tempted him with this devise, so secure for them as it could doe them no hurte in a thousand yeares, if they came not neere the place. And for him and such as he shoulde drawe into the action, a very pitfall and trappe in which their adversaries had them caught to theire handes, and might bring them forth when the tragedye should be acted, which (forsooth) should be neither sooner nor later but the very nyght before the parlament should beginne, and just in the occasion of the danger to be imagined, whereby to afreight so much the more, as well the king and the rest, whose consent was necessary to the lawes intended, as the common people of London and all others at home and abroade, to whose notice might come an interprise so strange, so newe, and so inexpected, as the authors of this tragedye desyred that it should appeare. As another not unlike to this coming (as it is saide) from the same or the like polititians was for a time esteemed, when the late Queene of Scotland was intangled with another devise of the like quality. For she was brought (being thene prisoner in England) by little and little to consent to certeine [363ᵛ] thinges ordeyned as it might seeme by her frindes for her liberty, but in deede intended by her enemyes for her destruction. For which little after they condemned her and cut off her heade, and tooke away the livings and lives of other certeine yong gentlemen.[65] Like to these whome now lastely they wounde into the bryers[66] and executed, adjudging their landes to the kinge by parlament to make sure worke for those that hope to enjoye them afterwardes.

58. This is the opinion that goeth currant, how thinges passed, God knoweth and tyme will discover. And in the meane season your Lordship may see that it wanteth not probability, and so much the more, that some of our adversaries esteeme much theire ability to bring about such like subtilties, and other thinges of theirs not unlike to this so publike as they cannot be denyed. And that letter without subscription sent by night to my Lord Monteagle,[67] in such a fashion and at such a tyme (where withall they woulde make the worlde beleeve that the conspiracye was discovered) smelleth of cunning dealing. And so much the more as it is constantly reported that all those that were privye to the action did affirme upon their salvation, that none of them had written any such letter. Yea, moreover I have understoode that a certeine protestant, a frinde and a depender of one of those that procured the tumult in Herefordeshire, saide in his comendations that N— (naming the party) had more witte then all the papistes and had over reached them all, suffering them to goe forwarde with that they had in hand many monethes, in which he knewe all the secretes to bring them forth and punish them when he sawe his tyme.[68] Yea, more then this: it is a thinge well known in London, how one Mr. Edwardes a neighbor to the parlament house observing the resort made in that house where the mine was amaking, advised a privy counselor at Whitsontide before the conspiracy was published, how there were caried many fagots and other things to that house, frequented by daye and by night with persons unknowen, and that it were convenient to examine what busynes they had there.[69]

The counselor not withstanding he was ready enough as his office (364ʳ] requireth to commande serches to be made upon far lesser occasions, yet seemed to make little reckoning of this, and for that time let it goe forwarde without more adoe. But afterwardes when the conspiracye was published and Mr. Edwardes told his nighbors what had passed with the counselor at Whitsontide before, inferring that they might have prevented it sooner if they had pleased, he was sent for before the counsell and rebuked, and he and his wife sent prisoners to the Fleete for two or three dayes, but after set at liberty.

All which thinges, and others reported to the same effect, togeather with the dispositions of the persons they name, and their manner of proceedings, make that which they saye not a little credible.

59. But how soever the matter did passe, and how culpable soever these gentlemen might be, for I will yeilde to your Lordship that you make them the authors and actors of the conspiracye, and of all that theire greatest enemies can imagine, yet what is all this to the purpose? Seing it is a particuler crime of a fewe, and what conextion hath it with these lawes which in consequence thereof they have made against all Catholikes, who had no more to doe with the conspiracye then those Catholikes which live in Japon. And this so evident and so notable injustice is the greatest presumption of all, that the grounde whereupon they founded them was but a devise contryved to abuse the king and the parlament, and a colour and occasion sought to persecute religion and to wrest out such barbarous lawes against it.

60. Amongst the which, not to speake of all nor to leave all untouched, that which forbiddeth under such great penaltyes that no man bring into the lande any Catholike bookes[70] (not so much as the histories and lives of saintes) sheweth that those which procured this lawe intende not to be saintes themselves and discovereth the weaknes and distrust of their superintendents and heades of their Sectes. Who now being no longer able to mainteine theire reputation with the people by any other meanes, doe shroude themselves under the seculer power. And seing all their follies and deceites laide open and confuted in the Catholikes bookes, which none of the wiser sorte [364ᵛ] of them dare take in hande to answere, though urged and commanded, seing they have no more to saye in so bad a cause, and that the slevelesse[71] answers and evasions of some silly companions (*qui ad pauca respicientes facile enunciant*[72]) be rather to theire discredite and losse then to any advantage, especially with such as have judgement to examine the force of the arguments and truth of the allegations on both partes,[73] they are forced for their laste refuge to make recourse to the parlament, and get the bookes forbidden and banished, that no indifferent reader maye come to see them and so they may have the more freedome to abuse the people without controlment.

61. The lawe also which maketh it treason for any man to suffer himselfe to be perswaded to be a Catholike, not only (as it was before) within England, but on the sea (as the lawe speaketh) or in any other cuntry abroade,[74] shewe how different a conceipt those that know us and our conversation holde of us, and of the holy Catholike faith which we professe and of our manner of proceeding with all men, from that which others conceive who knowe us not but by hearesaye, and many tymes the reporte of persons deceyved or that procure to deceive, and from that which our adversaries would be gladde that all men helde of us. Seing they barre them with so greate penaltyes and feare them with threatenings not to knowe us nor come neere us, because they finde by experience that as many as come out of that confusion of England, not being of their Statesmen and such as make reckoning of no religion, nor over much interested in the proceedings of the protestants, now over growen with vices and given over to licentious life (if otherwise they be men of capacyty and able to judge and distinguish betweene folly and truth) give over with greate facility the errors in which they were brought up, and (as our English natures be ingenious and sincere) imbrace most willingly that which they finde to be best, and become Catholikes. And therefore, this lawe made to the contrary testifieth evidently that those which procured it be *possessores malae fidei*[75] and know that theire religion is naught, seing they use so much violence insteede of argument [365ᵛ] for want of justice and reason.

62. And, not withstanding I know how little reason and truth prevayleth with such as have given themselves over to passion, yet I thought the labor well bestowed to set downe in wryting, with all sincerity and without offence to any man as neere as I coulde, what I thinke in all that is above saide intended only (in the presence of Almighty God) to give your Lordship light and information of that which I understand to be true, with as much desyre as I can have of anything in this worlde of the kinges prosperity, and the well doing of all that be under his charge. And I have set downe so much the more plainely what I thinke, for that (as I have saide in the beginning) I take your Lordship to be a man of honor and how soever deceyved in Religion, yet I hope so free of malice that you will not interpret in evill sense that which is spoken with good meaning and affection. And hereby your Lordship maye have occasion to enforme yourselfe of divers truthes and knowing them, you rest, by your office and the fidelity you owe to your prince, obliged to certifie him of them and so much the more as perhappes his magesty by other waies may not come to know them so plainely. And whosoever shoulde eyther wrest my wordes or meaning to other sense then I have saide, I appeal to a higher judgement where all our intentions, wordes, and actions must be revewed and judged with justice. And here I will adde an example much to the purpose worthy to be imitated of all princes, and specyally of his magesty, to the ende he may enjoye those kingdomes which God hath given him with quietnes and leave them with peace and benediction.★★★

63. The example mentioned is of the emperor Augustus set downe by Seneca in his first book of Clemencia,[77] the nineth chapter.

Augustus was by nature stoute and magnanimous, and ready to revenge himselfe in the beginning of his Empire, but afterwardes changed his condition, perceyving by experience that the use of rigor and punishment was no meanes for his owne quietnes, nor for the security he pretended. And the change happened uppon this occasion.

He having raigned fortye yeares, there was a conspiracye raysed [365ᵛ] against him by Lucious Cinna who had determined to kill him as he was doing sacrifice which with all the circumstances, the tyme, the place and the manner how it shoulde have bene

---

★★★Here the *Carta*, p. 37ʳ, adds:

"Among whom they say that the Prince[76] his son is of very rare talent and from him all manner of great things can be expected, for a good education is not lacking."

done, was discovered to him by one of the confederates themselves.

The emperor troubled with the newes, caled togeather his counsell and his frindes of moste confidence, who all agreed that Cinna and his companions shoulde forth with be apprehended, and receive the punishmentes due to so heynous an attempt.

64. Which consultation ended, the Emperor passing the night with care and perplexity, walked up and downe his chamber reasoning with himselfe *pro & contra* according to the different cogitations that disquieted his minde and at last broake out in these speeches. What shall I doe? Shall I live alwaies with this solicytude suffering so notable an enemy before mine eyes? How shoulde he be pardoned, who in tyme of peace hath gone about not only to kill but to sacrifice his emperor (so many tymes assalted in the civill warres and yet defended by the heavens) and in so many battles and dangers by sea and lande?

65. After awhile, having debated the matter in his owne minde, he broake out reprehending himselfe more then before he had Cinna, with these wordes. To what purpose shoudest thou live, if so many shoulde receyve profit and contentment to see thee deade? When shall we make an end of execution? How much bloude shall we shed? Muste thy heade be the only grindstone in which the men of most corrage in this commonwealth must sharpen their swordes and make tryall of theire valor? Thy life is not so much worth if so many must perish to save it.

66. The empresse Livia seing her husband thus perplexed, spoke unto him in this manner. Sir, will you take a womans counsell? Doe that which good phisitians are accustomed to doe, who having prooved one remedy many tymes and seing it doth no good, make tryall of the contrary. How many yeares have you spent in vaine using rigor and punishment? have you not put to death Salvidenus? Lepidus? Murena? Capion? and others that have conspired against you? Such and so many as it is a shame to remember them. Prove once how you shall speede by pardoning. Lucius Cinna being now discovered can doe [366ʳ] you no hurt, but maye doe you greate service for your reputation and authority.

67. The Emperor was gladde to heare this good counsell of his wife and gave her thankes, and forth with dismissing those of his counsell, gave order that Lucius Cinna should be sent for and another chayre set neere his owne. And being come he made him set downe and spoke unto him in these wordes.

The first thing Cinna that thou must promise me must be not to interrupt me, nor speake a worde till thou hast given me hearing of all that I have to saye, for afterwardes thou shalt have tyme to speake.

Thou canst not have forgotten howe I found thee in mine adversaries camp, not become but (as I maye saye) borne mine enemy, being nephew to Pompey. I gave thee pardon of thy life and all thy patrymony, so as at this daye thou art richer and in better estate then many of those which were my companions in the victory, who in these thinges come behind thee and envye thy prosperity.

Besides I have advanced thee since that time with those dignityes in the commonwealth which thy selfe hast required, preferring thee before many others, whose fathers did beare me company in my war, and having done all this for thee, how canst thou be so ungrateful as to seeke my life?

68. At which wordes, Cinna cryed out protesting that it was not so. Cinna (quoth the Emperor) thou keepest not promise for thou knowest that we agreed that thou shouldest not interrupt me. I saye thou hast made a conspiracy to kill me, such a daye, in such a place, with such and such companions, declaring unto him all the circumstances, and in what manner it should have bene executed. And seing him (now) convinced, and silent not as before by covenant but as guilty in his owne conscyence, he added. And to what purpose woudest thou have killed me? perhappes to have succeeded in the empire? Without doubt the commonwealth were but in bad taking, if only my life did hinder thee to governe. If I alone be the hindrance of thy hopes, what dost thou think of those Pauli? Fabii? and so many worthy men of noble families? Canst [366ᵛ] thou perswade thy selfe that these will have thee for their Emperor? And finally having added many thinges more to the same purpose, finally Augustus ended his speech in this manner.

69. Well, Cinna, now once againe I give thee thy life: the first tyme as to an open enemye, the seconde as to a secret traytor. From this daye forwarde let our frindship beginne, let us strive to shewe which of the two has done more, or whether I have given thee life with greater clemency, or thou hast receyved it with greater gratitude and loyalty. And afterwardes the Emperor made him *Questor* and *Consul* and did him many other favors, which Cinna himselfe durst not have asked, which withall he so obliged him, as he contynued alwaies after his faithful and gratefull frinde. In so much as when he died, he left all that he had to the Emperor, who passed all the rest of his life in greate security and quietnes, putting (with this heroycall act) an ende to all conspiracyes, so that there was never any more hearde of in all the residue of his reigne.

70. Hitherto be wordes of Seneca, where withall he setteth downe this worthy act of this famous Emperor and this prudent and profitable counsell of the Empris his wife. And truely, I have heard that some of those gentlemen lately executed did the king so greate service in procuring his peaceable entrance into England, that if his magesty had knowen of it in tyme, howsoever they might have deserved death for this other attempt, I am perswaded that he would have done with them (and perhappes with the rest) no lesse then Augustus did with Cinna. And not only Augustus but other princes have reaped benefits by this manner of proceeding more than anye have done by the contrary. As Aeneas Silvius writeth of the Emperor Charles the fourth, who in another like conspiracye a caled unto him the party chosen amongst the rest (for his valor and corrage) to strike the stroke, and shewing compassion, that his daughter come to womans estate was unmaried for her fathers poverty, gave him a competente some of mony for her dowry which he receyved with thankes as a benefite unexpected. And when afterwardes he was [367ᵣ] urged by his confederates to despatch the attempt, he answered them that when he undertooke it he was deceyved, not knowing the Emperor but that now his harte woulde not serve him to hurt so curteous, noble and bountifll a prince.[78]

71. These examples are antyent. But if your Lordship will have one more neere to our tyme and case, caste your eyes upon this present king of France, whome the Hugonotes and other ill disposed people of that cuntry kept (for some yeares) unquiet with the like suspitions and distrustes as these, with which others procure to enterteine his magesty of England: accusing, condemning, and putting unjustly to death inocent persons, as though they have bene confederates of the conspiracyes which at that time passed. And all this to give color to their wicked devises, with other mens publicke infamye, which they thought should have contynued for ever in France seing they had gotten it graven in stone, as these others have inserted their callumniations into the actes of parlament. But God almighty had far different cogitations from others, and his justice being now pacyfied in some parte for the sinnes of that kingdome, the punishment being now come to the highest was to decline. And the king being a man of valor and wisedome, after he perceyved the deceiptes of bad counselors shooke them off and opened his eares to such as proceeded with sincerity and truth.

Where withall he hath ended all those jelosies and suspitions, and resteth (since) peaceable lorde and king of his kingdome, not withstanding his subjectes be not all of one religion.[79] And his magesty of England if he be as well advised as the other, will do no lesse having far greater cause. For the Catholikes have alwaies bene well willers to him and his, and many of them lost theire lives in his service, where (to the contrary) they that gave him life and right to all he injoyeth, I meane his father and mother, were both of them pitifully murdered by conspiracye, publicke sentence, and bloudy handes of those which cale themselves protestants.

72. Greate mutations, being to be made by men, require commonly greater [367ᵛ] dispositions which must be longe adoing, but where and when God almighty putteth to his hande, neyther tyme nor labor is required. Who had looked upon France some yeares agoe, might with humane discorse have judged that that kingdome was beginning to fall from Christ to heresy and disolution.

But he in whose handes be the hartes of kings and subjects, and doth what he pleaseth in earth and in heaven, hath so changed the judgments and affections of men in that cuntry in fewe yeares, as it will quicly retorne to florish in Catholike piety with peace and concord as in olde tymes.

The meanes whereby God hath wrought this mutation were not thought of by men, not withstanding he served himselfe of mans industry and diligence and of theire different inclynations, permitting some thinges and aproving others, as much as they served to his purpose.

73. The like (infallibly) may be expected in the disposition of England, whose conversion, I thinke nothing hath hindered so much as over much confidence of some in humane meanes. Which now being removed, the tyme willeth us to expect his hande, who ever (for his parte) is ready to helpe in such cases as this, and nearest to succour his servants, when he seemeth farthest off, and they brought to greatest extremetyes. And so saide Philo to his companions when theire embassage was rejected,[80] and they rebuked by the Emperor Caligula, that theire busynes was then in best estate, seing it was given over by men that should have remedied theire wronges,★★★ and come into God almighties hands, who is a righteous judge, and though many tymes he defer when it is so convenient, yet never fayleth to doe justice, and hath infinite meanes to succour his servants, which neyther they nor their adversaries doe think of.

74. It is the course and order of Gods providence to suffer many tymes his servants to be afflicted, to refine and make perfect their confidence: yea, to increase their affliction, untill the tyme doe better instruct them and that they and others by experience come to understande that humane meanes and the power of creatures in which they had put their confidence, are not sufficyent to deliver them. And then he putteth to his hande to remedye [368ʳ] and comfort them with more abundance then they themselves could ever expect or thinke of.

75. In this sence the prophet David promiseth in behalfe of God almighty to the righteous man which in his afflictions trusteth in him, *quoniam in me speravit, liberabo eum: protegam eum quoniam cognovit nomen meum. Cum ipso sum in tribulatione eripiam eum et glorificabo eum,*[82] and is the same which passed with the patriarke

---

★★★The *Carta*, p. 40ᵛ, adds:

"And in our times another similar response is told about Father Master Juan de Avila, a most distinguished man of letters, counsel and sanctity, after he had been falsely accused and imprisoned by the Holy Office of the Inquisition. The lord Inquisitors, although examining his case carefully and wishing to release him for being such an eminent person, sent a message to him that, because his indictment was (in their opinion) so well founded in justice after all the witnesses had confirmed the testimony, they had failed to discover any human recourse for him.[81] To which he replied with great courage and satisfaction: "Blessed be God, for never has my case been in better state than at present, for I see it is taken out of the hands of men and placed in those of God." And so it was seen to be for, from then on, the falsehoods of the witnesses and the truth of his innocence began to be learned, until his release from that prison occurred with the greatest deference ever seen, whereby the Lord has proven in the case of this holy man and his accusers what he is doing every day on behalf of others."

Joseph soulde by his brethren, accused in Egipt and cast in prison without fault [Gn 37] and with others inumerable, and with the Sonne of God himselfe, when he lived in this mortall life, to leave us no just occasion nor color to complaine. And God proceedeth in this manner because it is convenient for our good and due to his glory that no man maye saye: *manus nostra excelsa et non dominus fecit haec omnia.*[83]

76. Whereby we maye learne that which God pretendeth to teach us with the affliction and persecution which he permitteth that not withstanding we maye and ought to helpe ourselves, with convenient and lawfull meanes yet our confidence must not be grounded on them, but in the power of his omnipotent arme, who serveth himselfe of such meanes and will have us to helpe our selves with them and use them as instruments of his divine providence and depending of his hande and disposition, and not otherwise.

77. Wherefore when such as men hoped should remedy their wantes doe faile them, it is not reason they should be disgusted, nor be out of charity or patience with them, because it is harde to judge who was in most fault, or whether God almighty without any fault on the one side ore on the other hath ordeyned thinges so, to rewarde more abundantly the patience and humility of those that suffer, and not to hinder the meanes appointed by his eternall providence for their salvation. Seing many are saved by adversity, and with persecution come to exceeding greate glory, who would have bene damned if they had lived in prosperity. And no tribulation can be long which endeth with our short life, nor any thinge greate that is holden in little roome [2 Co 4]. And if some tymes we feele it much, it may be for that our patience is little and because we would have thinges [368ᵛ] before theire tyme, and so we lessen our owne merite and the glory which our saviour with so liberall a hande would bestowe upon us who otherwise, of himselfe is so favorable and compassionate as he taketh no pleasure in our sufferings, nor would permit them for one moment if they were not to breede us greater comfort, and necessary to be permitted for the universall goverment and accomplishment of his divine purposes in which there faleth no imperfection.

78. For all which reasons, when those meanes where withall men would have remedyed our necessities become unprofitable, we ought not to discorage our selves nor is it reason that any man should be dismayed, but lifte up our hopes and fix them on God almighty, leaving it to his choise by what waye he will helpe us, seing he will doe it without faile. And when he doth it not by those meanes which men had disposed, he will doe it by others which shall be better, or by the same in another tyme more convenient, or will make choyse of other persons more fitte to bring to pass that which we have neede of. And he doth it many tymes by the waies that we least imagine and by them from whome we could looke for no good at all.

79. And by these demonstrations now and then he useth to give notice to the worlde of his infinite power, that we may learne to knowe him and that he can bringe to passe what he pleaseth by what meanes he list. Which not withstanding they be of themselves little to the purpose yet when he is pleased to use them they become both proportionate and profitable, and in a moment he lightneth the understandings most overclowded with darknes, and mollifyeth the hardest harts, and moveth with efficacy those to redresse the wronges of his servantes, that were farthest off from doing them any good. And infinite other meanes he hath to succour those that put their confidence wholy in him, which neither they themselves, nor their adversaries, are able to thinke of.★★★

80. Who would not have thought but that God had given over his people? When to trye their fidelity and manyfest his glory, he had suffered them to be brought to such a straight and perplexity as they had the Egiptian [369ʳ] army at their backes, and the red sea before them, ready to be murdered by the one, or swallowed up by the other, and who (I saye) could have imagined the remedye that God had prepared for their delivery!

81. The redresse and perplexity of the Christians (to omit other examples) was little lesse, when the Emperor Julian of whome we have made mention before, had made a vowe to sacrifice to his false gods the bodies of as many of them as shoulde be founde living at his retorne from the wars of Persya, and had

---

★★★The *Carta*, p. 42ᵛ, adds:
"Saint Bernard says that he read in a man of wisdom that the strong man does not exist whose spirit is not growing through adversities, then he added: but I say that he who would be steadfast despite the blows has to have greater faith and this one can have whose cause is just and has God before him."[84]

already commanded a publike place of spectacle to be builded in Jerusalem, that there the destruction of Christians should beginne from whence theire religion was derived. Which knowen, and they seing them selves forsaken and destitute of all humane helpe, turned (as St. Gregory Nazianzen writeth) their hartes and hopes wholy to God almighty importuning him with fervent prayers and fasting and with other workes of penance that it would please him to deliver his people condemned to death, and their religion which the Emperor meant to distroye.

This prayer, with this disposition, made in tyme of so greate necessity prevayled so much with God, as within fewe daies after he sent them remedy.

82. The intentions of our adversaries are nowe more declared then ever, and their presumption greater to destroy the Catholike religion, since it seemeth to them that by their policye they have deprived us of the temporall helpes wherein they imagine that our hopes were founded.

83. But your Lordship shall understand that such as looke not only upon the present and imediate state of things, but cast theire eyes further, consydering how these inferior mutations depend upon a superior immutable cause (which alwaies and infallibly directeth them to the greatest good) have now more hope and expectation of the remedy of that cuntry then ever, grounded not only upon the generall confidence which in such cases men ought to have in almighty God, but also in particuler and reasonable discourse. For Luther and Calvins heresyes long agoe have lost all credite in England, where they are violently supported (as a ruynous house readye to fale) with the favor donne to such as professe them exteriourly [369ᵛ] and with punishment of the Catholikes, to make them approve outwardly that which they doe not beleeve. But nothing so violent is durable, and these two proppes are over weake to upholde longe so heavy a burthen declyning dayly with the ruine of it selfe.

84. The prince is wise, and those that counsell him not without providence and will be wearied to stirre against God, and to trouble themselves and afflict their subjectes and scandalize their nighbors, making their goverment not only contemptuous, but offensive to the whole Christian world, which by many waies may bring inconveniences. *Sapiens* (saith the Holy Ghost) *timet et declinat a malo: stultus transivit et confidit.* And *Sapientis est mutare* *consilium*,[85] specyally when tyme discovereth and experience cryeth out that it is not factible which he hath taken in hande, and that his labors prove unprofitable.

85. Those which for the present governe England, desyrous to continue things as others had lefte them framed, have done as much as men could doe, pretending with the peace, the parlament, and their newe lawes so cunningly procured and contryved, to destroye religion and establish their errors and devises which be *ex genere privativorum*,[86] and therefore as they have no substance so can they have no stability. And on the other side, Catholikes are so warned as from henceforth none of them will easyly be drawn, to cooperate to their devises which would abuse the particuler zeale of some to the distruction of all, nor expect their remedye but from whence it is to come.

86. Wherefore, howsoever by these lawes they are made subject for the present to temporall inconveniences, and some weakelings may be brought to dissemble their conscyences, yet for one in this manner fayleth for a time, manye doe arise for ever. And the constant Catholikes which be the branches of the vine, and of whome it was foretolde by Christ in the behalfe of his Father, *purgabit eos ut fructum plus afferent*,[87] those with this newe tribulation are renewed in their olde fervor, charity and devotion. And those with care of their owne and desyre of other mens salvation, sprede out dayly and extend new branches that reach up to eternity: neither shall the gates of hell prevayle against these branches.

[370ʳ] **87.** The fall of the Kingdome of England had not the like beginning to the apostacy of other cuntryes, which did wilfully seperate themselves from Christ and his church by generall disorder and corruption of the people. But they of England were drawn unto it partly by force of violent lawes, and partly by the authority and practices of their princes and governers, who for their particuler interest have procured to set forwarde that which King Henry the eight so unhappily beganne, seduced by bad counselors, and overcome with a particuler passion to marrye Anne Boleyne during the life of his lawful wife Queen Katheren.

In which respect, as the Schisme beganne in greate parte with out fault of the kingdome and against the peoples will, so God almighty hath dealt mercyfully with them, more then with other cuntryes that have seperated themselves willingly from the obedyence of the church, giving to the priestes and Catholikes of this

95

nation the spirite of martirdome, which is a singuler and inesty-mable gifte, and from whence commeth the strength and con-stancye of our martirs. Like to that of the primitive church, where withall those glorious saints, *non resistendo sed perferendo*[88] (to use the wordes of venerable Bede) subdued the worlde to Christ, and is a sure pledge and godspennye[89] that his divine Magesty hath not forsaken our cuntry, nor given it over to infidelity and here-sye as he hath done to Africa and Greece and other cuntries for their wilful disobedience and other sinnes. But that being purged and refeyned with this persecution (which he permitteth) *ut reve-lantur cogitationes e cordibus utque probati manifesti fiunt.*[90] He will restore our ancestors faith, honor and vertue to prevaile againe in that kingdome, as it was wont in their happye dayes.

For which considerations among many others the priestes ban-ished seeke to returne, and can not, nor will not forbeare for dangers nor for threatnings to doe their dutyes. And he that fed Elias in the wildernes will not faile to provide for their mainte-nance, whilest he is pleased that they live and labor in his vin-iarde. And for one which our adversaries take awaye by martir-dome, he sendeth (as we see) a great [370ᵛ] sorte to supplye his place. And (as in the springe) with occasion of this winter storme, manye good purposes are renewed and strengthened, and others growe up that were not before, so as alreadye *vineae florem dede-runt odorem suum*[91] and as many plantes as have life are loden with flowers, and frutes of all the heroycall vertues above saide, and with many others, which promise plentie.

88. This newes I can give your Lordship for the present, that for two of our bretheren lately put to death in England, God hath raysed a greate number to desyre to enter into the Socyety that had no such cogitation before. And for the Semenaries, if all should be admitted that are fitte and offer themselves, specyally since these late rigorous lawes, the howses were to be doubled.

89. Finally seeing the kings high waye (by which so manye other princes and cuntries have returned from errors, and infidel-ity, and corruption of life to the Catholike truth) is made open and desencumbred, which maye we not hope of Gods mercy to our cuntry? Yea, we shoulde be blameworthy if we did not: see-ing that as many things as have bene guided by this waye since the beginning, have had prosperous successe above most expec-tations, and all other waies and meanes prooved unprofitable for the conversion of soules, which is and ought to be our only scope. And it could hardly be other wise, seing it implyeth contradiction and is impossible that men should be made goode against their willes. And here appeareth the excellency of Gods wisedome, so far beyonde humane policye, that the selfe same meanes which men ordeyne to suppresse vertue and truth, God almighty useth them as instruments to support them and to make them to be esteemed and desyred above all the riches in the world, even of the selfe same persons that (a little before) did not only contemn them, but abhorred them and pruned to roote them out. As in many successes might be exemplified, and specyally was seene in the sodaine conversion of the whole army of the Emperor Julian (so often mentioned) thought to be so confirmed in infidelity, as by it (according to the Emperors discorses and designements of state) Idolatry should have bene established and Christianity rooted out, forever.

[371ʳ] **90.** I remember I have reade in Sozamenus,[92] how the selfe same Emperor to intangle the Christians and give some color to his anger and their unjust persecution, and to bring the soldiers of the same army (insensibly by little and little) to yeilde to paganisme and become Idolators unawares, caused his owne picture to be set up in the middest amongest the pictures of Jupiter, Mars, and Mercury declaring that all those that would not doe reverence unto it shoulde be holden for his enemies. The Christians would have donne to the Emperor (by waye of civill curtesye) what honor so ever they might and was due to his place and person, and had bene done to other Emperors before him and to their pictures with better will then any others. And he knewe it well enough: but the drifte was to intangle them so as eyther he might charge them with treason, or make them commit Idolatrye.

91. After the same sorte, in this newe oath[93] the supposed harmes and dangers to the princes person and estate (which harmes and dangers the Catholikes detest much more then any of them that made it) are joyned with propositions of doubtfull and dangerous sence, bringing with them scrupple and perplexity to such as must sweare them, eyther to commit treason against Christ, or to be holden as disloyall to theire temporall prince.

What should Catholikes doe in such a case? But as their ancestors in the like have done, recurre for counsell to the Sea Apostolike who will unfolde this confused difficulty, and give to God his owne and to Cesar that which is his. And who shoulde counsell him to seeke for more, I assure your Lordship is not his frinde.

92. This letter I have indited, whiles I recover my health by peece meale as I could. And not withstanding the importance and variety of the matter hath made it longer then I purposed, yet I doubt not but your Lordship will take it in good parte, seing you know my custome to speake plainely (in all ocasions) what I thinke, submitting alwaies my thoughts and wordes to better censure without desire of contention, or any mans hurt, but only that truth mae have his place. And I hope in this letter your Lordship will perceyve (as in many other things you maye have perceyved) my sincere affection [371ᵛ] and good will which alwaies I have borne both to the king and to the kingdome, desyring to his Magesty, and to it, and to your Lordship, the same which I desyre to mine owne soule, truth, light and Gods grace in this life and afterwardes ever lasting felicyty: to which I beseech Him to bring us all that made us for it.

From Jesus dell monte, ettc.★★★

NOTES

1. "They seek after wickednesse in the house of the Just" (Pr 24:15).

2. Sir Edward Coke, the king's attorney, mentioned also in nos. 5 and 10.

3. I.e., to curry favor with another.

4. Robert Taylor, secretary of English letters at the Spanish embassy, wrote a report after attending Garnet's trial which reached the council of state, E 843, fols. 96–97, "Relacion de lo que se platico tocante a la condenacion del Henrico Garnet. . . ." Later Cornwallis heard this letter from "the embassys man" was circulating in Madrid (B.L. Cotton MSS. Vespasian C IX, fol. 585ᵛ, Cornwallis to Cecil, 16 Nov. 1606).

5. I.e., inaccurately.

6. Coke had stated that "Philopater," the pseudonym for Robert Persons in writing the *Responsio ad Edictum* in 1592, was a book by

---

★★★*Carta*, p. 42ᵛ, concludes:
> Right honorable my very good Lord
> Your true and faithful servant in Christ
> Joseph Creswell

Creswell. Cornwallis later assured Cecil that he was not "Godfather to Philopater" (B.L. Cotton MSS. C IX, fol. 408^v, n.d., ca. June 1606).

7. "An Act for the Attainders of divers offendors . . . ," the indictment of the conspirators of the Gunpowder Plot (*Statutes of the Realm*, vol. IV, *1547–1624*, pp. 1068–70, 3 Jac. I chap. 2).

8. When Creswell served briefly as a chaplain in Parma's command, he wrote an English proclamation with these same grievances in 1588; see A. Loomie, "Philip II's Armada Proclamation of 1597," *Recusant History* 12, no. 5 (1974), pp. 216–25; see also Colin Martin and Geoffrey Parker, *The Spanish Armada* (London: Hamilton, 1988), pp. 265–77, 290.

9. Philip secured the pardon of some who were associated with the conspiracies of Northumberland and Wyatt who later served in his campaigns in France in 1557, but did not have an effective role in Mary's council. Contemporaries said that he regretted later his failure to seek opportunities to have a larger role when in England. See David Loades, "Philip II and the Government of England," in Claire Cross, David Loades, and Jack Scarisbrick, edd., *Law and Government in Tudor England* (Cambridge: Cambridge University Press, 1988), pp. 177–94; M. J. Rodríguez-Salgado, *The Changing Face of Empire: Charles V, Philip II, and Habsburg Authority, 1551–59* (Cambridge: Cambridge University Press, 1988), pp. 201–4.

10. One of several allegations at the trial of Philip Howard, earl of Arundel (1559–95), was that he had earlier planned to join the forces of the League and the duke of Guise in France.

11. Sir John Perrot (1527?–1592), Elizabeth's natural half-brother, lord deputy of Ireland 1584–1588, had been unpopular in the Pale because of his enforcement of the penal laws against Catholics. Later under arrest in London, he was accused by an ex-priest, Denis Roughan, whom he had once prosecuted for forgery, of treasonous correspondence with Parma and Philip II. See Colm Lennon, *The Lords of Dublin in the Age of the Reformation* (Dublin: Irish Academic Press, 1989), pp. 157–58; Steven Ellis, *Tudor Ireland* (London: Longmans, 1985), pp. 285–88, 294; *Dictionary of National Biography*, *sub* Perrot.

12. It is possible that Creswell had recently heard this from someone in Nottingham's suite at Valladolid. Abdie Ashton, the chaplain of Essex, was said to have encouraged him to relate certain details of his plot which were not proven. Francis Bacon, the prosecutor, later published two short essays on Essex's treason. See Walter B. Devereux, *Lives of the Earls of Essex*, 2 vols. (London: Murray, 1853), II, 165–69, 201; Edwin Abbott, *Bacon and Essex* (London: Seeley, Jackson & Halliday, 1877), pp. 232–34.

13. The Spanish sources describing the activities of Thomas Wintour

and his circle are to be seen in A. Loomie, *Guy Fawkes in Spain: The 'Spanish Treason' in Spanish Documents, Bulletin of the Institute of Historical Research*, Special Supplement no. 9 (1971), pp. 10–16.

14. "A time to keep silence and a time to speak" (Qo 3:7).

15. I.e., abundance.

16. Piracy had continued during the recent war.

17. "Solitary grains fall to earth and a hundredfold are borne."

18. The sentence is not in the *Carta*; possibly to mean "when in life and when without it."

19. The *Carta* omits this paragraph.

20. "Our strength is delight in the Lord."

21. "We are clothed with strength from above."

22. "You have heard of the patience of Job and you have seen the end of the Lord" (Jm 5:11).

23. "Lay not this sin to their charge" (Ac 7:59).

24. "I am become foolish, you have compelled me" (2 Co 12:11).

25. This dates the manuscript to 1608, as distinct from the date in the *Carta*.

26. "Either that he may be corrected or through the good person be tested"; St. Augustine, *Enarrationes in Psalmos* (Ps 55:2), in *A Library of the Fathers of the Church*, 6 vols. (Oxford, 1847–1858), III, 29.

27. "Who taketh away the spirit of princes" (Ps 75:13).

28. "This is the seed which the Lord hath bestowed upon us"; the words seem to reflect Mk 4 in the parables of the seed as the word of God.

29. "Who before was a blasphemer and a persecutor and contumelious" (1 Tm 1:13).

30. "Yesterday, today and forever" (Heb 13:8).

31. A paraphrase from "A Sermon on St. Caesarius" and "A Sermon on St. Basil"; see Leo P. McCauley, ed., *Funeral Orations by Saint Gregory Nazianzen and St. Ambrose*, The Fathers of the Church 22 (New York: Fathers of the Church, Inc., 1953), pp. 13, 67–70.

32. Theodoret of Cyr, *The Ecclesiastical History* 4.16; see Blomfield Jackson, ed., *A Select Library of Nicene and Post Nicene Fathers in the Christian Church*, Second Series (Grand Rapids: Eerdmans, 1955), pp. 118–20.

33. Orosius, *Seven Books of Histories against the Pagans*, 6.33; see Roy J. Deferrari, *The Fathers of the Church*, vol. 50 (1964), pp. 339–40.

34. Sozomen, *A History of the Church in Nine Books, 324–440 A.D.*, 6.40 (London: Bagster, 1846), pp. 321–22.

35. From "A Sermon on St. Basil," (n. 31 above) pp. 72–75.

36. "There have they trembled for fear where there was no fear" (Ps 13:5).

37. It was well known that King James was encouraging a vindication of his mother's name; see Sharpe, *Sir Robert Cotton*, pp. 89–96; and nos. 57 and 71.

38. I.e., those who seek novelties.

39. "Would that the vengeance of the deity be delayed."

40. "The joy of the hypocrite is but for the moment" (Jb 20:5).

41. "Even a fly has its sting and an ant its bile."

42. The *Geuzen*, or "beggars," who led the resistance to Spanish authority.

43. "From rare circumstances."

44. Calvin's *Lectures on Amos, passim.*

45. Carlo Sigonio (1524–1584), *Historiarum de Occidentali Imperio Libri XI* (Bononiae, 1578), II, 39–40.

46. Eusebius, *The Life of Constantine*, 1.16; see *Select Library*, p. 486.

47. Gamaliel's speech as in Ac 5:34–39.

48. The next five lines are omitted in the *Carta*. Against the queen's supremacy continental apologists usually cited St. Paul: 1 Tm 2:11–15, 1 Co 11:9–11, Ep 5:22–24.

49. The treasons charged against Henry Brooke, Lord Cobham, and Walter Raleigh in 1604 were widely known; see Samuel R. Gardiner, *A History of England*, 10 vols. (New York: AMS Press, 1965), I, 108–14, 117–37.

50. B.L. Cotton MSS. Vespasian C IX, fol. 475, Salisbury to Cornwallis, 12 July 1606, related that a Captain William Nuse had reported a conspiracy against James's "safetie" and the "surprising" of the English cautionary town of Flushing. Nuse charged that a Tomaso Franceschi had arrived by ship with letters from Calais about this. On the same ship John Ball, the interpreter of the Spanish ambassador in London, had arrived and had to be defended from allegations of Nuse (P.R.O. S.P. 94/13, fol. 85). Later John Chamberlain reported "the treason is come to a cold sent and for ought I heare they can make nothing of yt" (*The Letters of John Chamberlain*, 2 vols. [Philadelphia: 1939]), II, p. 230.

51. The privy council's efforts to manipulate the queen are seen in Malcolm R. Thorp, "Catholic Conspiracy in Early Elizabethan Foreign Policy," *Sixteenth Century Journal* 15 (1984), 433–38; Christopher Haigh, *Elizabeth I* (London: Longman, 1988), chap. 4, "The Queen and Her Council," pp. 66–83.

52. Dr. Rodrigo Lopez from Portugal had been the queen's physician. The earl of Essex, intent on demonstrating his protection of the queen, had falsely accused him of planning to poison her on the orders of Philip II in 1594. There was widespread doubt of these charges. See Robert B. Wernham, *After the Armada: Elizabethan England and the Struggle for Western Europe, 1588–95* (Oxford: Oxford University Press, 1984), pp. 525–26; *Dictionary of National Biography, sub* Lopez.

53. Richard Williams and Edmund York, after brief service in the Spanish army in Flanders, were charged by Essex in August 1594 with planning to poison the queen (*Cal.S.P., Dom. 1591–94*, pp. 539–51). Thomas Fitzherbert, *A Defence of the Catholyke Cause* (Antwerp, 1602), part 2, pp. 25–27, wrote that Williams "was held but for a cold and weake Catholyke" and York "was suspected to be a protestant."

54. I.e., deceiver.

55. Creswell's friend, Martin Aray, who had lived in Seville in 1597–1598, had written of this third conspiracy to poison the queen in *The Discoverie and confutation of a tragicall fiction, devysed and played by Edmund Squyer* (n.p., 1599). See also Francis Edwards, "The Strange Case of the Poisoned Pommel: Richard Walpole S.J. and the Squire Plot, 1587–98," *Archivum Historicum Societatis Iesu*, 56 (no. 111) (1987), 3–82.

56. This is drawn largely from Sozomen, *History of the Church*, 5.18 and 6.4, 6, pp. 237–38, 254, 258–60.

57. I.e., disgraced.

58. See Philip Caraman, *Henry Garnet, 1555–1606, and the Gunpowder Plot* (New York: Farrar Strauss, 1964), pp. 348–429.

59. Henry Foley, *Records of the English Province of the Society of Jesus*, 7 vols. (London, 1882), IV, 61, has a letter of Henry Garnet to Claudio Acquaviva, 24 July 1605, about restraining restless Catholics; Caraman, *Henry Garnet*, p. 379*n*153.

60. I.e., a militant person. Later Cavalier officers who refused to surrender the royalist cause to parliament had the same name; see Richard Ollard, *Clarendon and His Friends* (New York: Atheneum, 1988), pp. 80, 89, 92, 183.

61. Paul V's policy at first had been to urge the courts of France and Spain to have their resident ambassadors in London plead for less rigor in the penal laws. After the Herefordshire riots (see no. 57 below), Nicolo Molin, the Venetian ambassador, reported that the pope wrote to the archpriest of the English Catholic clergy that "he is greatly displeased . . . as he is firmly resolved to deal very gently and cautiously with this question"; *Cal.S.P., Venet. 1603–7*, p. 280.

62. Local disturbances, in which religion was only one of the grievances, remained a serious concern to the privy council; see Anthony Fletcher, *Tudor Rebellions* (London: Longman, 1968), pp. 112–14; Roger Manning, *Village Revolts: Social Protest and Popular Disturbances in England, 1509–1640* (Oxford: Oxford University Press, 1988), pp. 330–40.

63. See Paul Hughes and James Larkin, edd., *Stuart Royal Proclamations* (Oxford: Oxford University Press, 1973), I, 123–31, for four proclamations for the arrest of Thomas Percy and others, November 1605.

64. See Roland Mathias, *Whitsun Riot: An Account of a Commotion*

amongst Catholics in Herefordshire and Monmouthshire in 1605 (London: Bowes & Bowes, 1963). Creswell was in correspondence with English Jesuits working in this region. The unrest began over the refusal of a local vicar to allow the burial of a recusant woman in his village church-yard. Other grievances kept the area in turmoil until the privy council ordered the earl of Worcester, a secret Catholic, to lead armed forces into the counties, where, according to Nicolo Molin, "he found the movement far inferior in importance to what had been represented"; *Cal.S.P., Venet. 1603–7*, p. 266.

65. The next sentence is omitted in the *Carta*.

66. "Lured into troubles."

67. William Parker, Lord Mounteagle, received an anonymous letter of warning about the opening day of parliament, but nothing was di-vulged about its authorship. See Mark Nicholls, "Investigating Gun-powder Plot," *Recusant History*, 19 (1988), 124–45 and note 137.

68. Thomas Hammond, *The Late Commotion of Certaine Papists in Herefordshire* (London, 1605), citing this unrest, urged a stricter enforce-ment of the penal laws and a rejection of any toleration of Catholic practice. To this Robert Persons replied in a *Treatise tending to Mitigation towardes Catholike-Subiectes in England* (St. Omer, 1607). Mathias, *Whit-sun Riot*, pp. 106–10, considers the presence of an *agent provocateur* un-proven but points out the informers present among recusants.

69. This sentence is omitted in the *Carta*. The story is hard to verify since the *Acts of the Privy Council* do not survive for this year. In all, 1,800 pounds of gunpowder were discovered; see N. A. M. Rogers, "Ordnance Records and the Gunpowder Plot," *Bulletin, Institute of His-torical Research*, 53 (1980), 124–25.

70. The penalty was 40 shillings for each book seized (3 Jac. I chap. 5, para. 15).

71. I.e., irrelevant.

72. "Who speak out with ease after looking at but a few things."

73. The first half of this sentence has been omitted in the *Carta*.

74. The penalty was remitted after conformity to the established church was proven (3 Jac. I chap. 4, para. 14).

75. "Owners in bad faith."

76. Cornwallis began corresponding with Prince Henry in early 1609 and on his return was appointed treasurer of his household. For his ed-ucation see Roy Strong, *Henry Prince of Wales and England's Lost Renais-sance* (London: Thames & Hudson, 1986), pp. 27–30, 83–84.

77. The seven paragraphs are a free translation of Seneca, *On Mercy* 1.9; compare with John W. Basore, ed., *Seneca: Moral Essays*, 3 vols. Loeb Classical Library (1932), I, pp. 381–87.

78. The last half of the paragraph is omitted in the *Carta*. This story

is not included in the "Historia Bohemica," chap. 33, of Pius II, *Aeneae Sylvio Piccolominei . . . Opera quae extant omnia* (Basle, 1551; repr. Frankfurt: Minerva, 1967), pp. 101–102.

79. For the legal protection of dissent under Henry IV, see Nicola Sutherland, *The Huguenot Struggle for Recognition* (New Haven: Yale University Press, 1980), pp. 301–32; David Buisseret, *Henry IV* (London: Allen & Unwin, 1984), pp. 121–25.

80. See E. Mary Smallwood, ed., *Philonis Alexandrini Legatio ad Gaium*, nos. 45–46 (Leiden: Brill, 1980), pp. 142–46.

81. Juan de Avila (ca. 1499–1569) was a popular Andalucian preacher, arrested by the Inquisition in Seville in late 1531 and released in July 1533, cleared of all charges. The narrative is available in Luis Sala Balust and Francisco Martin Hernandez, edd., *Obras Completas del Santo Maestro Juan de Avila*, 6 vols. (Madrid: Biblioteca de Autores Cristianos, 1970) I 23–35.

82. "Because he hoped in me I will deliver him; I will protect him because he knew my name" (Ps 90[91]:14–15).

83. "Our own hand is lifted on high; the Lord had not done all these things" (Dt 32:27).

84. From Epistola CCLVI, Bernard to Pope Eugene III; see J. Leclercq and H. Rochais, edd., *S. Bernardi Opera* VIII (Rome: Editiones Cistercienses, 1977), p. 163.

85. "A wise man feareth and declineth from evil: the fool leapeth over and is confident" (Pr 14:16); "to change his advice is the sign of the wise man."

86. "From the category of things lost."

87. "He will purge it that it may bring forth more fruit" (Jn 15:2).

88. "Not by resisting but by choosing."

89. An agreement sealed by a coin, or earnest money.

90. "That out of many hearts thoughts may be revealed" (Lk 2:35); and "That they also who are approved may be made manifest among you" (1 Co 11:19).

91. "The flowering vines gave forth their fragrance" (Sg 2:13).

92. Sozomen, *History of the Church*, 5.17, pp. 234–36.

93. The oath is part of the statute 3 Jac. I chap. 4, paras. 8–9. This was already translated into Spanish in *Las Leyes* in 1606 and known to the court of Philip III. Creswell reflects the contemporary Catholic writings; see J. P. Sommerville, *Politics and Ideology in England, 1603–40* (London: Longman, 1986), pp. 195–99. The first stage of the controversy is analyzed in Thomas Clancy, "English Catholics and the Papal Deposing Power, 1570–1640," *Recusant History* 6 (1962), pp. 114–40, 205–27; 7 (1963), pp. 2–10.

Carta Escrita al Embaxador de Inglaterra

Iluſtriſsimo Señor.

VIENDO Viſto la moderacion con que V. S. Iluſt. procedio llegando a eſtos Rey nos, es fuerça que confieſſe la opinion que entonces concebi, de la pru dencia de los que auian hecho eleccion de perſona tan diſcreta, que aunque no concordaſſe con noſotros en Religion, ſupieſſe con ſu buen termino lleuar adelante, la concordia comen çada entre Principes y perſonas de diferentes profeſſiones, cumpliendo con el oficio de Em baxador (que es de Angel de paz) y no como al gunos otros, que por no tener de ſu coſecha los reſpetos honrados que V. S. Iluſtr. ha heredado de ſos paſſados, ni la conciencia que ſuelen te ner muchos hombres moralmente buenos, aūque engañados en materia de Religion, con o caſiones, y ſin ellas, *Quærunt iniquitatem in domo iuſti,* cõtra el precepto del Eſpiritu ſanto: y por *Preu. 24.* captar beneuolécia a coſta agena, y no parecer eſteriles en ſus informaciones, echan mano de qualquiera chiſmeria que les llega à los oydos, y faltandoles materia, fingen la que no ay, y las

A 2   coſas

cosas buenas, y indiferetes, tuercen à malos fen
tidos, con que ponen à los que las creen en mu
chos engaños: como se vee cada dia por sus o-
bras, y en lugar de ganarles autoridad. y amigos
con el trato llano, noble, y digno de los que re-
presentan las personas de sus Príncipes, les pier
den el respeto, y la buena volutad, que otros les
auian ganado, con notable daño suyo, y inquie
tud del bien publico.

2 Y porque (demas de otras experiencias passa
das, de la lealtad y verdad con que V. S. Illustris.
como caballero, procede) he entendido por car
tas de Inglaterra, de buenos originales, recebi-
das en Roma, que V. S. Ilust. auia testificado a su
Rey y Consejo, la sincera voluntad que en mi
auia hallado, de hazer todos los buenos oficios
que pudiesse para conseruar la paz, y quan age-
no estoy de hazer agrauio a nadie: para que V.
S. Ilust. sepa que no se engañò en esta buena o-
pinion, y pueda mejor dar razon de la dicha informacion suya, quando fuesse menester, me pa
rece estar obligado, en cierta manera, por la ley
de deuido agradecimiento, y buena correspon
dencia, à darle satisfacion en las cosas que algunos, ò por liuiandad han creydo, ò inuentado
con malicia, para que la buena informacion de
V. S. Ilust. y de otros, no hallasse cabida en el a-
nimo de su Magestad. Pero como quiera que es
to

to aya fido,quedo a V.S.lluft. con la mifma o-
bligacion,como fi tuuiera efeto fu buena volũ-
tad,y con deffeo que fe entere de la verdad,ha-
ziendo poco cafo de lo que fienten , ò dizen
otros que no la tratan,ni bufcan,fino lo que fir-
ue à fus intentos , fea verdadero , ò falfo,como
bien fe vee por muchas cofas acomuladas contra perfonas aufentes , è inocentes , fin fundamento,en el proceffo del padre Garneto, y con
todo effo encarecidas harto fuera de propofito,
por quien tiene la lengua vendida ya muchos
años ha:y no menos en eftos decretos del Parlamento,tan violentos , y tan contrarios à las leyes diuinas,y humanas,que quitan la autoridad
de aquel tribunal,que folia tener tanta, quando
en el fe juntauan verdaderos y legitimos Obifpos,hombres de ciencia y conciencia; y titula-
dos tan zelofos de fu honra , que no permitian
affomaffe en aquel lugar cofa que olieffe à in-
jufticia,y menos que fe condenaffe à nadie por
fofpechas de efpias,y malfines, fin oirle , ni co-
nocerle; y Procuradores de Cortes , quales el
Parlamento requiere , Eclefiafticos y feglares,
no entrefacados por negociaciones,fino nom-
brados por libres y legitimos fufragios de fus
Ciudades y Prouincias, ni atados à las pafsio-
nes de nadie,fino con la libertad ḡ fe folia guar
dar en aḡl tribunal,de hablar cada vno (fin per-
juy-

juyzio) lo que sentia conuenir al bien comun? Pero tal es la mudança de los tiempos, y de los que han dexado la Religió de sus ante passados, que no es mucho q̃ con ella ayan mudado tambié de costumbres, ni ay de que marauillar, que los que no guardan ley con Dios, no la tengan, ni guarden justicia con los hombres.

3 Llegando à Guadalajara cansado de tan largo camino, y tan enfermo que no podia passar adelante, con la caridad de los buenos Duques del Infantado, y la comodidad, y cuydado de sus Medicos, me entretuue en aquella ciudad algunos dias para cobrar salud: adonde llegò à mis manos la relacion de todo lo que auia passado con la santa memoria del padre Enrique Garneto, y con otro de la Compañia que han martirizado en Inglaterra. La qual ley con tanto gusto y consuelo, que fue gran parte para abreuiar la enfermedad : admirado por vna parte de la paternal prouidencia de Dios para con sus santos, y por medio de quantas dificultades, trabajos, y agrauios, los lleua à la participacion de su gloria; y por otra, de la ceguedad y temeridad de los q̃ se atreuen à oponerse à Dios, y porfiar contra la verdad, la qual siempre vence, y descubre las inuenciones y los inuencioneros, y los dexa tiznados, y notados como merecen.

4 Llegando despues à Iesus del Monte, recebi

cebi los decretos deste vltimo Parlamento, en
que se vee el blanco à que tiran, y la fragua de
donde salen todos estos enredos, en que han
puesto, y procuran poner al buen Rey, los que
no le aman ni à sus hijos y casa con amor de
beneuolencia, sino se siruen del, y de su nóbre
y autoridad, para sus particulares designios y
prouechos; haziendole andar al retortero, como otros hazian a la Reyna Ysabel, con las sospechas, assombros, y miedos que le ponen, y
apartarse del cumplimiento de su fee, y palabra
Real, dada à diuersos Principes (como de algunos dellos mismos he sabido) y à sus vasallos tambien, y agrauiar à las personas à quien
mas deue en esta vida: Y finalmente, poner la
mano en sangre inocente, cobrando en todo
el mundo, y con la posteridad, opinion, y nombre tan contrario à su condicion, y tan aborre-
cido del, como se ha visto por su modo de proceder en tiempos passados, antes que cayesse
en las manos de los que agora le quieren gouer
nar, conforme a sus passiones, y trazas, que no
pueden parar en bien.

5 Pero para llegar à lo que à mi me toca, quie
ro que V. S. Ilustrissima sepa, que me han hecho notable agrauio, y lo puedo prouar con
euidencia, y con testigos mucho mas graues,
que los autores destos decretos: y el Procurador

dor del Rey (como en otras muchas cosas,
assi en el cargo que à mi me hizo) no supo lo
que dixo. Porque yo no fuy autor de aquel libro, en el qual funda toda su quexa contra mi
en el dicho processo, y quantos han visto alguna cosa mia en Latin (y pueden juzgar) testifica-
ran que aquel libro no es mio, pues los hombres se conocen y se pueden distinguir, no
menos por los estilos que por las caras. Pero
que digo desta imprudencia del Procurador!
quando el mismo Parlamento errò tan palpa-
blemente como se verà, ò por lo menos los que
(por comission del) escriuieron, y compusie-
ron estos vltimos decretos, en los quales se vee,
que no supieron la verdad de lo que dizen. Y
por esso, no es mucho que ayan errado en su
sentencia, y atreuidose contra personas de menos calidad, quando se atreuieron con tan poco respeto à su Magestad Catolica, en materia, que (aunque fuera como ellos querian que
se creyesse) en ley de hombres cuerdos, auian
de dissimular, y no tocar aquella tecla, y mas no
siendo verdad.

6 Porque, aunq̃ no ayan faltado, ni falten personas de mucha autoridad y letras, que aprueuã
y defienden el derecho de su Magestad à la Corona de Inglaterra: con todo esso, afirmo à V. S.
Ilust. con toda verdad, que es mentira y calumnia

ñia lo que dixo el procurador delante del Tribu
nal, y se apunta en el decreto segundo del Parla
mento, que Tomas Vvinter, ò otra qualquiera
persona aya venido à España para solicitar su
Magestad à tal efeto, ò que yo les aya ayudado
en tal pretension, ò que su Magestad, ò sus ministros ayan jamas dado oydos àtal proposiciò,
ò mostrado tal desseo.

7 Antes al còtrario, se acordarà su Magestad,
y el Duque de Lerma tambien (cuyo testimonio, ò de qualquiera dellos deue ser preferido à
mil decretos semejantes, fundados en falsas informaciones, sospechas, y passiones de particulares) que el dia de santa Leocadia, a nueue de
Diziembre, en el año de 1599. auiendo su Magestad recien heredado, le dixe en Aranjuez,
para preuenir qualquiera opinion diferéte que
pudiesse auer, que los Catolicos de Inglaterra,
aunque estimauan y amauan à su Magestad co
mo era razon, en ninguna manera le queriá por
su Rey, aunque pudiesse pretender derecho à la
Corona: porque no estaria biè a ellos, ni à su Ma
gestad que ya tenia hartos Reynos, y de Inglaterra sacaria mucho mas prouecho, con tener
la confederada y amiga, que con ser señor della:
y que los Catolicos por esse mismo respeto pre-
tendiá, solo, que muerta la Reyna Ysabel, se qui
tassen los latrocinios, y otras desordenes que

B   auian

auian dado principio à las guerras, y las yuan fo
mentando, y que tuuieſſen Principe que les go
uernaſſe como Padre, con juſticia y amor, y có
feruaſſe la buena correſpondencia que ſolia tener aquel Reyno, y ſus Reyes en otros tiempos,
con los demas de la Chriſtiãdad. La qual propo
ficion ſu Mageſtad (con ſu grã prudécia, y zelo
del bien publico) aprouò, y tuuo por bien: y el
dia ſiguiente el Duque (en cuya preſencia tambien eſto ſe dixo) confirmò lo miſmo con palabras harto graues. Y por lo que ſu Mageſtad ha
hecho deſpues, viniendo en las pazes en la forma q̃ ſe ha viſto, bien ſe puede entender q̃ eſto
ha ſido ſiempre el intento, aſsi ſuyo y de ſus miniſtros, como de los Catolicos de Inglaterra: de
lo qual V. S. Iluſtr. ſe podra informar mas enteramente quando fuere ſeruido.

8 Antes, mas quiero dezir à V. S. Iluſt. y có la
miſma aſſeueracion, que nunca he podido deſ-
cubrir, que la glorioſa memoria del Rey don Fe
lipe Segundo tuuieſſe intencion de hazerſe ſeñor de Inglaterra, ni pretendieſſe otro fin, aun
con el armada del año de ochenta y ocho, mas q̃
atajar las ſinrazones que ſe hazian à ſus vaſallos,
por los piratas Ingleſes, y por los que fomenta-
uan à ſus rebeldes è inquietauan ſus Indias; y re
duzir aquel Reyno al Eſtado honorifico que ſo
lia tener en tiempos antiguos; y cumplir en parte

té con su conciencia, pues (por ventura) le podia parecer que la mucha clemencia que su Ma
gestad auia vsado con personas delinquentes, q̃
despues se lo agradecieron poco, estoruando, y
anulando las sentencias de la Reyna su muger,
y su Consejo contra ellos, y algun descuydo de
ministros, en no acudir con tiempo à cosas que
se deuian preuenir quando el reynaua en Ingla
terra, huuiessen sido parte (entre otras cosas) para que aquel Reyno y su Reyna Ysabel, cayes-
sen en manos de los que la aconsejaron, y ayudaron despues, à apartarse à si y à sus vasallos de
la obediencia de la Yglesia, y de las antiguas y
honrosas amistades de aquella Corona, y à con
federarse con rebeldes y gente ruin, y à comen
çar aquellas sangrietas tragedias en su casa, que
algunos querriá que su Magestad (que agora es)
continuasse, y finalmente à intentar muchas o-
tras cosas no acostumbradas en aquel Reyno, y
tan molestas à los vezinos del, que pedian obligar, no a quien huuiesse sido tan irritado dellos
como fue la Magestad Catolica, sino à qualquie
ra otro Principe Christiano, à procurar el reme
dio. Y estas han sido, y son las verdaderas causas
(segun yo he podido entender) de la buena voluntad que la dicha Magestad mostrò siempre
à los Catolicos de nuestra nacion, y de la com-
passió de sus trabajos, y de la merced que el y su

hijo

hijo(digno heredero de sus virtudes y obligaciones)les han hecho y hazen,de cuyaReal libe
ralidad no ay nacion debaxo delSol que no par
ticipe. Y las mismas causas han ocasionado las
guerras,que los mismos Reyes Catolicos há he
cho para defensa de sus Estados cótra los cossa-
rios y Piratas;y no codicia alguna , ni desseo de
hazerse señoresde aquelReyno.Como algunos
han procurado que el pueblo entendiesse,alegá
do informaciones d espias,y cófessiones depre
sos,q son harto flacosoriginales:pues los vnos
por sus interesses se alargan, por hablar à gusto
de quien se lo paga,y à los otros sacan con tormentos lo que muchasvezes,ni saben,ni sienté,
y confiessan por redemir su vexacion.Demas,q
se suelen publicar por algunos de nuestros con
trarios,cófessiones,y sucessos de personas pré-
sas,antes,y despues que los ayan quitado las vidas,sin fundaméto de verdad, alegádo testigos
muertos.Como se hizo con el Conde de Arun
del,de ilustre memoria,cargandole con cartas
escritas al Duque de Guisa,y có otras cosas que
despues se aueriguaron ser falsas,y inuenciones
de sus enemigos.

Y de lamisma manera fue infamado elVirrey
de Irlanda don IuanParret sobre el dicho de vn
predicador Caluinista,que huydo de Inglaterra
por delitos,y preso en Irlanda , mientras estaua
en

en la carcel maquinò la muerte del mismo Virrey: y siendo contra derecho que se admitiesse por testigo persona infame, y mucho mas conocida por capital enemigo del reo; con todo esso condenaron al Virrey à muerte por su testimonio, publicando como cosas verdaderas y aueriguadas las inuenciones del otro.

Y aun es mas al proposito lo que hizieron cõ el Conde de Essex, a quien estando preso embiarõ vn Capellã suyo Puritano, llamado Ashton, con titulo de consolarle. Y despues de su muerte le hizieron al mismo publicar vna confession que dezian ser del Conde, llena de cosas fingidas y falsas; como el pobre hombre declarò con lagrimas, à diuersos amigos del mismo Conde que le hizieron cargo, alegando por su disculpa la autoridad de las personas que le obligaron à hazerlo, con promessas de acrecimiento y remuneracion, y amenazas sino lo quisiesse hazer, y me lo refirio persona de autoridad, que lo supo de boca del mismo Ashton. Y siendo este modo de proceder tenido por licito de nuestros contrarios, y como regla de su Estado, y pan cotidiano tan vsado dellos, como se sabe y se ha visto aora en este vltimo caso, no se deue hazer ninguno de quanto publican, sino còstar le por otros caminos ser verdad. Y assi quanto V.S. Ilustrissimo huuiere oydo de los interesses de las

Reyes Catolicos diferentes de lo dicho, sepa que no ha sido otro que inuencion y calumnia.

9 Cóforme à esto V.S.Iluf. sabrà, q̃ la venida de Tomas Vuinter à España en los vltimos años de la Reyna Ysabel, fue solo à procurar algũ medio licito y cõueniéte, para q̃ al tiépo de su muerte della los Catolicos no fuessé oprimidos cõ violencia de sus contrarios, que podia parecer cosa justa, y prudẽteméte pensada por los que le embiaron, para su propria seguridad, y de muchos otros, y en beneficio del mesmo Reyno, y de quien huuiesse de suceder por Rey, y à que qualquier Principe Christiano pudiera con mucha justificacion y alabança acudir. Y los otros que vinieron despues, vinieron à dar cuenta de lo q̃ en la muerte de la Reyna, y despues della auia sucedido en Inglaterra. Adonde auian concebido esperanças de su remedio, con la entrada del Rey Iacobo (que fue, no solo con aprouacion, si no con aplauso de los Catolicos) por las muestras que su Magestad auia dado de que le hallarian Principe benigno, justo, y indiferente con todos, y no se podia presumir menos de hijo de tan buena madre; fuera de que ya tenia prendada su fe y palabra Real de tratarles bien. A estas consideraciones se añadia la memoria de la buena correspondencia que siempre los Reyes Catolicos

tolicos auian tenido con el siendo Rey de Escocia, la qual su Magestad se resoluia de continuar
por su parte, como con hijo de tal madre; y de
las muchas buenas obras que el dicho Rey auia
recebido en su persona , para preseruarse de o-
pression de susvasallos quando era de menos e-
dad; y de las que auia tambien recebido la dicha
su madre de feliz memoria, no solo desta Corona, y de la Sede Apostolica, sino de los mismos
Catolicos de Inglaterra, en orden à que viniessen a suceder en aquel Reyno. Los quales respe
tos, aun en sola ley de humanidad y natural agra
decimiento, aunque otro no huuiera, eran bastantes à obligar a vn hombre gentil , quanto y
mas à vn Principe Christiano, y por esto se pre-
sumia que en ninguna manera podia dexar de
mostrarse agradecido. Estas razones hazian tan
grande fuerça à quantos las consideauan con
prudencia, que se persuadian auia la Magestad
diuina proueydo bastantemente, assi para la seguridad de los Catolicos, como para la quietud
y buen Estado de aquel Reyno.

10 Vea V. S. Illustr. como le hablo claro, perq̃
(segun dize el Espiritu santo:) *Est tempus loquen* *Eccles. 3.*
di , & tempus tacendi; y agora lo es de hablar. Y
como quiera que proceden otros que juzgan, y
sospechan, segun lo que ellos mismos suelen ha
zer, los Catolicos, assi Principes como los de-

mas

mas que se gouiernan con conciencia, no admi
ten, ni consienten en cosa, por secreta que sea, q̃
à su tiempo no se pueda publicar con justifica
cion. De donde se puede ver quan mal auisado
fue el Procurador del Rey, y à que proposito v-
so de aquella palabra, *Traycion Española*, tan mal
sonante y tan contra razon y verdad; y contra la
grauedad de aquella Audiencia; que assi el, como quien se la puso en su instruccion (porque
parece que vino con la leccion decorada) se de
clararon por enemigos de la paz con España, y
consequentemente de su Rey y Reyno. Y assi
me espanto como los señores del Consejo presentes no le reprehendieron, y pusieron silécio
à quien con tan mal lenguage, y tan descomedi
da, y sediciosamente hablaua.

11 Pero de lo que en publico hazen y dizẽ se
puede colegir algo de lo que traçan en secreto,
y estos mismos, que por los mismos fines querrian, si pudiessen, deshazer la paz, y reboluer o-
tra vez el Reyno con robos y guerras, son los q̃
procuran poner en el Rey, y en los de su Consejo, tan errados conceptos de sus vasallos Catoli
cos, y del Vicario de Christo, y de otros Principes, y en particular de los Sacerdotes de los Seminarios y Iesuitas, como si no fuessemos mas
amigos del Rey y del Reyno cien vezes q̃ ellos:
y à la prueua me remito, pues todo lo que traba
jamos

jamos,y padecemos,hasta dar las vidas en la de-
manda,es solo por la caridad, y por su bien dellos,y de los mismos perseguidores, si lo quierē
entender:y sin esperança (como es euidente) y
aun sin possibilidad de premios temporales.En
los quales solos,se funda la professió de beneuo
lencia y lealtad,que à su Rey hazen muchos de
los que agora le rodean y siguen con sumissio-
nes y lisonjas,y andan por ay tan gordos,ricos,y
bien tratados de los despojos agenos, y procurā
ponerle mal con todo el mundo, à trueco de
triunfar ellos, y de que en esta confusion y re-
buelta,vnos se harten de la hazienda de los po
bres Catolicos de su Reyno,ya que no pueden
embiar sus nauios à hazer presas como soliã, pa
ra sustentar su prodigalidad con haziédas de los
estrangeros,y otros traguen la de la Yglesia, de
que lleuariamos en paciencia gozassen , có que
dexassen de peruertir las almas de los della.

12 Por estas causas,es cosa tã criminal có ellos
el ser Catolico, y tantos testimonios leuantan
por este titulo contra personas inocentissimas,
y contra el Vicario de Christo,como si su Santidad les fuera enemigo,ò les quisiera quitar algu
na cosa,y no les diera mas hazienda, como la
diera de buena voluntad,con tal que ellos fuessen buenos.Pero esto siempre ha sido,y siempre
serà de vna misma manera,por ser cosa natural,

que

que las ouejas amen y ſigan, y los lobos y otras fieras aborrezcan al paſtor. Haganſe los que hablan mal del Papa y perſiguē a los Catolicos, o-uejas de Chriſto como los otros, y veran como (luego al momento) todo eſte odio que tienen à ſu Vicario ſe muda en amor y reſpeto, y la rapina en inocencia y miſericordia, y ceſſaran todos los deſaſſoſsiegos del Rey, y las ſoſpechas que agora leuātan, ceſſando la malicia de ſu parte, y trocandoſe en caridad.

13 Lo qual para ꝗ ſuceda como fuera razon, y que V. S. Iluſt. mejor entienda quan errados andan y quan inutilmente ocupados, inuentādo nueuos vocabularios, y mudando la ſinificacion de palabras vſadas, con llamar los miniſterios Eccleſiaſticos, inſtituydos por Chriſto, trayciones, y la adminiſtració de los diuinos miſterios, y elvſo de los ſantos Sacramentos (ſin las quales coſas no puede auer Religion, Chriſtiandad, ni Ygleſia) crimenes de leſàMageſtad, los Sacerdotes traydores, y otros ſemejantes diſparates: traſtrocando no ſolo el verdadero ypro prio modo de hablar, ſino todo el antiguo gouierno, para enredar los pobres vaſallos en ſus redes, y quitarles à ſu voluntad las haziendas y las vidas, y quan deſproporcionado medio es to do eſto para el fin que los perſeguidores preten den, ſi con ello pretenden deſterrar la Fè Catolica

lica de aquel Reyno: Sepa V.S. Iluſtr. en primer
lugar, que la ſangre de los Martyres es, y ſiempre ha ſido, *Semen Eccleſiæ*; porque *Grana ſingu-*
la cadunt, & centuplicata naſcuntur. Y ſegundo, q̃
eſte miſmo fue el deſuario de los Emperadores
y tiranos Gentiles, y de hereges antiguos, que
vnos dellos con violencia, y otros con maña, y
otros (como Valente, y Iuliano el Apoſtata) con
entrambas juntas, penſauan cada vno en ſu tiépo de acabar con los Chriſtianos : pero acabò
Dios con todos ellos, como ha acabado ya con
muchos de nueſtros perſeguidores en Inglaterra, y quedan todos depoſitados para el dia del
juyzio, adonde pagan y pagaran eternamente
la pena de ſu mala voluntad, mientras la Ygleſia,
cobrando fuerças y aumento, queda ſiempre y
quedarà, purificada y renouada: con las miſmas
perſecuciones, como todas las hiſtorias, y mas
ſu grandeza y Mageſtad preſente, teſtifican, y ha
zen euidencia, à quié no quiere cerrar los ojos
con voluntaria ceguedad.

14 Por eſto no podemos perder la cõfiança, cõ
la qual nueſtros antepaſſados deſde el principio
han vencido todos los enemigos de la verdad,
ni temer el enojo de los que *Quando han quitado* Luc. 12.
la vida temporal, no pueden mas; ſiendo ella de las
coſas que los Catolicos, que por miſericordia
de Dios tenemos Fè ſobrenatural, eſtimamos

C 2   en

en poco, por ganar con ella la eterna, y la corona de Martyrio: y tal es la caufa por la qual pade
cemos, que fin perder nada podemos perder en
fu defenfa, no vna fola fino muchas vidas fi las
tuuieffemos: fabiendo que ni los hombres, ni to
da la potencia del infierno, pueden hazer mas
de lo que Dios les permite, y que no les permiti
rà, fino lo que finalmente ha de feruir para mayor bien de los fuyos, y para fu mayor gloria. Y
por effo nos holgamos fiendo perfeguidos , y
nos tenemos por honrados y dichofos, quando
por efta caufa nos calumnian y leuantan tefti-
monios, porque fon prendas de nueftra predef-
tinacion, y rogamos à Dios por los que nos per
figuen y tienen mala voluntad, pidiendo al Señor de todo coraçon, y con las mayores veras
que podemos : *Vt non ftatuat illis hoc pecca-*
tum.

15 Y por dezir à V. S. Iluft. algo mas en particu
lar en efta materia, y certificarle mas quan vanas fon las fofpechas de los otros, y quan lexos
de la verdad, y de mi difpoficion y penfamientos, y quan fin fundamento fon aquellas cofas
que los mal intencionados han querido que el
Rey, y otras perfonas graues creyeffen de mi:
quiero dezir a V. S. Iluft. aqui confidentemente
(à gloria de Dios) algunas mercedes que fu diuina Mageftad me ha hecho defde muchos a-
ños

ños atras , antes, deſde la niñez muy ſobre mis
meritos, con que he viuido (por ſu miſericordia) ſin ofenſa ni agrauio à nadie , como tãbien
viuen muchos otros que padecen perſecucion
y calumnia de los miſmos: y dirè lo que es no-
torio à muchos, y en preſencia de quien todo
lo ſabe, y no ſe agrada ſino con la verdad: y aunque holgàra de no hablar de coſas proprias,
aqui es forçoſo: *Et ſi in hoc fuero inſipiens, vos me* 2.Cor. 12.
coegiſtis.

16 V.S. Iluſtr. en parte ha viſto quan lexos de
pretenſiones temporales (por miſericordia del
miſmo Señor) yo viuo: porque ſi en Eſpaña tuuiera alguna, no huuiera partido della los me-
ſes paſſados como parti, ni tampoco de Roma
agora, ſi tuuiera alguna pretenſion por alla, a dõ
de perſonas graues procuraron detenerme, y ſu
Santidad huuiera guſtado dello. Y mucho menos las he tenido, ni tengo en Inglaterra: adonde no me faltauan amigos quando ſali della , y
en particular la perſona que entonces mas podia en aquel Reyno, y otros ſus iguales , no ſa-
biendo que era Catolico, me hazian merced: y
conforme à mi eſtado, tenia mas que auia meneſter. Aſsi que ſi yo eſtimara coſa alguna , ò q̃
tenia, ò que pudieſſe tener en aquel Reyno, no
lo huuiera dexado tantos años ha con tales pren
das ſin alguna neceſsidad; pues ſolo el deſſeo de
gaſtar

gaftar bien el tiempo(no hallando los Eftudios
de Inglaterra à mi propofito, fiendo Catolico
recufante)y de poder gozar mas libremente de
mi Religion,y de los Sacramentos y otros be-
neficios della,fue la primera ocafion para facar-
me de alla. Y cierto en efto quedo con tanta o-
bligacion y tan agradecido à la Reyna defunta,
y à los Confejeros que ayudaron (aunque indi
rectamente con la perfecució de los Catolicos)
à mi refolucion de falir de Inglaterra,que fi pudiera con la vida temporal facarlos de dóde eftan,lo hiziera de entera voluntad : pues por fu
medio dellos,he gozado yamas de veinte años
en la cafa de Dios, con el contento que V.S.
Iluftrif.por ventura aura aduertido,de muchos
y tá ineftimables bienes y cófuelos,que no tro
càra el menor dellos en todo efte tiempo por
diez Coronas de Inglaterra. Tanta es la eftima
que fe deue tener del patrimonio que no fe acaba, y tan poca de todo lo que paffa con el tiempo,que no puede fer cofa grande por mucho q̃
parezca. Y con lo mifmo podra V.S.Iluftr. entender,quan diferentes fon los penfamientos y
los deffeos de los hombres en efta vida , de cada
vnoconforme à la luz y gracia que Dios le da:
el fea bendito para fiempre.

17 Pero,con todo efto,no puedo negar vna
pretenfion que he tenido, y todavia me queda
en

en Inglaterra, la sola que he tenido en mi Reli
gion, como sabe el Superior della. A quien he su
plicado muchas vezes que me embiasse alla du
rante la persecucion, y es la sola gracia particular que me acuerdo de auerle pedido para mi,
en veinte y cinco años que soy su subdito, y mas
de quinze dellos con protestació, que si no me
embiasse durante esta necesidad, el dia que la
Yglesia tuuiesse paz en aquel Reyno, quádo no
hiziera falta persona de tan mediocres talentos
como los mios, de aquel dia en adelante la renú
ciàra por patria, ofreciendome desde entonces
para la India, ò para el Iapon, ò para qualquiera
otra parte del mundo, adonde los Christianos
tuuiessen mayor necesidad de ministros del E-
uangelio. La qual agora me parece que tienen
los Catolicos de Inglaterra, y que por esto hizie
ra algun seruicio al Señor, cuyos son, y que los
comprò con su preciosissima sangre, si pudiesse
en alguna manera, aunque fuesse à costa de la
mia, ò de qualquier otro trabajo ò peligro personal, consolar à gente tan fiel, y tan quérida de
su diuina Magestad, y tan benemerita de la Igle
sia, y de su misma nacion y patria, que por ellos
y por su constancia es mas estimada en todas
las otras, que por quanto en aquel Reyno ha a-
uido despues que es habitado de hombres. Y af
si si yo fuera dueño de mi voluntad, bien presto
me

me hallara entre ellos, no obstante estas nueuas leyes, y todo el mal q̃ me pudiesse venir, à truecco de seruirles, y cooperar, sino fuesse à mas que à la saluacion de vna sola alma, de las muchas q̃ alli passan peligro agora por falta de socorro espiritual.

18 Y no piense V.S.Ilust. que digo cosa extra ordinaria, ni que este desseo es singular en mi; porque lo mismo dessean otros muchos, assi de la Compañia, como de las mas Religiones, y con mayores veras que antes, despues destas nueuas leyes, conforme à la gracia y luz sobrenatural q̃ Dios da à cada vno para hazer verdadero concepto destas cosas: y no solo Ingleses (que mas obligacion tenemos que otros à dessear el bien de aquel Reyno) sino tambien muchos estrangeros, zelosos de la gloria de Iesu Christo y saluacion de las almas, dessean lo mismo. Pero que digo Religiosos? pues à quantos se crian en los Seminarios dà Dios estos mismos azeros, y desde niños los tienen, y con ellos salen de Inglaterra, no có mal animo à nadie, y menos à su Rey ò à su patria: porque no cabe tal cosa en su inocencia y poca edad, y de pensarlo fuera, ò grande malicia, ò grande inorancia; sino vienen para ser instruydos en verdadera y Catolica dotrina, huyendo (como otros han hecho) los juramentos ilicitos, y las molestias que padecen los

Catolicos

13

Catolicos en las Vniuerſidades de Inglaterra, y para alcançar virtudes heroycas, las quales tienen ſu prueua en coſas dificultoſas.

19 Como (por exēplo) vna *Fè heroyca*, q̄ nos haze creer las palabras y promeſſas diuinas, aūque no las alcāçamos con nueſtro corto entendimiento, y es el fundamento de todas las demas virtudes Chriſtianas.

Eſperança heroyca, fiandoſe mas del ſocorro de Dios en las mayores dificultades.

Caridad heroyca, que dà animo à los hōbres de ofrecerſe a la muerte por la ſaluacion de los proximos.

Paciencia heroyca, que arma el alma y el cuerpo con fortaleza inuencible.

Heroyca humildad, que ſujeta los entendimientos, y las voluntades humanas enteramente, a la de Dios, y por el, no ſolo a los que juſtamente nos pueden mandar, ſino a los iguales, è inferiores, y à todos quando es meneſter.

Longanimidad heroyca, que nace deſta otra virtud, y nos da conſuelo, y fuerças para aguardar las viſitaciones diuinas, y à no canſarnos aū que nos parezca que tardan: Porque ſolo Dios ſabe los tiempos y las coyunturas, y haze todo para mejor, y como mas conuiene.

20 *Heroyca manſedumbre*, con la qual, no ſolo perdonamos, ſino queremos bien a los enemi-

D   gos,

gos, no procurando (como inuent a la malicia) de abreuiar sus dias, sino de alargarlos, paraque tengan lugar a penitencia, sabiendo que no viuen, ni que Dios les permitiera viuir, sino para algun buen fin; *Aut vt corrigantur* (como dize san Agustin) *aut vt per eos boni exerceantur.* Assi que es mas que agrauio, querernos cargar con conjuraciones cótra personas poderosas, pues por nuestra parte no son menester, y fuera en nosotros grandissima imprudencia, no digo có sentir, sino pensar en ellas, ya que tenemos por nosotros, y en nuestra defensa al Señor de la vida y de la muerte, que quando el quiere, sin trabajo alguno, *Aufert* (como dize el Profeta) *spiritum Principum*, y quando vee su tiempo no ha menester que nadie le ayude, y lo haze infalibleméte cada y quando q̃ assi conuiene. De manera, que el querer intentar los hombres vé gáça cótra el orden y voluntad de Dios, y preuenir sus juyzios diuinos, fuera notable yerro, y pecado muy graue. Y esta es Catolica dotrina, y no la que sueñan, y fingen, y nos querrian imputar los hijos de la mentira.

In Psalm. 54.

Psal. 75.

21 Finalmente, vienen a los Seminarios para aprender y alcançar aquella *lealtad y fidelidad heroyca*, que los nuestros Catolicos en Inglaterra tienen y exercitan el dia de oy, mas que ninguna otra gente del mundo, sufriendo vnos lo que

que dize san Pablo de los de la primitiua Iglesia, *Rapinam bonorum suorum cum gaudio;* y otros, Hebr.
que les infamen, atormenten, y les hagan peda-
ços, hasta dexarse arrancar los coraçones leales
de los cuerpos, por no apartarse vn punto de cò
sa que su Señor les ha dexado encomendado, y
à sus antepassados mil y seiscientos años ha: *Et* Isai. 1.
hoc est semen, quod dedit nobis Dominus, que no està en poder de los hombres estoruar que no
nazca, y dè fruto.

22 Y para que assi se haga, y con exemplos de
tal fidelidad y constancia se despierten y animé
muchos, y se conuiertan hasta sus mismos jue-
zes y verdugos, como cada dia acontece, con
alegria y edificacion de toda la Iglesia, y gloria
de Dios autor de tantos bienes: No es mucho,
que aunque faltassen otras razones mas superio
res de la eterna prouidencia, que los hombres
no alcáçamos, permita la diuina Magestad que
dure por algun tiempo esta persecucion (como
duraron otras, que con todo esso se acabaron)
y la passion tan grande de los perseguidores, y
los varios engaños en que caen por medio della. Pues por su culpa dellos mismos les vienen,
y en pena de otros pecados, y sin ella, y su caida
y obstinacion, no huuiera lugar para las dichas
virtudes, en grado tan eminente como le ay, ni
los Martyres alcançaran corona sin vitoria, ni

D 2   ruuie-

tuuieran vitoria fin efta guerra efpiritual, ni tal
guerra pudiera fer fin enemigos, y finalméte en

Ioan. 17. efta guerra no perecen fino *los hijos de perdició.*

23 Y afsi, los que agora en aquel Reyno fe vá
al infierno por perfeguir los fantos, es muy pro-
uable, que aunque eftuuiera Catolico, lo fueran por otros fus vicios y pecados: y los efcogi
Ioan. 10. dos de Dios(*los quales nadie con fraude, ni con vio*
lencia puede facar de fus manos) fe faluan con mu
chas ventajas, y mucho mayor gloria que de o-
tra manera tuuieran de prouidencia ordinaria,
por la qual todas las criaturas fe gouiernan, con
marauillofa fabiduria y diftribucion de jufticia.
Y al modo que fe permite mueren los anima-
les menos nobles, para que fe conferue la vida
del leon, y para el fuftento temporal del hombre, vemos quantas y quan diferentes criaturas
fe confumen y perecen. y (generalmente hablando)las criaturas mas viles, fe ordenan y fir
uen a la perfecion y conferuacion de las mas
nobles: afsi ha paffado y paffa en el cafo prefen
te, y con mucho mas fundamento de razon y
jufticia,y con mas particular prouidencia entre
los reprobos y los efcogidos de Dios.

24 Cóforme a efto, y fupuefta efta verdad, el
deffeo que tenemos que ceffe la perfecució, no
es tanto por los Catolicos conftantes, que participan de aquella *fupereminente fciencia de la ca-*
ridad

ridad de Iesu Christo, y han gustado la suauidad Ephes. 3.
de su Cruz, en los quales a la medida de lo que
padecen por el, y mucho mas *abundan los consue* 2.Cor. 1.
los celestiales, que sobrepujan a todo el mal que
los hombres les pueden hazer, quanto el cielo
y tierra; y a los quales, por la misma razon y la
ocasion que tienen de padecer por Christo, los
Catolicos de otras naciones les tienen vna san
ta embidia: sino por los flacos, que por temor
humano doblan y se rinden a los perseguidores, y sobre todo por los perseguidores mismos;
a los quales tenemos muy grande lastima y có-
passion, y en ninguna manera mala volútad, co
mo ellos imaginã. Porq̃ a los dellos que persecu
raren en su error, harto mal les queda, y mucho
mas q̃ les querriamos, y de ninguno dellos en
particular, por muy descaminado q̃ ande, pode
mos desconfiar, pues vemos q̃ ordenò Dios có
su infinita misericordia, la muerte *de san Esteuã,*
à la conuersion de san Pablo, que de lobo se hizo
cordero, y de perseguidor Apostol y coluna de
la Iglesia, quando menos se pensaua, como a innumerables otros ha acontecido en otras per-
secuciones, y en esta misma de Inglaterra.
Adonde (como de passo) se ha de notar, que
andan casi siempre vnidas aquellas tres calida-
des, que el mismo santo Apostol reconocio en 1.Timo.1.
si mismo antes q̃ recibiesse el espiritu de Dios,

Blaf:

1.Timo.1. *Blasphemus, persecutor, & contumeliosus* : porque ſon propriedades del eſpiritu contrario , atizador de las perſecuciones, que reboluio el mundo en otros tiempos. Y aſsi nadie ſe ha de eſpátar, que algunos lleuados del miſmo eſpiritu en eſtos nueſtros, hablen con táto deſacato de los diuinos myſterios, y con tan poco reſpeto de los Principes Chriſtianos mas ſeñalados en potencia y bondad , y del miſmo Vicario de Chriſto : ni que ſobre tan flacos fundamentos leuanten tantas maquinas contra la verdad y perſonas innocentes: porque no ſon ellos los q̃ hablan y hazen eſtas coſas, ni tanta malicia puede ſer de hombres, ſino *eſt ſpiritus nequam qui lo quitur in eis*; como al cótrario, *el eſpiritu de Chriſto* es el que gouierna y encamina a los ſantos, y endereça todas ſus palabras y obras.

Matt. 10.

25 Y ſi V.S.Iluſt. quiſiere oyr hablar a vno dellos a eſte nueſtro propoſito, y como reſpondio en eſta miſma cauſa , pueſta en controuerſia ya muchos ſiglos ha, verà que Chriſto nueſtro Señor en ſus ſieruos es (como dize el Apoſtol) el miſmo, *Heri, & hodie, & in ſecula*. Y porque la platica es digna de ſer entendida, pondrè aqui las miſmas propueſtas y reſpueſtas, como paſſaron, y como ſan *Gregorio Nazianzeno* las refiere.

Hebræ.13.

Horat. in laudem Baſilij.

En la perſecucion del Emperador Arriano

Valen-

16

*Valente,*vno de fus Lugartiniétes, por nombre *Modefto,*pero en las obras Barbaro, y cruel perfeguidor de los Catolicos, no tanto por creer que hizieffe bien, quanto por lifonjear a fu Emperador,como hazen muchos en Inglaterra el dia de oy.EfteModefto auiendo llamado delante fu tribunal a *San Bafilio,*defpues de auerle tétado otros debalde con promeffas y amenazas, le hablò defta manera.

Que razon teneis Bafilio que atreueys a oponeros a tan grande Mageftad, y folo entre tátos otros perfiftir en efta vueftra obftinacion?

A que propofito (refpondio Bafilio) me hablays defta manera? que nouedad es efta ? porq́ no la entiendo.

Porque(dixo Modefto) no profeffais la Religió del Emperador,a la qual todos los de mas han confentido?

No lo hago(dixo el Santo)porque el Emperador a quien yo firuo,no la aprueua,ni tendria por bien que yo fiendo fu criatura, y reprefentádo fu perfona en el cargo que tengo, adoraffe a otro que a el.

Y nofotros (dixo Modefto) que os mandamos,quien penfais que fomos?

En verdad (refpondio el Santo)foys nonada quando mandais cofas injuftas.

Pero dezidme (dixo Modefto) no penfais q̃ fuera

fuera cosa mucho mas honrosa para vos, y mas para vuestra autoridad, hazeros de nuestra parte y tener a nosotros por compañeros, que resistir desta manera?

A lo qual respondio san Basilio; No puedo negar que soys personas grandes, y mandays en la Republica, pero en ninguna manera os podreys comparar con Dios. A mi me fuera consuelo y honra teneros por compañeros, con otros muchos que estan a mi cargo, criaturas tã bien de Dios todo poderoso y en esto yguales a vosotros; porque en la religion Christiana, iuzgamos que la honra se deue mas a la entereza de Fè, que sin ella a la calidad de las personas.

Modesto, enojado con esta respuesta, se leuã tò del tribunal, y començo a tratar al Santo có mas aspereza: y con mucha colera le dixo: Como no temeis nuestra autoridad?

Porque (dixo el Sáto) la he de temer? que me podeis hazer? que cosa padecerè?

Que cosa? (dixo el) qualquiera de muchas q̃ estan en mi mano de hazeros.

Y que son essas? (dixo San Basilio) oygamos las os ruego.

Confiscacion de vuestros bienes (dixo Modesto) destierro, tormentos, muerte.

A lo qual respondio el Santo, si ay otra cosa que amenazar, oygamos la; porque estas que aueis

ueis dicho, no son al proposito.

Como no: (dixo Modesto) Porque (dixo san Basilio) no està sujeto a confiscaciones, quien no tiene bienes; si por ventura no quereis esta ropa pelada, y vnos pocos de libros, que son todas mis riquezas. Y quanto al destierro, no entiendo que cosa sea: porque no hago diferencia de tierras, ni esta en que agora viuo, hago cuenta que es la mia mas que otra qualquiera adonde me pudieredes embiar. Antes (para hablar mas propriamente) toda la tierra es de Dios, y yo peregrino y huesped para pocos dias passando por ella, a priessa, como han hecho mis antepassados. Y quanto a vuestros tormentos, que pueden hazer faltando el cuerpo? si por ventura no hazeis caso del primer golpe, porque aquel solo està en vuestro poder. Y finalmente, me hareis buena obra con la muerte, embiádome tanto mas presto a mi Señor, a quien viuo y siruo, y he andado ya la mayor parte del camino para adóde està, y me doy la priessa que puedo para acabar lo que queda, con desseo de hallarme con el.

El Lugarteniente espantado con estas palabras, respondio: En verdad (Basilio) nadie me ha hablado en esta manera hasta el dia de oy, ni con esta libertad.

Por ventura (dixo el Santo) no aueis topado

E　　　con

con quien tuuieſſe la miſma obligacion de hablar, pues ſi huuieredes encontrado con ellos, y
apretadoles como a mi aueis hecho, os huuieran reſpondido de la miſma manera. Porque
en otras coſas ſomos manſos y humildes, y nos
ponemos debaxo de los pies de todos, como
Chriſto nueſtro Maeſtro con ſu palabra y exé-
plo nos enſeñò, y eſtamos tan lexos de reſiſtir
al Emperador, que no lo hazemos al mas mini
mo del pueblo: Pero quando ſe trata de la cauſa
de Dios, y nos apretais para que le dexemos,
entonces, menoſpreciamos a todo lo demas, y
en el ſolo ponemos los ojos. Vueſtras eſpadas,
vueſtras beſtias fieras, vueſtros eculeos y inſtru
mentos con que nos atormentays, y deſpeda-
çays las carnes, no nos ponen miedo, ſino gran
diſſimo conſuelo: y por eſſo (Modeſto) maltra-
tadnos, amenazadnos, atormentadnos, hazed
lo que quiſieredes, vſad de toda vueſtra potencia, (y lo miſmo digo al Emperador) no nos po
dreys vencer, ni hazer que conſintamos en eſta
vueſtra falſa y impia dotrina, aunque nos pu-
dierades amenazar con otras coſas mucho mayores que eſtas.

26 El Lugarteniente oyda eſta reſpueſta, y
viſta tal reſolucion y conſtancia en el ſanto varon, y que no le podia eſpátar, ni poner miedo,
le deſpidio: no como antes con palabras aſpe-
ras,

ras,fino con refpeto y comedimiento , y dando fe la prieffa que pudo para llegar al Empera
dor,le hablò defta manera. Señor,vécidos que
damos. Efte Bafilio ni fe ablanda con promeffas,ni fe efpanta con amenazas; auemos de aco
meter a algun otro mas flaco,y a efte,o echarle
mano, y vfar de violécia,con el,ò dexarle eftar:
porque con el palabras no firuen de nada.

27 El Emperador entendiendo quanto auia
paffado,quedò admirado de la finceridad y có
ftancia del fanto varon , y reprehendio al Lu-
gartiniente,por auer paffado tan adelante có el.
Y con efta ocafion començo a proceder mas
blandamente con los Catolicos , y en la enfermedad del Principe fu hijo, acudio con muef-
tras de humildad y arrepentimiento a las oraciones de fan Bafilio , y defpues con otras oca- *Theodore:*
fiones alçò el deftierro a diuerfos Obifpos Ca- *lib.4.cap.*
tolicos , y (como otro Faraon) dio efperanças *17.*
de fu emienda , mientras le dolia el açote de
Dios.Pero,porque fe auia enfrafcado demafia-
damente en la heregia Arriana,y entregado fus
oydos y fu coraçon en poder de gente ruin, y
que algunas vezes los Principes y perfonas gra
ues,toman por menofcabo de fu reputació no
ça por adelante,aunque fepan que van fuera del
camino;demas que es caftigo deuido a alguna
fuerte de pecadores, que Dios les permita (co-

E 2   mo

mo dize el Profeta) *paſſar adelante en ſus inuenciones*:El Emperador, perſeuerãdo en aquel miſerable eſtado,vino a acabar la vida miſerabiliſſimamente.Porq̃ fue vencido por los Gothos, que en ſu tiempo acometieron aquella parte del Imperio, y por los miſmos herido y perſeguido,y finalmente quemado viuo en vna choza adonde auia huydo para eſconderſe;paſſando,deſta manera,delos tormentos del fuego téporal,à los del eterno que no tendra fin. Y nota *Oroſio* el juſto juyzio de Dios en el caſo deſte Emperador,que perecieſſe temporalmente por las manos de aquellos miſmosque eſpiritualmé te auian perecido por las ſuyas, porque por ſu medio fueron inficionados con la heregia Arriana los Gothos, pues pidiẽdo ſer inſtruydos en la Fê de Ieſu Chriſto, les embiò *Valete* falſos Profetas y maeſtros, que les enſeñaron la ſuya,es a ſaber,la heregia Arriana.

28 Otra coſa tambien ſe halla enlas hiſtorias, digna de ſer ſabida deſte Emperador, y como Dios nueſtro Señor ſuele juſtificar ſus caſtigos, auiſando a los pecadores con tiempo,para que no les quede eſcuſa, como lo hizo con Valen-
te.Porque inſpirò a vn ſanto ermitaño por nóbre *Iſaac*,a ſalir del deſierto, y (como otro *Daniel*) a encontrarle en el camino por donde paſſaua con ſu exercito,y hallando comodidad,le hablò

habló desta manera. *Bolued(señor) à los Catolicos
sus Iglesias que les aueis mandado quitar, y Dios todo poderoso os darà buen suceffo en esta jornada:* à lo
qual el Emperador no respondio nada.

Otro dia Isaac tornò a encontrarle, y al mismo proposito que antes, le dixo, *O Emperador a-
brid las Iglesias de los Catolicos, y Dios os prospera-
rà en esta batalla, y boluereis con victoria y paz.* El
Emperador mouido con estas palabras oídas ya
dos vezes, y con el aspecto y grauedad de la per
sona, juntò su Consejo, con proposito de resti-
tuir las Iglesias; pero algunos se lo desuiaron, di
ziendo, que perderia mucha reputacion si lo hi
zieffe : y el que mas insistia que no se hizieffe,
fue su Lugartiniéte del exercito, herege Arriano, el qual reprehédio asperamente al santo varon, y le mandò que no hablaffe mas en aquella materia.

Pero el otro que fue embiado de Dios, no hi
zo caso de sus mádamientos, y se puso a seguir
el exercito, y alcançando al Emperador echò
mano del freno de su caualio, y le hizo parar, y
tornò a hablarle al mismo proposito, pero con
mas eficacia que las otras vezes. Có que enojado el Emperador, mandò que le echaffen envn
hoyo grande que auia alli cerca, y de tal manera encubierto con espinas y çarças, que huma-
namente no podia salir del : pero Dios le facò
lue-

luego fin daño, y el corriendo por vn atajo fe pufo en el camino por donde el exercito auia de paffar, y encontrando otra vez con el Empe rador (que quedò pafmado de verle, porque fé faua que le auia dexado muerto) le hablò con e ftas palabras. *Penfaftes (ò Emperador) que yo auia de morir adonde me mandaftes echar, mas los Ange les de Dios me facaron luego, y fin lefion alguna, co mo lo podreis ver: por effo oydme, y abrid las Iglefias y vencereis à vueftros enemigos, y bolvereis con glo ria.* A las quales palabras el Emperador no dio refpuefta, porque tenia el coraçon apartado de Dios; pero mandò a los dos Senadores *Saturni no*, y *Victor* q tuuieffen al fanto varon prefo con muy buena guarda, hafta q el boluieffe en paz, y mádaffe caftigar a fu infolencia. A lo qual re plicò Ifaac (como hizo *Micheas* al Rey *Acab*) *Si os bolueis (ò Emperador) en paz, entonces podreis de zir que Dios no me ha embiado à hablaros : pero en contrareis y peleareis con los vueftros enemigos, y quedareis vencido, y huyreis dellos, y al fin os pren deran, y quemaran viuo.* Todo lo qual fucedio po co defpues, al pie de la letra como el fanto auia dicho, y los dos Senadores dexaron la heregia Arriana, y fe hizierò Catolicos, y no folo le die ron libertad a Ifaac, fino perfeueraron deuotif fimos del fiépre defpues hafta la muerte, y por fu confejo y medio hizieron muchas buenas

obras,

obras, en recompenſa de ſus erros paſſados. Y
eſtos ſon los caminos de Dios que el ſolo ſabe,
para ſaluar a vnos y caſtigar a otros, ſiempre có
juſticia y miſericordia, y ordenádo todo al mayor bien.

29 Noto (Iluſt. ſeñor) q̃ aqui ſe vee como vn
ſolo ſieruo de Dios Iſaac auiſó al Emperador, y
huuo Dios con eſte ſolo auiſo por juſtificada ſu
ſentencia y caſtigo: y lloro que aya tantos ſieruos de Dios que auiſen a Inglaterra, y que les ſe
pulten (hablado al modo humano) en tan extra
ordinarias eſpinas y çarças de perſecuciones. Y
lloro tambien, porque temo que alargarſe el caſtigo, y juſtificarlo el Señor por tantas vias, es pa
ra hazer demoſtracion de ſu juſticia, tanto
mas ſeñalada con los obſtinados, quanto es ma
yor la miſericordia que con ellos ha vſado.

30 Eſta hiſtoria de Iſaac, ſe lee en *Simeon Me-*
taphraſtes, y como el Lugarteniente del exercito, que dio el mal conſejo al Emperador, murio quemado viuo con el en la miſma choça. Pe
ro (para boluer a ſan Baſilio y al otro Lugarteniente Modeſto) el, deſpues de algun tiempo
cayendo enfermo, y deſauziado de los Medicos, conociendo ya a ſi miſmo, y humillado có
la viſitacion de Dios, embió a llamar al ſanto
Obiſpo, y con muchas lagrimas le habló deſta
mrnera. Mirad (Baſilio) Dios me çaſtiga por reſ
peto

peto vuestro y por vuestro medio he de salir de mi trabajo, por esso rogad por mi al Señor, paraque vse conmigo de su misericordia, y me perdone mis pecados. Hizolo san Basilio, oluidandose de los agrauios recebidos, y por sus oraciones el enfermo cobrò salud, y quedò siēpre despues muy reconocido por tal beneficio. De otra manera que el Emperador su amo, el qual tambien embiò a llamar a san Basilio (como se ha dicho) en la enfermedad del Principe su hijo, q̃ de la misma manera por las oraciones del santo hallò aliuio, pero tornò a perderlo, y la vida por el desagradecimiento de su padre, q̃ sin respeto a la misericordia que Dios le auia hecho, por mal consejo de los suyos dexò q̃ ciertos Obispos Arrianos visitassen al enfermo, que recayò, y murio luego despues que los hereges le fueron a ver.

Orat. in laudem Basily. 31 Otra cosa refiere san Gregorio Nazianzeno del mismo san Basilio semejante a la dicha, como saluò la vida a otro Lugarteniente llamado Eusebio, librandole de vn tumulto del pueblo q̃ le queria matar, al mismo tiempo que Eusebio le auia llamado a su tribunal, y maltratado con amenazas, y le queria dar tormétos: Y estan llenas las historias de semejantes exemplos; sucessos. Todos los quales, y el diferēte modo cō q̃ proceden siempre y en todas partes, los hijos de

de Dios, y los hijos deſte ſiglo, particularmente
los que hazen reſiſtencia à la verdad conocida;
y las miſericordias de Dios para con los vnos, y
ſus caſtigos para con los otros, ſe pueden aco-
modar al caſo preſente, y confirman en grã manera quanto arriba ſe ha dicho.

32 Pero aunque algunas de las coſas dichas
ſon tã prouadas y aueriguadas, y otras en ſi miſmas tan claras y euidentes, que nadie de los que
viuen en la luz de la Ygleſia Catolica puede de
xar de creerlas: con todo eſſo, puede ſer que à
V.S.Iluſt. à la primera viſta le parezcan Algara
uia, y mas pareceran à quien mas apartado eſtu-
uiere deſta luz, y mas metido en las tinieblas, las
quales ſon otra cauſa de eſſe mal. Porque ellas
por ſu miſma naturaleza ſuelen cauſar temo-
res, y leuantar ſoſpechas de mal donde menos
lo ay: y por eſto, y de los tales que caminan en ti
nieblas, dize el Profeta: *Trepidauerunt timore, vbi* Pſal. 13.
non erat timor. Aſsi que nadie ſe deue eſpantar,
que anden ſiempre deſaſſoſſegados y inquietos,
y tan ſugetos, como vemos y ſiempre ſe ha viſto, à recebir qualquiera impreſsion ò ſoſpecha
contra los hijos de la luz, ni que los vnos, y los
otros, hagan tan diferentes conceptos y juyzios
de las miſmas coſas, teniendo tan diferentes diſ-
poſiciones, y gouernandoſe por tan diferentes
principios.

                    F   33 De

33 De aqui nace, que algunos mal afectos à nuestra santa Religion, ayan preualecido con el Rey de Inglaterra, para que admita desconfiança contra los que siempre le han amado: *Incidès in Scyllam, dum vult vitare Caribdin*. Pues por remediar sospechas vanas, se ponen contra su propria inclinacion, su honra, y el bien de su Reyno, en vn laberinto de confusion y cuydados con perpetuo desassossiego de su coraçon, obligandole à proceder con sus subditos, tan diferentemente de lo que suelen otros Reyes que se tienen por magnanimos y justos, que es lastima de pensarlo: solo porque professan la Fê de sus antepassados (porque si buscáran nouedades como hazen los otros, no tuuieran escusa) la misma Fê en q han viuido y muerto, todos los buenos Reyes que han gouernado bien aquel Reyno; y por medio de la qual, los primeros moradores del se reduxeron de costumbres fieras y barbaras, y de la inorancia de la Gentilidad, al conocimiento del verdadero Dios, y al gouierno tan concertado y apartado de toda violencia, con que se ha conseruado tantos siglos en grande felicidad; y finalmente, por la qual su misma madre la Reyna doña Maria padecio muerte, y podemos en toda ley y buena razó pensar, que Dios, en premio de tal fidelidad, aya hecho merced à su hijo, de la Corona que ella quiso
antes

antes perder, que apartarse de la Fê que el agora
en sus vasallos persigue, con pretexto de no se q̃
seguridad suya y de su Estado, siendo ella el me
dio mas seguro parala conseruacion de los Rey
nos y de sus Reyes que en este mundo puede a-
uer, y con la qual (sola) hallaria su Magestad mas
descanso, y quietud de cuerpo y de alma, que có
todas las inuenciones que (sin ella, ò contra e-
lla) podrá hallar los amigos de nouedades. Pues
con ella sola, *Ipse facto*, y sin otra industria algu
na, quedan los vasallos con la mayor obligació
possible, de reuerenciar y obedecer à sus Princi
pes como à substitutos y lugartenié́tes de Dios,
y à serles fieles y leales como à los que les mádá
en nombre del mismo Dios, à quien todo amor,
fidelidad, y obediencia se deue.

34 Conforme à esto, vemos que los Reyes y
Principes, que professan esta Fê y gouierná por
las leyes y reglas della, viuen ellos y sus subditos
con grandissimo descanso, consuelo, y seguridad, creciendo cada dia la mutua beneuolencia, con las obligaciones reciprocas que esta Fê
y ley pone, entre los Reyes (que lo son de nombre y obras) y sus subditos, y que de entrambas
partes se han de guardar. Yla razon de todo esto
es, porque el Rey santo y justo, en quien estan
libradas las voluntades de sus vasallos para ser
dirigidas por la suya, tiene en su voluntad bue-

F 2

na y vniuerfal, en cierta manera, prefas y encar-
celadas las malas voluntades y inclinaciones, y
los vicios de muchos, y con fu jufticia, y voluntad concertada haze à muchos concertados y
juftos, que de otra manera no lo fueran, eftoruã
do con fu bondad inumerables males cada dia
y hora, y caufando otros tãtos bienes en fus fub
ditos. Y por efto, como vn arbol frutifero de
preciofas y faludables frutas, y como vna fuen-
te manantial de vida, y vn bien general, es en fi
mifmo preciofo, y por fi mifmo amable fobre-
manera, y mas que fe puede encarecer digno de
honra y refpeto, y que por fu conferuacion y fe
guridad, los vafallos no folo gaften fus haziendas, fino pongan fus vidas quando es menefter:
cuyos coraçones y voluntades (naturalmente, y
fin violencia) atrahe à fi con grandifsima fuaui
dad y fuerça, y lo que mas importa, la de Dios
todo poderofo, que es Rey de los Reyes, y da y
quita, alborota y conferua en paz, los Reynos co
mo el es feruido, y con particular proteccion af
fifte y ampara à los buenos Reyes, amigos de ju
fticia y paz, y q̃ tratan bien à fus vafallos. Y en
efto (principalmente) eftriba fu feguridad, pues
haziendofe amables, como efta dicho, fin faltafe
ran amados: y quien es amado defta manera, y
por eftos refpetos, ni recibe, ni tiene que temer
mal alguno de los que afsi le aman.

35 Al

23

35 Al contrario, el Rey ò Principe que tenien
do (como se ha dicho) las volũtades de muchos
libradas en la suya, las encamina à fines no deui-
dos, siguiendo errores y vicios, sea por mal consejo, ò de propria inclinacion por sus gustos y in
teresses, como *Ieroboam*, que por aquella regla   3.*Reg.*
engañosa, que en algunas partes, contra toda ra
zon se llama razon de Estado, imaginando que
assi los diez Tribus quedaran mas sugetos à el y
à sus descendiẽtes, los apartò del verdadero cul
to de Dios. Este tal Rey ò Principe, como tiene
en prisiones la virtud y los santos desseos de mu
chos, y la verdad oprimida, abriendo campo li-
bre y dando fuerças à la lisonja y mentira, y à
inumerables desordenes que dellas se siguen, se
haze como vn mal general, y vna fuerte manan
tial de agua ponçoñosa, inficionando su Reyno
y confundiendolo con vna inficion y confusiõ
tan abominable, que ningun entendimiẽto pue
de alcançar, ni lengua, ni pluma encarecer, quã
grande sea su pecado, ni quan aborrecible queda (consiguientemente) à Dios y à los hombres
por su culpa. De cuya malicia participan los que
le aconsejan mal, como tienen parte en la bondad y amabilidad del otro, los que le dan buen
consejo, y por esto son en gran manera dignos
de premio y honra, y de todo respeto, y la justicia diuina à los vnos esta infaliblemente orde-
nando

nando y disponiendo premios, y castigos à los
otros, desde la hora que comiençan à ordenar,
ò desordenarse. Y aunque parezca (algunas vezes) *Quòd sit sera Numinis vindicta,* y que tarda el
castigo, no por esto estan los malos mejor libra
dos, porque quanto mas se alça la mano, mas pe
sado y mas penoso descarga el golpe: y al fin, co
mo quiera que los hombres engañen à si mismos: *Gaudium hipocritæ ad instar puncti.*

Iob. 20.

36 Pero, por dezir algo para los q̃ no se acuer-
dan de Dios ni de sus juyzios: desseo que consi-
deren vn poco sin passion (con sola razon y pru
dencia humana) en quanto peligro ponen à su
Principe, mayormente si es estrangero, nueuo, y
aun no bien assentado en su gouierno, quando
obligan à sus vasallos, con malos tratamientos,
à prouar lo estremo de lo que pueden, apretan-
doles de manera con agrauios, que les pongan
en desesperacion; lo que aun con los enemigos
no se deue hazer, y mucho menos con los do-
mesticos: y fue el consejo de los moços, al qual
3. Reg. 12 permitio Dios que el Rey *Roboan* diesse oydos,
quando le quiso castigar, y quitarle la mayor par
te de su Reyno. Y no bastan juramentos força-
dos, ni otras protestaciones extrinsecas de fidelidad, à remediar este mal, quando no la huuiesse en los coraçones. Antes, el mal quanto mas
oculto y dissimulado, tanto mas peligroso se ha
ze,

ze,y mas dificultoso d curar,y peores efetospro
mete. Porque el temor fin amor, y el agrauio
fin efperança de juſticia, cauſa notable paſsion
y aflicion en los animos de los hombres, la
qual perſeuerando,y (poco à poco) aumentan
doſe,y trocandoſe finalmente en aborrecimien
to,y odio(al parecer)juſto,de los que cauſan los
agrauios,haze que los agrauiados anden conti-
nu imentepenſando en lo que no deuiã,è imaginando modos como ſe puedan deſagrauiar.
Y adonde ay muchos afsi afligidos y ocupados,es caſo peligroſo,y impoſsible moralmente,que tarde ò temprano alguno no acierte cõ
lo que otros no penſauan,ni puede viuir ſeguro,
ni baſtantemente guardado con ningun pertre-
cho,quien es odiado de muchos,y ſugeto à tales inconuenientes. Y aduierto a V.S.Iluſtriſ.
que lo que ſe platica en gentes de diferente ley,
conquiſtadas,ò con eſtrangeros admitidos en
algun Reyno ò Eſtado debaxo de pretextos ef
pirituales ò temporales,no tiene lugar en los va
ſallos naturales Catolicos Ingleſes,ſi ſe examina
eſto como conuiene. Y lo miſmo digo en pro-
hibirles las armas,y en otras vexaciones que l.s
hazen.

37 Eſto es lo que paſſa entre hombres *Ex natura rei*,porque los hombres ſon hombres. Antes *Habet muſca ſplenem,& formica ſua bilis inſt.*
                              Y pue-

Y pueden hurgar tanto à las criaturas mas man
sas, y inocentes, que se azoren, y procuren defen
derse. Y por esto *Neron, Domiciano, Comodo*, y o
tros tiranos fueron de corta vida: y grandes de
sastres suelen seguir à grandes violencias. Y en
la balança dela diuina justicia, adonde se guarda
admirable proporcion y à cada cosa correspon
de su peso deuido, por fuerça ha d ser assi, y Chri
Matt.26. sto nuestro Señor lo dexò aduertido: *Qui gladiũ*
accipit, gladio peribit. y antes del el Profeta Da
Psal. 54. uid, *Viri sanguinum & dolosi non dimidiabunt dies*
Hebr. 11. *suos.* Y solos los Catolicos, *que estiman los denue-*
stos de Iesu Christo, mas que los tesoros de Egypto,
son los que en todos tiempos y lugares han te
nido paciencia y sufrimiento en casos semejan
tes, confortados con la gracia sobrenatural, y có
los consuelos interiores que el fiel Señor les da,
y con la consideracion dela causa por que padecen, y testimonio de su buena conciencia, y prin
cipalmente con el exemplo de su Señor y Mae
stro, que de la misma manera padecio por nosotros, *Sin culpa y con paciencia*, para darnos exemplo y desseo de padecer por el, y no quiso entrar
en su proprio Reyno sino mediante su cruz: y
con estas y otras muchas ayudas de costa, de que
carecen todos los demas que padecen por otras
causas, son consolados los Catolicos en esta oca
sion: y assi son solos los que con el Apostol pue
den

den dezir, *Persecutionem patimur , sed non angu-*
stiamur:porque a todos los trabajos hallan sali
da, entendiendo con cierta y verdadera per-
suasion, que es honra y prouecho perder las ha
ziēdas, la libertad, y las vidas por Iesu Christo
y por su santa religion. Y conforme a esta verdad, deuia mas la Reyna Isabel a los religiosos
y sacerdotes, que enseñauan esta verdadera do
trina, por la quietud de que ella gozò quaren-
za años en su Reyno, que a los que la aconseja-
uã muchas cosas bastantes a alborotarlo , sino
estuuierã de por medio estos otros principios
pacificos, y las personas que enseñauan que la
persecucion a nadie trae daño, que con constã
cia y paciencia la sabe lleuar.

38 Y para mayor prueua desto, V.S.Ilust.po
drà considerar, si los Luteranos de Alemania,
ò los Guezes de Holanda, ò los Hugonotes de
Francia, ò los Caluinistas de Escocia, ò los Puri
tanos de Inglaterra, huuieran sufrido la menor
parte dela opression, que con paciencia han su
frido, por las causas arriba dichas, los Catolicos
de Inglaterra. Antes el mismo Turco tenido
por el mayor tirano del mundo, nunca se ha a-
treuido a imponer a sus vassallos(por barbaros
que sean) carga tan pesada, como la que estos
Catolicos lleuan:sino que permite a los Grie-
gos, y a otros muchos,que pagandole su tribu

to, y

to,y en lo demas prestandole obediencia, vi-
ua cada vno en su rito, por los grandes inconuinientes que le pudieran nacer de lo contrario en sus Reynos. Y sabemos los alborotos, y
rebeliones, que los otros referidos han intenta
do contra sus Principes muchas vezes, por le-
ues causas; y có todo esso no solo justificados,
sino ayudados por otros de su misma professió; siendo *ex raro contingentibus*, q los Catolicos, confortados có la luz y gracia y persuasio-
nes arriba dichas, ayan procurado remediar có
fuerça, agrauios que se les han hecho con titu
lo de su religion.

39 Por todas estas causas, menos temor pue
de y deue tener el Rey de los Catolicos recusantes (contra los quales se arman todos estas
leyes, lazos, y penas) que de otros innumerables no comprehendidos en ellas; antes de
qualesquiera que negassen la Fè que tienen
por verdadera, sean Catolicos ò otros. Porque los tales trayendo las conciencias mole-
stadas, y escozidas de escrupulos, y cargadas
con sacrilegios, y sin el consuelo del cielo que
reciben los Catolicos recusantes en recompen
sa de sus daños téporales, estan mas próptos, y
mas instigados a remediar vna violencia con
otra, para librarse de las congoxas y tormétos
de sus conciencias, y de la seruidumbre q sus
almas

almas padecen:y mayor comodidad tendran
para hazerlo,por muchas vias, que los Catolicos declarados. Y de perſonas deſta manera o-
primidas,y mal ſatisfechas , todos los Reynos
de Inglaterra, Eſcocia,y Irlanda eſtan llenos.

40 Por eſto,no ſè en que prudencia ſe fun-
dan tantas cautelas contra los Catolicos recu-
ſantes,echādolos preſos, areſtādolos en ſus ca
ſas,y vedandoles que no viuan en Londres,ni
lleguen cerca a la Corte : y por otra parte, ha-
ziendoles fuerça por tantas vias que vayan a
ſus preces,aunque no ſientan deuocion a ellas;
y coman de ſu pan por fuerça,aunque no tengan hambre , y juren que el Principe ſeglar es
cabeça de la Igleſia (lo que ſu maeſtro y autor
de ſu ſecta Caluino no podia lleuar,y reprehen   *Preſac in*
dio como arrogācia del Antichriſto en el Rey   *Amos &*
Henrique Octauo) y otras coſas ſemejantes.   *alibi.*
Pues ſi ya las creen y las tienē por verdaderas,
es ſobrado el juramento que les hazen tomar:
y ſi no las creen,aunque juren y perjuren y va
yan mil vezes a ſus ygleſias,no ſirue para nada.
Antes es dañoſo para lo miſmo que los perſeguidores pretenden , y contra la regla de buenos Medicos , que jamas procuran meter
dentro del cuerpo lo que eſtà de fuera y querrian curar;y contra la coſtumbre de todos los
Principes ſabios , que hallan graues inconue-

nien-

nientes en obligar a sus vassallos a mentir, fin-
gir, y ocultar sus enojos sin remediarlos.

41   Y esto digo, no solo por los Catolicos, sino por todos los demas, Puritanos y otros, que
no creen la dotrina, ni aprueuan los ritos de
los Protestantes que les obligan a jurar. Y assi,
mas me fiara mil vezes, y mas se puede fiar el
Rey o otro qualquiera, de quien (aunque fuesse con conciencia erronea) recelasse de jurar, ò
protestar exteriormente lo que tiene por falso, que del que traga juramentos por temor,
o por otro respeto niega su religion quando està obligado a professarla. Porque quien
se rinde a vna passió, ofreciendose la ocasió se
rindira a otra: y quien para redimir su vexació
dissimula, y engaña con escrupulo de conciencia, no lo tendrà pudiendo a su saluo librarse
de quien se obliga a el.

42   Y si V. S. Ilust. quiere ver que no hablo
sin exemplo y razon (dexando a parte lo que
escriue *Sigonio* del Rey *Theodorico* y otros exé-
plos, que ay muchos en las historias) se sirua de
acordarse de aquel nobilissimo y prudentis-
simo *Constancio Cloro*, padre de nuestro gran
Constantino, el qual (si viuiera) pudiera pretender voz en el Parlamento y Cósejo de Estado,
como quien pacificò y gouernò bien aql Reyno, y por lo que hizo entóces reprueua lo que
agora

Sigon. lib.
6. de Occi
dent. Imp.
Euseb. de
Vita Con-
stantin. li.
1. cap. 11.
Sozom. li.
1. cap. 6.

agora hazen los nueſtros contrarios,y apruciua
y cõfirma por bueno lo que arriba eſtà dicho.
Porque,eſtando informado que diuerſos miniſtros ſuyos y criados de ſu caſa ſe auiã hecho
Chriſtianos,echò bando debaxo de grauiſsi-
mas penas,que todos los que no quiſieſſen ſa-
crificar a los Idolos ,ſe fueſſen luego de la Cor
te,como ſe fueron los Chriſtianos conſtātes,
dexando ſolo a los que por temor de daños
temporales no temieron ir contra ſus conciencias. Y como lo huuieſſe entendido el
Emperador, contra la expectacion de todos
mandò echar de ſu caſa y ſeruicio a eſtos,
y que boluieſſen a ella los Chriſtianos conſtantes,a los quales honrò y hizo mercedes , y
ſiempre deſpues ſe ſiruio dellos en los pueſtos
y cargos de mas confiança,aſsi cerca de ſu per
ſona como del gouierno de la Republica: dã
do por razon,que los que eran tan conſtantes
en ſu religion,y tan fieles a ſu Dios, ſerian de
la miſma manera leales y fieles a ſu Emperador . Y en eſto juzgò prudentemente, como la eſperiencia deſpues moſtrò,y que lo có
trario que agora vſan en Inglaterra es engaño:
y mucho mayor lo que algunos dellos pienſan
de poder có fuerças humanas atropellar la ver
dad de Dios.Porque lo que es de Dios (como
dixo *Gamaliel* en el Conſiſtorio de los Fari-
ſeos,

seos, *ha de preualecer* : y querer los hombres e-
storuarlo con protestaciones violentadas, ò có
otros qualesquier artificios, es imitar a los mis
mos Fariseos que por este camino perdieró su
Republica; y tan gran desatino, como fuera ha
zer reparos de sal contra el agua, ò cótra el fue
go de cera, ò estopa; y muestran euidente-
mente en lo que hazen, que ò no saben ò no
consideran la fuerça de la verdad, ni la naturaleza del juramento: pues en confirmacion de
vna verdad ya conocida y creida por tal, el juramento es la obligacion mas forçosa que pue
de auer; pero el quererlo torcer y trocar a contrarios efetos, es inorancia y trabajo perdido.

43 Assi, que jamas he podido hallar, ni pien
so que V.S.Iluftrif. ni nadie hallarà otro fundamento real y verdadero, de los juramentos
y protestaciones exteriores, y otras cosas a que
procuran (por fuerça) induzir los vassallos en
Inglaterra, mas que la malicia del demonio,
que sin otro proposito gusta de hazer a los hóbres pecar. Pues todas estas demostraciones
son totalmente inutiles para los intétos de los
mismos que los procuran, si ya no pudiessen jú
tamente persuadirles, lo q es impossible a personas que tienen entendimiento, que es buena y verdadera la religió que por fuerça les ha
zen professar. Demas que la violencia con que
les fuerçan a cosas tan inutiles, y las ficciones y
tre-

tretillas de que se siruen para dar color de justi
cia, a violencia tan injusta, no solo quitan la re
putacion a los autores, y desautorizan mucho
el gouierno adonde se permiten, pero abren
camino a los mismos inconuinientes que por
estos medios deshonrosos querrian preuenir.
Y pudiera alegar a V.S.Il. *exēplos en otros Rey-*
nos, q̃ cōuencen por indubitable esta verdad.

44 Pero porq̃ V.S.Il. en cōtrario desto (por
vētura) alegarà las cōjuraciones q̃ auemos oydo
en Inglaterra cōtra su Magestad, se puede respō
der, q̃ la primera se imputò a personas a quien
auiā tomado hartos juramētos, y yuā a las ygle
sias, y comiā el pā de los Protestātes, y bien se sa
be q̃ no erā Catolicos. Y oxala q̃ todos los dis-
gustos en aq̃l Reyno fuerā solo por materia de
religion, y q̃ los Protestantes tambien y otros,
no tuuieran los suyos por otras causas harto
mas dificultosas de remediar que el sentimien
to de los Catolicos. Porque assi algunos q̃ por
allase preciō de politicos y de hōbres de Estado,
con menos peligro de daños publicos, pudierā
passar adelāte cō la cōfusion q̃ en aquel Reyno
han començado. Pero confio q̃ el Señor vsarà
de su misericordia con ellos, y les abrirà los o-
jos, ò por lo menos a su Magestad paraq̃ mo-
dere la vehemēcia y precipitaciō de personas
apassionadas, pues tanto le importa q̃ se haga.

45 Y

45 Y quanto a esta vltima sospecha de la có
juracion, que (segun ellos dizen) se tratò en Flá
des, aqui se tiene por cierto que fue patraña, in
uétada por aquel Nuce, y por los que le sobor-
naron para hazer tiro al Embaxador de España. Y parecen euidentes los testimonios que
ay por la innocécia de los presos, acusados por
personas enemigas de la paz. Y si el Rey da
oydos a algunos, y se muestra espantadizo, cada dia le leuantaran conjuraciones en el ayre,
como hazian sus passados por algun tiempo a
la Reyna Isabel, como a Reyna, que a Rey no
se permite en ninguna manera. Porque seria
mostrar poco respeto y estima de su persona
y valor: Y por la misma razon, no oymos que
se hable con este lenguaje y chismeria a otros
Reyes ni Principes. Y lo que haziá con la Rey
na Isabel era, para lisongearla, y entretener al
pueblo con nouedades, y irritarlos contra los
Catolicos, y por preambulos de sus Parlamen-
tos para alcançar las contribuciones, seruicios,
y emprestitos que pretendian; y que mucho
mejor se alcançàran por otros medios licitos y
vsados. Aunque ninguno es tan facil como e-
ste, para los q no tienen conciencia ni temor
de Dios, ni tan a su saluo y sin costa, pues todas
las vezes que quisieren, pueden inuentar las sos
pechas y testimonios que se les antojare, contra

tra qualquier innocente, y (segun el refran) có
tra sospechas no ay armas, ni se vsa en Inglaterra en nuestros dias pedir cuenta, ni castigar a
los autores dellas, como se acostumbra en o-
tros Reynos, y por alla en tiempo de sus Reyes
Catolicos se solia hazer.

46 Por esto, y para dar aparencia de verdad a
lo q̃ en si no tiene ninguna, vsã tãtos destos ar
tificios, y en cierta manera estando ellos en sus
principios, no pueden hazer menos. Porque
como la verdad se sustenta con verdades, assi
el artificio no se puede sustentar sino con artifi
cios, los quales, por mucho que les procuré au
torizar personas poderosas, no dexan por esso
de ser lo q̃ son, ni de parecer mal a todos quan
do se vienen a descubrir. Desta suerte eran las
patrañas que (mientras auia guerra con España
ña) inuentaron tan a menudo, sacando a luz
vnos hombrezillos que fingian ser embiados
por la Magestad Catolica, y por sus ministros y
personas en su nombre, para matar la Reyna
Isabel Como *El Doctor Lopez* Iudio, que a la
hora de su muerte protestò, que era falso lo q̃
le imputauan, y que queria mas a la Reyna, que
a Iesu Christo nuestro Señor.

47 Lo mismo fue de los mancebos *Guillams*
Torque acusados de la misma manera falsamente, como todos vieron al tiempo de su

muer-

muerte. Y por dexar otros muchos desta suer
te, basta por todos aquel de *Esquire*, conocido
por hombre sin verdad, y embustero, a quien
para que parecieffe verdadera su confesfion,
mandaron dar la muerte, y acabar de presto
con el, atajandole la palabra, quãdo (visto que
el negocio yua de veras) se queria desdezir.

43 Eftos, por entonces que auia guerra, erã
los artificios para hazer los Efpañoles odiofos
con el pueblo, y deftos mifmos medios comié
çan otra vez a vfar, los que querriã deshazer la
paz, aunque no pueden agora tener la fuerça
que folian, conociendolos todos por enredos.

49 Pero, que digo deftos enredos particulares, de los quales otros han efcrito lo que ba
fta? quando con la cara defcubierta fe atreuen
algunos a afirmar que en Inglaterra no mole-
ftan a nadie por fu religion, publicando por
otra parte, las leyes que teftifican lo contrario,
y lo confirman los proceffos y las fentencias
de los martires, y todo fu modo de proceder
contra ellos. Y aunque algunas vezes, pareció-
doles que el pueblo fe efcandalizaria fi mataf-
fen a tantos con folo titulo de religion, han leuantado tambien contra ellos femejantes te-
ftimonios, con todo effo, pues les huuierã per
donado las vidas, y aũ hecholes mercedes por
                                                    folo

solo ir a los templos de los Proteſtantes, es e-
-uidente que eran fingidas las trayciones : pues
no ſe ſuelen perdonar tan facilmente, tan graues delitos como a ellos les imputauan.

50 Deſta miſma manera fue la perſecucion
del Apoſtata Iuliano (como ſe ſaca de ſan Chri-
ſoſtomo, ſan Gregorio Nazianzeno, y de las hiſtorias Ecleſiaſticas) que para quitar a los martires
la honra de ſu martirio, les hazia leuantar teſti-
monios de leſa Mageſtad, y los atormentaua y
quitaua las vidas por titulo de varios delitos.

In SS. Mar-
tyr. Iuſti.
& Maxi.
tom. 3.
Orat. I. in
Iul.

Aſsi a los ſantos *Iuuentino y Maximo* mandò
tentar por todas las vias que ſupo, con promeſ
ſas y amenazas, y que rindiendoſe ellos a rene
gar de Chriſto, los ſacaſſen con honra y publi
cidad, pero no lo queriendo hazer, que les ma-
taſſen con titulo de traydores, ſin hazer men-
cion alguna de ſu religion.

A los Obiſpos y ſacerdotes conſtantes, y a
otros Catolicos de valor, y de vida exemplar,
perſeguia y embiua deſterrados; diſsimulan-
do con otros cuya vida podia deſautorizar a ſu
religion.

Fauorecia a los *Arrianos*, a los *Aecianos*, a los
Donatiſtas, y a todas las ſectas que por entonces auia debaxo de nombre de Chriſtianos, y
a los *Iudios*, y a qualquiera que quiſieſſe o pudieſſe ſer contrario a los Catolicos.

Ha-

Haziase Compromissario de las diferencias
que el mismo auia sembrado entre los Christianos, para penetrarlas y hazerse mas capaz
dellas, y poderlas fomentar como lo hazia por
varias vias. Acusaua los Obispos y sacerdotes
al pueblo, para ponerle mal con ellos, y a los
vnos y a los otros infamaua.

Sus leyes contra la religion Christiana eran
las mismas que (con lastima y compassion) vemos sacadas a luz en Inglaterra en nuestros
dias. Ponia pechos y confiscaua las haziendas
a los Catolicos, eximiendo solos aquellos que
se rendian a sacrificar a sus Idolos. A los *Recusantes* de aquellos tiempos mandaua echar de
su casa y Corte, vedando que pudiessen tener
oficios en la Republica, y mucho menos ser
Magistrados, Capitanes, ni soldados Pretoria-
nos, si primero no negassen a Christo, por lo
qual *Iouiano*, que despues del fue Emperador,
arrojò en su presencia la insignia militar, como lo hizieron tambien otros.

Quitò a los Christianos las escuelas, y no solo de enseñar o aprender las ciécias en ellas, sino toda comodidad en quáto el podia de criar
bié sus hij s, hasta quitarles el vso de los libros
que en aquellos tiempos se enseñauá, con que
fue causa de que san Gregorio Nazianzeno y
otros varones doctos hizesse otros mejores para ellos.   Tan-

31

Tanta anſia tenia de hazerles pecar, que por
fuerça procuraua que entraſſen en ſus tēplos,
y aſiſtieſſen a los ſacrificios de ſus falſos Dio-
ſes, y no lo queriendo hazer ellos, hizo ofrecer
a los miſmos Idolos el pan y los mantenimien
tos que ſe auian de vēder en las plaças, paraque
los fieles, o participaſſen en alguna manera de
ſu maldad, o no tuuieſſen que comer. Pero e-
llos ſe ſuſtentaron de trigo cozido en lugar de
pan, haſta alborotarſe los miſmos Gentiles, y
canſarſe el Emperador deſta violencia.

Finalmente, de los conſejos Euangelicos ſa
caua ocaſiones para deſpojar, agrauiar y mal-
tratar de mil maneras a los Catolicos: Negan-
doles el beneficio y defenſa de las leyes que a
los mayores facinoroſos no negaua, y todo re
medio a las vexaciones que recebian de los Gē
tiles, y de ſus miniſtros, por cuyas manos les
perſeguia.

51 Eſte miſmo ha ſido el modo de proceder
en Inglaterra por eſpacio de muchos años cōtra los vaſſallos Catolicos de aquel Reyno. Los
quales no han ſentido menos las calunias que
les han leuantado, que los robos de ſus hazien
das, y daños perſonales que han ſufrido, y con
todo eſſo por las razones arriba dichas, han tenido paciencia, y viuido pacificamente. Adon
de, ſi los que mandan huuieſſen procedido de
la

la mifma manera con los Puritanos, o hecho
el menor de tantos agrauios a los Proteftátes,
tuuieran no folo fofpechas en que entender, fi
no verdaderos peligros,y verdaderas caufas de
temor,y por faberlo muy bien no fe atreuen a
meter con ellos.

52   Pero que diremos a la conjuracion q̃ pre
cedio efte vltimo Parlamento? Digo,que aun
que fueffe como fe ha publicado,y fuponien-
dola como cofa traçada por Catolicos (aũque
los mas cuerdos fon de otra opinion) con todo effo, *Vna hirundo non facit ver*, vna golondri
na no haze verano,como dize el refran. Y aun
que los autores de la perfecucion quifieran ef-
tender efte hecho,como el pecado original a
toda la generacion humana,y en el Decreto 4.
del Parlamento,dizen al mifmo propofito cótra toda verdad,que fe hizo por inftigacion de
los Iefuitas,y facerdotes de los Seminarios(en
lo qual defcubren fu buen animo,y el blanco
a que tiran) y en otros libelos que han facado
de molde fin nombres de autores, fingen que
el Papa tambien tuuo parte en ella, hablando
contra fu Santidad con tan grande defacato,
que caufa admiracion ; pero la verdad ya publica y fabida en Inglaterra es,que folos aquellos feis o ocho caualleros que interuinieron
en la mina fueron los conjurados, y por fu pro
ria

pria seguridad la ocultaron a todos. Y assi es
muy grande injusticia, hazer consequécias ge
nerales deste hecho particular, y sacar leyes tá
rigurosas contra todos los Catolicos, por causa destos.

53 Ni haze al caso que los contrarios preten
den, que vno o dos sacerdotes sin procurarlo
ellos lo viniessen a entéder, de tal manera q̃ no
lo podian descubrir. Pues viniendo a su noticia no consintieron en el hecho, antes lo afea-
ron y disuadieron, y alegaron las razones que
pudieron contra el: que era quanto por su par
te podian hazer, en Reyno adonde el Magistra
do no tiene respeto a los Sacramentos. Porque
en vn Reyno Catolico pudierá y hizieran mas,
adonde no les apretaran a descubrir las personas, ni a violar el sigilo de la confession, en la
qual los sacerdotes oyé muchas vezes cosas q̃
no quisieran, como son o todas o las mas de
las q̃ oy en, pero con obligació de *derecho diui*
no (a que ninguna ley humana puede perjudi-
car) a no manifestarlas sin licencia del penite-
te, y mucho menos la persona, por ningun ca
so. Y este es el caso del bué *Padre Garneto*, cuya innocencia descubierta al tiempo de su publica acusacion y muerte, tanto mas cófundio
a sus perseguidores, quanto las calunias que le
auian leuantado y diuulgado con malicia, se

conο-

conocieron mas claramente ſer falſas , y muchos que antes las auian creydo, quedaron admirados de ſu modeſtia, y con láſtima dela ſin razon que padecia, y eſcandalizados de la poca conciencia de ſus cótrarios, y de ſu mal modo de proceder.

54 Y para mayor euidencia del agrauio que hizieron a eſte ſanto varon, y de ſu inocencia, V.S.Iluſt. ha de ſaber, que agora eſtando yo en Roma, vi algunas cartas ſuyas, eſcritas con harta aflicion y perplexidad, laſtimádoſe mucho que con ocaſion de las vexaciones y exorbitancias cotidianas que ſufrian los Catolicos, algunos dellos (que llamaua hóbres de eſpada) quedaró tan eſcandalizados y ofendidos, que aquel enojo y ſentimiento, podria con el tiempo parar en algun inconuiniente. Y que aunque el por ſu parte, auia ſiempre procurado de induzir a todos a paciencia y ſufrimiento , como hazian los demas ſacerdotes, y que le parecia que ſus palabras tendrian fuerça con las perſonas que tratauan con el ; pero porque los agrauios eran muchos en todo el Reyno , y los ſacerdotes no ſe podian hallar en todas las partes y ocaſiones para irles a la mano, que para ſoſſegar los animos, y aſſegurar que ninguno dellos hizieſſe coſa que pudieſſe irritar al Rey, o alguno de ſu Conſejo en daño de todos, pedia
y juz-

y juzgaua por necessario, que su Sátidad embiaf
se vn precepto general à todos los Catolicos,
exortandoles que guardaffen la diuina difpoficion para falir de fus rrabajos, y que en ninguna manera intentaffen otra nouedad, como fe
hizo, y algunos de los contrarios (que prefumé
faberlo todo) no lo pueden inorar.

55 De donde es euidente, lo primero, có quã
ta inocencia padecio efte fanto varon, que me-
recia premio y no caftigo: y el grande cargo de
conciencia que tienen los que le quitaron la vida. Lo fegundo, que ni fu Santidad, ni otra perfona graue, ò de confejo y prudencia, fabia defta conjuracion. Lo tercero, à que defdicha ha
venido aquel Reyno, y quan mal gouierno es, y
quan peligrofo, reduzir las cofas à tal eftremo, ã
los vafallos pienfen (no digo con razon, fino có
la menor fombra della) que por falta de quié les
haga jufticia, quedan libres del derecho de las
naciones, y pueden remediar fus agrauios por
fus manos, y valerfe del derecho natural, atajan
do vna fuerça con otra; que en ningun cafo fe
deuiera permitir, ni que las cofas fe reduxeffen
à tal eftremo: y finalmente, por las mifmas razo
nes queda prouado, que no menos culpa tienen
los ã có las cótinuas vexaciones y agrauios que
hizieron, dieron caufa à la dicha conjuracion, ã
los mifmos que interuinieron en ella.

I   55 Y

56 Y cierto quando yo la supe, à los 11. de Diziembre con el correo que truxo la nueua à España, me parecio cosa tan peregrina, y tan fuera de las costumbres y pensamientos de los Catolicos, que sabiendo los tiros que les suelen hazer sus contrarios, y los falsos testimonios que muchas otras vezes han leuantado contra otras personas, en Inglaterra, Flandes, Francia, Alemania, y en todas las partes donde ay falta de Fê, aunque vi los vandos impressos, y diuersas cartas aquí y en Italia, que hazian relacion del caso, con todo esso no acabè de creerlo hasta llegar à Roma. Antes, pensè que todo aquel apercebimiento de poluora, &c, se huuiesse hecho por otros, y la culpa despues se echasse à los Catolicos, por parecerme casi impossible, que ellos pudiessen juntar tanta cantidad de poluora y de otros pertrechos en aquel lugar tan publico, y (auiendo passado tanto tiépo, como dezian las cartas) sin que alguno del Consejo lo supiesse y dissimulasse. Ni parecia (como he dicho) cosa de Catolicos, ni medio proporcionado para algun buen fin que pudiessen tener, ni traçado con alguna prudencia, por los daños que les podian seguir à los mismos que los tratauan siendo descubiertos, y mucho mayores si tuuiesse efeto con tanto daño de tantos inocentes, y otras razones que al mismo

mo propoſito ſe me ofrecieron entonces.

57 Pero deſpues de auer viſto eſtos decretos
del Parlamento, juntado (ſegun parece) ſolo pa
ra deſtruyr los Catolicos, pues en el no ſe ha he
cho otra coſa de momento que leyes contra e-
llos, y redes para prenderlos: y el blanco adonde
tiran los inuentores deſtas leyes, y toda ſu traza, y la trabazõ della trazada (como ſe vee claramente) antes de la conjuracion: y con todo eſſo que la ſupone, auiendoſe de fundar en ella ò
en otra coſa ſemejante : y conſiderando la anſia
que los miſmos mueſtran de eſtender la culpa
de aquellos pocos (como ſi fuera el pecado de
Adan) à los nacidos y por nacer: me inclinã las
miſmas razones dichas, à penſar que puede ſer
verdad lo que algunos afirman con grandes
fundamentos, que aunque aquellos Caualleros
fueron los inſtrumentos, pero que la traza tuuo por autores à los miſmos que el año antes,
(por perſonas ſobornadas) auian procurado al-
borotar à los Catolicos en la Prouincia de Here
fordia, para que tomaſſen las armas, y con tal o-
caſion perſuadir al Rey continuaſſe la perſecucion contra todos: y que eſtos conociendo à v-
no de los Caualleros culpados en eſta conjura
cion por hombre de grandes brios, y (aunque
Catolico) mal ſufrido en ſinrazones, le cebaron
con eſta traza, harto ſegura para ellos que no co

I 2   rrian

rrian peligro no acercandofe al lugar de la mina en cien mil años,y para los engañados,como
vna trampa en que los tenian cogidos, para facarlos fuera quando huuieffe de comécar la tra-
gedia,que auia de fer,ni antes, nidefpues, fino
la mifma noche precedente al Parlamento,y en
la mifma coyuntura del peligro imaginado,pa-
ra mas affombraral Rey,y al pueblo, y à todos
los demas à cuya noticia huuieffe de venir vn
fuceffo(al parecer)tan repentino, como queriã
los aurores de la traza que efto pareciele,y pare
cio por algun tiempo otro cafo femejante, que
(dizen)falio de la mifma fragua,quando ceuarõ
y enredaron à la fanta memoria de la Reyna de
Efcocia madre defu Mageftad con otra traza
defta fuerte,para que eftando ella prefa en Ingla
terra,confintieffe en cofas ordenadas (al parecer)por fus amigos para fu libertad , pero traza-
das por fus enemigos para fu deftruycion , por
las quales(defpues)à ella,y à algunos Caualleros
moços femejantes a eftos, quitaron las haziendas y las vidas.

58 Efto es lo que dizen,fabe Dios fi es afsi,pe
ro no dexa de tener grande prouabilidad, porq̃
algunos de nueftros contrarios fe precian def-
tas finezas;y otras cofas fuyas defta calidad ya
han falido à luz tan clara,que no las pueden ne
gar. Yaquelvillete fin firma embiado de noche,
en

en aquella forma y ſazon , al Baron de Monte-
gel,con que pretendian ſe penſaſſe que la conju
racion ſe deſcubria,huele à artificio; y de la miſ
ma manera muchas otras circunſtancias del ne
gocio:fuera de que todas las perſonas que ſabiã
de la conjuracion proteſtaron deſpues, que nin
guno dellos auia eſcrito aquel villete; y no faltò
Proteſtante,amigo de vna de lasperſonas ſobre
dichas que procuraron aquel tumulto enHere-
fordia,que dixo en ſu alabança,que fulano (nõ-
brádole)ſabia mas que todos los Papiſtas, y que
auia ſabido hazerles tiro dexandoles paſſaſ adela-
lante cõ lo que tenian entre manos muchos me
ſes,ſabiendo todos los ſecretos , para ſacarlos à
luz en la ocaſion,y hazerles caſtigar,como ſe hi
zo por medio del villete.Todas las quales coſas,
y otras que dizen al miſmo propoſito, juntamẽ
te con las condiciones de las perſonas que nom
bran,y ſu modo de proceder,hazen lo que ſe di
ze muy creyble.

59 Pero como quiera que aya paſſado (que el
tiempo lo deſcubrira)y por muy culpados que
ayan ſido los dichos Caualleros , que los doy à
V.S.Iluſtriſ.por los autores y execuroics deſta
conjuracion,y de quanto mandaien los contra
rios.Pero todo eſto que haze al propoſito?ſien-
do culpa particular de pocos. Y que tiene que
hazer con las leyes que en conſequencia della
han

han sacado à luz cõtra todos los Catolicos? que
no tiené mas que ver con la conjuracion que los
que viuen en el Iapon. Y esta tan euidente y tã
notoria injusticia, es la mayor presunció y prue
ua, de que el fundamento sobre el qual se fabri-
caron estas leyes, fue vna artificiosa inuencion,
trazada para engañar al Rey y al Parlamento, y
ocasion buscada para perseguir la Religion Catolica, por sus contrarios, y para sacar con algun
color tan barbaras leyes y prematicas contra
ella.

60 Entre las quales (por no hablar de todas)
aquella que prohibe con tan grandes penas los
libros buenos , hasta las historias y vidas de los
Santos, que no entren en aquel Reyno, muestra
que los que procuraron esta ley no lo pretendé
ser, y la flaqueza y desconfiança de sus superin-
tendentes y cabeças de su secta, que no pudiendo mas sustentar la opinion della por otras vias
acuden al braço seglar: y viendo todos sus desati
nos y engaños ya descubiertos y conuencidos
en los libros de los Catolicos, y que está tan ago
tada (años ha) su sciencia, que ni se atreuen, ni sa
ben que responder à ellos, handado en este arbi
trio de desterrarlos por ley del Parlamento, para
que no vengan en manos de algun indiferente
lector, y puedan ellos mas libremente hazer lo
que suelen, sin que se descubran sus enredos.

61 La

36

61 La otra tambien, que pone crimen de tray
cion y lesa Mageſtad, à los que ſe dexan perſuadir à hazerſe Catolicos y reconciliarſe à la Y-
gleſia, no ſolo en Inglaterra como era antes, ſino
en la mar, como dize la ley, ò en qualquier otro
Reyno, mueſtra quan diferente concepto ha-
zē de noſotros, y de la ſata Fê que profeſſamos,
y de nueſtro modo de proceder, los que nos conocen y tratan de cerca, del que tiené otros que
no nos tratan ni conocen, y el que nueſtros ad-
uerſarios querrian que todos tuuieſſen. Pues có
tan grandes penas les quieren eſcarmentar que
no nos traten ni conozcan, viſto que quantos ſa
len de la confuſion de aquel Reyno, que no ſon
hombres de eſtado intereſſados en las opinio-
nes y modo de proceder de los Proteſtantes,
ſiendo perſonas de capacidad, y no muy prenda
das en los vicios, la dexan facilmente y abraçá
la Religion Catolica, como la mejor. Y eſta miſ
ma ley haze euidencia contra ſus autores, que
ſon *Poſſeſſores malæ fidei*, y que ſaben que ſu ſecta
no vale nada pues en lugar de argumentos ſe ſir
uen de violencias, por faltarles la juſticia y la ra
zon.

62 Y aunque entiendo quan poco pueden la
razon y la verdad con los que ſe han entregado
à ſus paſsiones, con todo eſſo he juzgado por tra
bajo bien empleado el poner en papel, con toda
ſinceri-

sinceridad y sin ofensa de nadie en quáto he podido, lo que arriba está dicho, sin otro intento, (como sabe Dios) que de certificar à V.S.Ilust. lo que entiendo es verdad, con el mayor desseo que puedo de la prosperidad y verdadero bien del Rey, y de quantos tiene a su cargo. Y he escrito con tanta claridad lo que siento, porque téngo à V.S.Ilust. (como ya he dicho) por persona de ta ta honra, y de tan buena intenció, q̃ (auñq nos diferenciamos en Religion) no interpretará en mal sentido lo que se dize llana y sinceraméte con buen animo y voluntad. Y de aqui podra tomar ocasion de informarse de muchas verdades, las quales sabidas, queda V.S.Ilustr. por razon de su oficio y de la fidelidad que deue à su Rey, obligado à certificarle dellas de la manera q̃ las entédiere, fuera de que su Magestad (por vétura) jamas las podra saber por otro camino con tanta claridad. Y en caso que alguno quisiesse torcer mis palabras, à diferente sentido del que acabo de dezir, apelo de tal interprete à otro juyzio mas recto, y al supremo Tribunal, a donde las palabras, obras, y intenciones de todos se han de examinar, y sentenciar en reuista con justicia y equidad. Y assi acabare esta materia con vn exemplo muy al proposito, y digno de ser imitado de todos los Principes, y en particular de su Magestad, para que goze de los Reynos q̃

Dios

37

Dios le ha dado con quietud, y los dexe cõ paz
y bendicion à sus descendientes. Entre los quales dizen, que el Principe su hijo es de muy rara
abilidad, y de quien se puede esperar qualquiera cosa grande, no faltandole buena educa-
cion.

63 El exemplo es del Emperador *Augusto*, re-
ferido por *Seneca* en el primer libro, y capitulo
nono de su libro de clemencia.

Fue *Augusto* en su mocedad bullicioso, y amigo de vengarse en el principio de su Imperio. Pero despues mudò estilo, por ver que el rigor y el
castigo no eran medios para su seguridad: y se
mudò con esta ocasion. Viuiendo en la Galia, y
auiendo ya quarenta años que gouernaua, le
fue descubierta vna traycion que le auia apercebido Lucio Cina, y como le querian matar mié-
tras estaua sacrificando, y todas las circunstancias de la conjuracion, el tiempo, el lugar, y el
modo cõ q̃ se auia de efetuar, por vno de los mismos complices della. El Emperador alborotado
cõ la nueua, jũtò cõsejo de sus mas intimos amigos, y todos fueron de parecer que Cina y sus
complices se prendiessen y castigassen luego, cõ
la pena deuida à tan atroz delito.

64 Passando despues Augusto la noche sin
dormir, y con el animo inquieto de varios pensamientos, algunas vezes (hablando consigo mis-

K   mo

mo)dezia : *Pues que hare? viuire siempre con este cuydado, dexando viuir enemigo mio tan capital? Como no se ha de castigar à quien ha querido no solo matar, sino sacrificar en tiempo de paz à su Emperador? cuya persona tantas vezes acometida en las dissensiones ciuiles el cielo ha defendido, y guardado en tantas guerras y peligros por tierra y por mar.*

65 Despues de vn rato (auiendo discurrido secretamente entre si) con mas fuerça que antes auia hablado contra Cina, reprehendio à si mismo con estas palabras: *Para que has de viuir, si à tantos trae gusto y prouecho tu muerte? Que fin aurà de castigos? Quanta sangre se derramarà? Ha de ser vuestra cabeça la sola, en que todos los moços nobles desta nobilissima Republica han de afilar sus espadas, y prouar sus fuerças y valor? No vale tanto vuestra vida, si para que no perezcais tantos han de perecer.*

66 Viendole *la Emperatriz Liuia*, tan congoxado y perplexo, le dixo desta manera: *Si quereis (señor) cōsejo de muger: hazed lo que suelen los Medicos, que auiendo vsado mucho tiempo de vn remedio, y viendo que no aprouecha prueuan lo contrario. En tantos años no aueis hecho nada con los castigos y rigor. No aueis muerto à Saluideno, à Lepido, à Murena, à Cepion, y à otros que han conspirado contra vuestra vida? tantos, que es verguença de nombrarlos: Prouad vna vez como os sale el perdonar. Lucio Ci-*

na

ma ya esta descubierto, ya no os puede dañar, y puede
aprouechar mucho para vuestra reputacion y autoridad.

67   Holgòse mucho el Emperador del buen
consejo, y agradeciosele à la Emperatriz, y mã-
dò que se fuessen los de su consejo, y que le lla-
massen luego à Lucio Cina, à quien hizo poner
otra silla, y assentar junto à si, y le començò à ha
blar con estas palabras. *Lo primero que os pido (Ci
na) es, que no me interrumpais, ni hableis palabra haf
ta auerme oydo: porque despues tēdreis tiempo de ha
blar. Ya os acordais como os halle en los reales de mis
contrarios, no hecho, sino en cierta manera nacido
mi enemigo, sobrino de Pompeo. Os perdonè la vida, y
os hize merced de todo vuestro patrimonio, de manera que el dia de oy estais tan prospero, y tan rico, que
muchos de mis compañeros en la vitoria os quedan in
feriores, y os tienen embidia. Despues os he honrado
con los cargos que aueis querido en la Republica, an-
teponiendoos a muchos otros, cuyos padres me acom-
pañaron en las guerras: y auiendo hecho todo esto cõ
vos, como desagradecido me quereis matar?*

68   A estas palabras dio vozes Cina, protestan
do que no era assi. *No me guardais, ò Cina, la palabra (dixo el Emperador) porque me prometistes de
no interrumpirme. Digo pues, que procurado aueis
quitarme la vida, en tal parte, con tales compañeros,
y tal dia, declarandole como la conjuracion se auia de*

executar. Y viendole ya conuencido y callado, no como antes por concierto, ſino por acuſarle ſu propria conciencia, añadio: *Y con que intento quereis hazerlo? por ventura para que me ſucedais en el Imperio? Cierto, la Republica Romana eſtuuiera en muy mal eſtado, ſi otra coſa no os eſtoruára el mandar, ſino mi vida. Si yo ſolo impido vueſtras eſperanças, que penſais de los Paulos, de los Fabios, y de tantos otros nobiliſsimos varones de iluſtriſsimas familias? penſais que os querran eſtos por ſu Emperador?* Y auiédole dicho muchas otras coſas al miſmo propoſito, concluyò finalmente Auguſto la platica, deſta manera.

69 *Cina, ya ſegunda vez os doy la vida. La vna como a enemigo declarado, la otra como a traydor. De oy adelante comience nueſtra amiſtad: andemos a porfia los dos, para moſtrar ſi yo os he dado la vida, ò vos la aueis recebido, con mayor lealtad.* Y deſpues deſto le hizo Auguſto Queſtor y Cóſul, y muchas otras mercedes que el miſmo Cina no ſe atreuiera à pedir: con que le quedò ſiempre muy fiel y agradecido amigo, y táto, que muriendo le dexò por ſu heredero. Y paſsò lo demas de ſu vida Auguſto con grandiſsima quietud, auiendo có eſte hecho tan heroyco pueſto fin à todas las cójuraciones, demanera, que no huuo deſpues ninguna contra el, en todo lo reſtante de ſu Imperio.

70 Haſta

39

70 Hasta aqui son palabras de Seneca, con q̃ declara este hecho, digno de tan digno y magnanimo Emperador, y el cósejo acertado y prouechoso de la persona que mas bien le queria. Y cierto, yo he entendido que algunos de los que han muerto agora en Inglaterra (digo de los Caualleros, que mataron por esta conjuracion) aunque por ella merecieſſen la muerte, con todo eſſo deuiales tanto el Rey por la quietud có que fue recebido en el Reyno, que si lo supiera con tiempo, no dudo sino que huuiera hecho con ellos(y por ventura con los demas) lo que hizo Augusto con el otro.

71 Este exemplo es antiguo: pero si V.S Iluſt. quiere otro, mas cercano à nueſtros tiempos y à nueſtro caso, ponga los ojos en el Rey que agora es de Francia, à quien los Hugonotes y géte mal intencionada de su Reyno truxeron por algun tiempo deſaſſoſſegado, y con los miſmos aſſombros y rezelos con que otros procurá entretener al Rey de Inglaterra, haſta deſterrar en su nombre y dar la muerte à perſonas inocentes, acumulandoles que auiaſido complices en las conjuraciones que entonces auia, con nota de publica infamia : la qual penſauan los perſeguidores que auia de durar para ſiempre en Francia, pues la tenian ya eſculpida en las piedras, al modo que eſtotros han entremeti do y mezclado

do otras calumnias semejantes entre los actos de su Parlamento. Pero Dios tenia muy diferen tes pensamientos: y estando ya aplacada en grá parte su diuina justicia por los pecados de aquel Reyno, la pena (llegada ya à su colmo) auia de declinar. Y el Rey, por tener prudencia y valor, vistos los engaños, supo sacudir de si ruines có sejos, y abrir los oydos à personas que le amas sen y tratassen verdad. Con que se le han acaba do los desassossiegos y sospechas, y queda paci fico Rey, y señor de su Reyno, aunque sus vasa llos no sean todos de vna misma Religió. Y ha ra lo mismo el Rey de Inglaterra, teniendo tan to valor y prudencia como el de Francia: y aun deue hazerlo con mucha mas razon, pues los Catolicos siempre han querido bien à su Mage stad y à los suyos, y à algunos dellos les ha costa do las vidas, adóde al cótrario los que à el le die ron vida y ser, y el derecho à los Reynos que possee (que fueron su padre y madre) entram bos perdieron las suyas, con muertes violentas, por conjuracion, sentencia, y crueles manos de los que se llaman Protestantes.

72 Grandes mudanças (si las han de hazer los hombres) piden comunmente grandes disposi ciones, que no se pueden aparejar sino en mu cho tiempo: Pero adonde Dios todo poderoso mete la mano, ni tiempo ni trabajo es menester.

Quien

40

Quien huuiera mirado con ojos humanos
à Francia, algunos años ha, pudiera auer penfar
do que aquel Reyno fe auia de affolar de todo
punto, pues fe yua apartando de Chrifto, y
dando à la heregia y diffolucion. Pero el en cu
ya mano eftan los coraçones de los Reyes y de
los fubditos, y haze quanto quiere en el cielo y
en la tierra, de tal manera ha trocado los ani
mos en pocos años, que fe puede efperar, que
boluera prefto à florecer alli la piedad Catolica, con toda la pureza que folia en otros tiempos.

Los medios por donde encaminò Dios efta mudança, no los defcubrio defde el principio, aunque fe quifo feruir de la induftria y dili
gencia humana, y de las diferentes inclinaciones de los hombres, permitiendo algunas cofas, y queriendo otras en quanto venian a fu
propofito.

73 Lo mifmo fe puede efperar fin duda en la
difpoficion de Inglaterra, a cuya converfion
pienfo que ninguna cofa ha eftoruado tanto,
quanto la demafiada confiança que algunos há
tenido en medios humanos.

Pero, eftado eftos ya en alguna manera apar
tados, el mifmo tiempo nos combida a efperar, que el Señor ha de poner (particularmête)
fu mano, pues eftà apercebido fiêpre para dar
la

la en casos semejantes , y muchas vezes tanto
mas cerca para el socorro de los suyos, quanto
parece estar mas lexos , y ellos en mayores a-
prietos. Assi lo dixo *Filon* a los demas Embaxa
dores sus compañeros (quando el Emperador
Caligula les echò de si con aspereza, en otro caso semejante) que estuuiessen de buen animo,
porque ya que los hombres no querrian reme
diar los agrauios, tocaua a Dios el hazerlo, y
boluer por su causa. Y en nuestros tiempos, se dize del Padre Maestro *Iuan de Aui-
la*, varó muy insigne en letras, consejo, y santidad, otra respuesta semejante; que siendo acusa
do falsamente, y estado preso por el santo Ofi
cio de la Inquisicion, y visto su negocio cō mu
cho cuydado y desseo de librarle, por ser perso
na tan eminente; embiandole a dezir los señores Inquisidores, que por estar el processo tan
fundado(al parecer)en iusticia, y todos los testigos contestes, no hallauan para el remedio
humano: respondio con grande animo y con
tento. Bendito sea Dios,que nunca mi negocio
cio tuuo mejor estado que agora, que lo veo
fuera de las manos de los hombres, y puesto en
las de Dios. Y viose ser assi: porque desde aql
punto, se començò a descubrir la falsedad de
los testigos, y la verdad de su inocencia, hasta
salir de aquella prision con la mayor honra,
que

que se ha visto, mostrando el Señor en el caso
deste santo hóbre, y de sus acusadores, lo q̃ cada dia haze en otros, que sus juyzios son re-
ctos è infalibles, y aunque muchas vezes dila-
ta la justicia, porque assi conuiene, pero nunca jamas falta de hazerla.

74 Es estilo y orden de la diuina prouidencia, dexar(muchas vezes)crecer la tribulacion
a sus sieruos, por apurar y perficionar su esperança, hasta que el tiempo les desengañe, y con
la experiencia ellos y todos acaben de entender, que los medios humanos y la fuerça delas
criaturas en que tenianpuesta su confiança, no
son bastantes para librarles: y entonces acudo
a remediar y consolarles, con mayores ventajas que ellos mismos esperarian.

75 En este sentido dixo el Profeta Dauid, en *Psal. 90.*
nombre de Dios, y del hombre justo atribula-
do qué confia en el: *Quoniam in me sperauit, libe*
rabo eum: protegam eum, quoniam cognouit nomen
meum. Cum ipso sum in tribulatione, eripiam eum
& glorificabo eum. Y es lo que passò con el Pa-
triarca *Iosef,* y có innumerables otros: y sufrio *Genes. 37.*
trabajos el mismo hijo de Dios, quando viuió
en carne mortal, para que no nos podamos
quexar. Y hazelo Dios desta manera porq̃ assi
cóuiene a nuestro bien, y se deue a su gloria q̃
nadie pueda dezir, *manus nostra excelsa, & nõ Do* *Deut. 32.*
minus fecit haec omnia.   I.

76 De donde auemos de apreder, lo que el Señor con la tribulacion pretende enseñarnos, que aunque para salir della podemos y deuemos valernos de medios humanos licitos y conuenientes: pero, que la cõfiança nuestra no ha de estriuar en ellos, sino en la virtud de su braço todo poderoso, que se sirue de los tales medios, y quiere que los hombres se siruan de llos como de instrumentos de su diuina prouidencia y pendientes de su mano, y no de otra manera.

77 Por esto, quando algunas personas de quien esperauamos que nos auian de remediar en nuestra necessidad nos faltaren, no es justo dessabrirnos, ni perder la caridad ni paciécia con ellos: porque puede ser que la falta o alguna ocasion della aya procedido de nuestra parte, por la dicha razon, ò que (sin falta de nadie) lo aya ordenado assi nuestro Señor, por premiar mas colmadamente nuestra paciencia y humildad, y no estoruarnos los medios ordenados por su eterna predestinacion para nuestra saluacion: pues muchos se saluan por la aduersidad, y con muy grande gloria, que con la prosperidad perecieran eternamente: y ninguna tribulacion puede ser larga que se acaba có Momenta neũ & leue 2. Cor. 4. vida breue, ni cosa grande la que cabe en pequeño lugar. Y si algunas vezes el sentimiento

es

es mucho, puede ſer, porque la paciencia es po
ca, y porque queremos las coſas antes de ſu tié
po, y apocar nueſtro merecimiento, y la glo
ria que el Señor con larga mano nos quiſiera
dar, que es tan piadoſo q̃ en ninguna manera
guſta de nueſtras penas, ni las permitiera por
vn ſolo mométo, ſino cóuinierá para nueſtro
mayor conſuelo, y por el gouierno general, y
cumplimiento de ſus diuinas traças, en las qua
les no puede auer falta.

78 Por todas las quales cauſas, quando los
medios con que los hombres penſauan ſoco-
rrer a nueſtra neceſsidad ſalieré vanos, no nos
deuemos deſmayar, ni es razon que nadie pier
da el aliento : ſino que auiuemos nueſtra confiança, y la pógamos en Dios, dexádo en ſu libertad la manera có q̃ nos aya de ayudar. Pues
ſin falta lo hara; y quando no ſe haga por los
medios que los hombres auian traçado, ſe hara por otros mejores, ò por los miſmos en o-
tro tiempo, ò por otras perſonas acudira a lo
que auemos meneſter; y lo haze muchas vezes
por caminos por donde menos lo aguardaua-
mos, y por perſonas de quien ningun bien parece podiamos eſperar.

79 Y eſtas mueſtras de quádo en quádo ſue
le dar al múdo deſu infinito poder, paraq̃ enté
damos q̃ puede obrar por los medios que quie

F 2   re,

re, y aunque de fuyo fean inutiles, queriendo
fu diuina Mageftad feruirfe dellos, los haze pro
porcionados y prouechofos. En vn momento
alumbra los entendimientos mas ofufcados
con tinieblas, ablanda los coraçones mas em-
podernidos, y los mueue con eficacia, para que
remedien a las necefsidades de fus fieruos, los
que mas lexos eftauan de hazerles bien, y cien
mil otros medios tiene, para ayudar y confolar
a los que ponen fu confiança enteramente en
el, que ni ellos, ni fus contrarios llegan a entender.

Epif. 256. Dize fan Bernardo, que auia leydo en vn
fabio, que no es varon fuerte a quien no le cre-
ce el animo en medio de las dificultades: y aña-
de, Pero yo digo, el hombre fiel entre los aço-
res ha de eftar mas confiado. Y lo puede eftar
quien tiene caufa jufta, y a Dios delante.

80 Quien no huuiera penfado que fu diuina Mageftad tenia ya oluidado fu pueblo? quádo por prouar fu fidelidad, y librarles (defpues)
con mayor demoftracion de fu gloria, les dexò reduzir a tanto eftremo, que tenian a las ef-
paldas vn exercito poderofo de los Gitanos, y
el mar Bermejo delante: y eftauan a punto de
fer muertos con la efpada de Faraon, ò ahoga-
dos en la mar. Y quié diera jamas en tal medio
como el que Dios tenia traçado para librarles?

81 El

43

81 El aprieto y sobresalto de los Christianos erapoco menor, quando el Emperador Iuliano de quien hablamos arriba, tenia hecho voto, de sacrificar a sus Idolos a quantos dellos hallasse viuos, boluiendo el de la guerra dePersia: y auia ya mandado fabricar vn Teatro en Ierusalem para que començasse el assolamiento de los Christianos, en el mismo lugar adonde tuuo principio su religion. Lo qual sabido, y viendose ellos desamparados de todo socorro humano, boluieron (como refiere *san Gregorio Nazianzeno*) sus coraçones y sus esperanças enteramente a la Magestad de Dios, importunádole con oraciones, ayunos, y otras obras de penitencia y piedad, que tuuiesse misericordia de su pueblo condenado ya a muerte, y sin otro refugio que el suyo, y boluiesse por la defensa de su santa religion, que el Emperador pretendia destruyr. Esta peticion hecha con la disposicion dicha, y en tiempo detan estrema necessidad (a la qual parece que permitio Dios que llegassen las cosas, para disponer los animos de los Christianos a recebir tá grāde misericordia como les queria hazer) mouiode suerte el coraçó delSeñor, q détro de pocos diasles librò de todo púto de aquel trabajo y peligro.

Orat. 1. in Iulianum.

82 Los intentos de nuestros contrarios está ya tan declarados que no pueden estar mas,

pues

pues son querer, si pudiessen, destruir la religió Catolica. Y su presuncion ha llegado al colmo, despues que les parece nos han despojado (con sus ardides) de los medios humanos, en que imaginauan teniamos fundadas nuestras esperanças.

83 Pero la verdad es, que los sieruos de Dios, que no ponen la mira en solos los sucessos y circunstancias de las cosas presentes, sino miran mas de lexos a las consequencias venideras, considerando como estas mudanças temporales cuelgan de vna causa inmutable y superior, que las encamina siempre con justicia al mayor bien, tienen agora mayores esperanças, y mas ciertas prendas que nunca del remedio de aquel Reyno: y estriuan no solo en la cōfiança general que en casos semejantes los hōbres han de tener de Dios, y de su diuina bondad, pero tambien en particular y muy fundado discurso de razon.

Porq̃ años ha q̃ la heregia ha perdido su credito en Inglaterra, adōde se sustēta por fuerça, como casa apuntalada, con la merced que se haze a los que la professan exteriormente; y con el castigo de los Catolicos recusantes que no quieren ir a sus yglesias. Pero las cosas violentas no pueden ser durables, y estos dos puntales tan flacos, no son para tener por mucho
cho

cho tiempo tan grande peſo,cargandoſe cada
dia mas ſobre ellos con ſu propria ruina.

84 El Principe es prudente:y los que le acó
ſejan no ſon tan faltos de prouidencia,que no
echen de ver en que há de parar eſtas coſas. Y
ſe cáſará,de porfiar cótra Dios,y de ſu miſmo
trabajo,y de la aflicion de los vaſſallos,y del eſ
candalo general con que ſe quita el luſtre de
ſu gouierno , y de otras coſas que hazen tá en
ofenſa de toda la Chriſtiandad , ǧ podra qualquiera buen iuyzio barruntar,los malos ſuceſ
ſos que ſemejantes deſordenes prometen,al
largo andar.

Sapiens (dize el Eſpiritu ſanto) *timet,& de-*   *Prouc.*14.
*clinat à malo:ſtultus trãſilit,& confidit.*Y aquel
dicho tan recebido , *Sapientis eſt mutare conſi-*
*lium,*aqui tiene lugar:mayormente,quando el
tiempo deſcubre,y la experiécia da vozes, que
lo que pretenden no ſe puede hazer , y que el
trabajo que ponen es embalde.

85 Los que al preſente gouiernan en Inglate
rra, deſſeando lleuar adelante lo que otros les
dexaró traçado y coméçado,han hecho quan
to los hombres(con fuerças humanas)podian
hazer,por medio deſta paz,y de ſu Parlaméto,
y de las leyes que han ſacado y acomodado a
ſu propoſito,para acabar con la religion Cato
lica,y eſtablecer el error y la maldad en aquel
Rey-

Reyno. Pero siendo estas cosas *Ex genere pri-uatiuorum*, como no tienen sustancia ni ser, no pueden tener estabilidad: y por otra parte, los Catolicos quedan tan escarmentados, que para adelante ninguno dellos se dexara facilmente engañar, con los enredos de los que procurã seruirse del zelo de algunos para la ruina de todos, ni aguardaran su remedio, sino de donde les ha de venir que es de Dios.

86 Por esto, aunque queden por agora sujetos a daños temporales con estas leyes, y que algunos flacos por temor dellas podrã encubrir sus conciencias, con tan poco prouecho a los que lo procuran como arriba queda dicho: pero por vno que caiga desta manera por algun tiempo, muchos otros se leuantan para siempre. Y los Catolicos constantes (que son los sarmientos viuos vnidos a la vid, de quien di-

Ioann. 15. xo Christo, *Que se auian de limpiar, y podar, para que diessen mas fruta*: Con esta nueua tribulacion se han renouado en su antiguo feruor, de uocion y caridad, y con el cuydado de su propria saluacion, y desseo de la agena, cada dia echan fuera renueuos y pampanos que crecen para la eternidad.

87 La Apostasia del Reyno de Inglaterra, no tuuo el principio que la de otros, que se hã apartado de Iesu Christo por corrupciõ y culpa ge-

pa general de los vaſſallos, ſino introduxoſe
por fuerça de las iniquas leyes, y por la induſ-
tria y potencia de ſus Principes y cabeças, que
han querido lleuar adelante, lo que el Rey Hē-
rique Octauo començò, vencido de vna paſſiō
particular, para poderſe caſar con Ana Bole-
na, en vida de la Reyna doña Catalina ſu legi-
tima muger. Por eſto, como la ciſma comē-
çò ſin culpa del Reyno y contra ſu voluntad,
le ha hecho Dios particular merced, mas que
à algunos otros que ſe han apartado de la Igleſia, y dado à los ſacerdotes y Catolicos deſta
nacion el eſpiritu del martirio, don ſingular y
de ineſtimable precio, en que ſe funda la conſtancia de los martires, como en el miſmo ſe
fundò la de los que huuo en la primitiua Igle-
ſia, con la qual, *Non reſiſtendo, ſed perferendo* ſu   *Beda ſerm*
jetaron el mundo à Ieſu Chriſto. Y es prenda   *18. de ſan*
ſegura, que Dios no ha dexado de ſu mano a-   *Etis.*
quel Reyno, como dexò la Africa, la Grecia y
otras tierras que ſe apartaron voluntariamente
de ſu obediencia: ſino que deſpues de purgado
el Reyno, y perficionado con eſta perſecucion
(mediante la qual *Reuelātur ex multis cordibus*   *Lucæ 2.*
cogitationes: & probati, manifeſti fiunt) ha de   *1. Cor. 11.*
boluer la Fè y la virtud à preualecer en el, co-
mo en tiempos paſſados ſolia.

Por eſta razon, los ſacerdotes agora deſte-
M   ra los

rrados de Inglaterra procuran boluer a su
labor, y no dexaran de hazer lo que deuen por
amenazas, ni por peligros. Y el que apacentò
a su Profeta en el desierto, no faltara de pro-
uerles de lo que huuieren menester, y darles
ración, mientras fuere seruido que viuan y tra
bajen en su viña: y por vno dellos que permite
que se nos quite con el martirio, embia (como
vemos) muchos otros que suplan su lugar. Y
de la manera que se renueuan las plantas en la
primauera, assi con ocasion deste inuierno y
tempestad, vemos vna primauera espiritual y
celestial en aquel Reyno, adonde se han renouado los buenos propositos de muchos, y o-
tros nacido de nueuo, que antes no auia, y el a-
nimo crecido à los fieles mas que se puede de-
Cantic. 2. zir. *Vineæ florentes (ya) dederunt adorem suum*, y
quantas plantas quedan viuas, estan cargadas
de flores y frutas de todas las virtudes heroycas arriba dichas, y de muchas otras que prometen cosecha abundante.

  88 Esta nueua puedo dar à V. S. Ilust. de pre
sente, que por dos de los nuestros que estos
dias martirizaron en Inglaterra, ya han salido
de alla cinco o seys de grande expectacion : y
el superior que ha sucedido al Padre Garneto,
ha embiado los nombres de otros dezyseis,
que dessean y merecen ser recebidos en la Có-
pañia.

pañia. Y quanto à los Seminarios, ſi ſe recibieſ
ſen à todos los que tienen las partes requiſitas,
y deſpues deſtas tan riguroſas leyes, piden ſer
admitidos en ellos, fuera meneſter doblar las
caſas.

89 Y finalmente, el camino real por donde
los Reyes y Reynos, dexando ſus errores y vicios, ſuelen ſeguir al reſplandor de la Catolica
verdad, eſtà ya deſembaraçado y abierto. Y
quãtas coſas ſe han endereçado (deſde el prin
cipio) por eſte camino, hà tenido mas proſpe
ros ſuceſſos de lo que los hombres penſauan:
y todos los demas caminos y medios han ſalido inutiles para la conuerſion de las almas, que
es, y ha de ſer nueſtro fin. Y apenas pudiera ſu-
ceder de otra manera, pues implica contradi-
cion, y es caſo impoſsible, que los hombres
ſe hagan buenos, no lo queriendo ſer. Y en
eſto cápea ſobre manera la grandeza y la exce
lécia de la diuina ſabiduria, y ſobrepuja tanto à
la aſtucia de los hombres, que de los miſmos
medios que ellos inuentan, y de las traças que
maquinã, para oprimir la virtud y eſcureccer la
verdad, ſe ſirue Dios por inſtrumentos para en
ſalçarlas, y darles luſtre y autoridad, para que
ſean eſtimadas, *y libremente deſſeadas* ſobre
todas las riquezas del mundo, por los miſmas
perſonas ỹ (poco antes) no ſolo las menoſpre-

ciauan

ciauan y aborrecian, ſino que las procurauan arrancar de los coraçones de otros.

Como ſe puede ver en muchos exemplos, y particularmente en la repentina mudança y conuerſion de todo el exercito del Emperador *Iuliano*, tan confirmado y arraygado (a ſu parecer) en la infidelidad, que por medio del miſmo exercito, ſe auia de eſtablecer la idolatria, y arrancar la Fè y memoria de Ieſu Chriſto para ſiempre jamas, ſegun las vanas traças de Iuliano.

Soʒom. li. 3. cap. 3.

90 Acuerdome de auerle leydo en la hiſtoria de *Soʒomeno*, como el miſmo Emperador, para enredar à los Chriſtianos, y dar color à la injuſta perſecucion con que les oprimia, y encaminar (poco à poco) los ſoldados del miſmo exercito al paganiſmo, hizo pintar ſu retrato en medio, entre los de Iupiter, Marte, y Mercurio, echando vãdo, que todos aquellos que no quiſieſſen haʒer reuerencia al dicho retrato, fueſſen tenidos por ſus enemigos. Los Chriſtianos eſtauan mas prõptos que nadie, à haʒer al Emperador todo la honra humana que ſe le deuia y le pudieran haʒer, y que ſe ſolia à los retratos y inſignias de los otros Emperadores, y biẽ lo ſabia el. Pero el poner aquellas pinturas de aqlla manera fue treta, para haʒerles caer en Idolatria, ò achacarles de traycion.

Soʒom. li. 5. cap. 16.

91 De

47

91 De la miſma manera, en eſte nueuo juramento, los daños y peligros que ſuponen co
mo poſſibles à la perſona del Rey y à ſu Eſtado, ſon coſas que los Catolicos aborrecé, mas
que los miſmos que traçaron el juramento: pe
ro el mezclarlas con propoſicio nes de ſentido
dudoſo y peligroſo, que traen anexo el ſcrupu-
lo, y perplexidad de conciencia à los que las hã
de jurar, es enredo, para hazerlos caer en leſa
Mageſtad de Chriſto, ò parecer desleales à ſu
principe temporal.

Que pueden hazer los Catolicos en un caſo como eſte? ſi no lo que han hecho ſus antepaſſados en otros ſemejantes, acudir por conſejo al Vicario de Chriſto, que deſemboluerà
la maraña, y declararà eſta dificultad, dando a
Dios nueſtro Señor lo que es ſuyo, y à Ceſar
lo que a el le toca: y quien le aconſejare pretender mas, no es ſu amigo.

92 Eſta carta he dictado à ratos como he podido, por entretenimiento de mi conualecen-
cia, y aunque (por la importancia y variedad
de la materia) aya ſalido mas larga que pide la
forma de carta miſſiua, con todo eſſo confio
que V. S. Iluſt. la recibira con el animo y volũ-
tad que ſe ha eſcrito, reconociendo en ella, como puede en otras muchas coſas, la verdad y
llaneza con que procedo, y la buena voluntad
que

que siempre he tenido y tengo al Rey, y à todos los suyos, y à los demas de su Reyno, def-
seandoles à ellos, y à V.S.Iluft.lo que desseo pa
ra mi mismo, que es verdad, luz, y gracia de
Dios en esta vida, y despues la bienauenturan-
ça eterna:ala qual nos lleue el Señor que nos
crió para ella. De Iesus del Monte,&c.

De V. S. Iluftrifsima

Verdadero y fiel sieruo en Chro.

Ioseph Cresuelo.

Appendix

A Letter of Joseph Creswell to Robert Cecil, Earl of Salisbury, 20 June 1605

This brief personal letter was written shortly after the ceremonies for the ratification of the treaty of peace at Valladolid. It is of value in that it anticipates a major idea which Creswell would develop a year later in his public letter to the ambassador in Madrid. The time for coercion of the English Catholics is past, he suggests to the principal adviser of King James, now that the war with the leading foreign Catholic power is over. Since the earl had labored successfully to secure peace abroad, it is time to bring relief to those still harassed in the kingdom. His opening lines repeat one of the rumors circulating in 1598 at the time of the death of his father, William Cecil. Francis Peck, *Desiderata Curiosa* (2 vols. [London, 1735], I, 42), recorded a contemporary story that on his deathbed William Cecil said the Lord's Prayer in Latin, "whereupon some inferred he was popish, but God knoweth the contrary." It was also known that William and his son Robert were at times attended by a physician, Thomas Frear, who was a recusant (Historical Manuscripts Commission, Cal. Salisbury MSS, Vol. 18, p. 400). There is no evidence that William had sought a "reunion" with Christendom; he did, however, seek a peace with Spain at Vervins in 1598 (see R. B. Wernham, *After the Armada* [Oxford: Oxford University Press, 1984], pp. 556–58).

This transcription is from the original autograph letter, with abbreviations expanded, in P.R.O. SP 14/14, fols. 109^r–109^v. Later Robert Cotton had a copy made from this letter when it was in the custody of the Keeper of the Records Thomas Wilson, Salisbury's former secretary. This is now in Vespasian C XIII, fols. 207^r–207^v, the same volume where he kept the letter to Cornwallis.

Right Honorable

I have heard that my Lord Treasuror yor late father beinge
upon his deathbed, did leave much comended to the Quene that
then lived and her councellors to procure to reunite the kingdome of Ingland to the rest of the body of Christendome, which
as a prudent and Christian councel yt seemeth yor honor hath
followed, in beinge so principal an instrument and meanes in the
continuinge of this peace now so happely concluded, whose
frutes, I beseche God, you and the rest that have procured yt may
enjoy longe with all trew and permanent felicitie. Wherunto a
short and secure way will be, yf by the same good meanes, wher
with you have made peace with straungers, yt will please you to
procure that the subjects at home may have peace amongest them
selves, and those be favored who have peaceable mindes with out
forcinge them to more daungerous intrinsecal warre with God
and with their owne consciences, or beinge subject to the moles-
tacion of such as for their particuler gayne, under pretence of the
princes and councells comandment, use many insolencies, which
may not be thought according to his majesties meaning, nor so
grave a councells consent, seing that it reaped no publike benefite, but much offence and scandal at home and abrode; and those
that yeild to the oppression, and seeme to conforme themselves
are never the nearer to the purpose pretended, but further off, by
doinge that whych they doe with interior hart burninge, repugnance and mislike. Wherin I cannot be perswaded but that yor
Honor with yor wisdome doth forsee how much the hurt is and
wil be, more then the benefite, seinge yt can be none to any
prince or estate to afflict and disgust their best subjectes without
other effect then to oblige them to feyne, dissemble, and cover
their greves, which by violence used, with oppinion of injustice
must nedes dayly encrease more and more, wher (otherwise) they
desire to live in peace, and in all obedience and love to their
prince, as in all ages and cuntries they have done more then men
of any other profession. For which they have bene favored of the
very heathen emperors; and those that have sought to oppresse
them have perished. Which (in this happy beginning of peace,
that hath given me this occasion and desire to write to yor
Honor, to give you thankes) I have thought not amisse to remember, with all deutyful affection, as one more obliged for his

owne particuler to the late Quene and those that governed in her tyme then can be expressed, seing that by occasione of their resolucions, he hath enjoyed more then 20 yeares an inestimable treasure, and holdeth him selfe more beholding to them for yt, then yf they had given him the crowne of Ingland and all the crownes in this worlde. And so, with this supposicion, yt may please yor Honor to thinke of my good will and gratitude, desiringe Almighty God to prosper yor Honor and to bringe you to the participacion of his glory for which you wer created, wher yf yt please him that we may mete *olim haec meminisse juvabit.*[1]

Valladolid the 20 of June 1605
Yor Honors in al dewty
Joseph Creswell

NOTE

1. "Perhaps it will be a pleasure to recall these things . . ." Vergil, *Aeneid* 1.203.

Manuscripts Consulted

A. Anglo–Spanish Relations, 1605–1612

Archivo General de Simancas, Sección de Estado

842, 843, 844, 8341, letters concerning English affairs, "*avisos*," drafts of *consultas* (i.e., advisory opinions) of the council of state. 2022, 2023, 2024, 2025, *consultas* on correspondence from the Low Countries which also include English affairs.

2512, 2513, original copies of the debates of the council of state on letters of Cornwallis and Creswell, with the comments of Philip III.

2571, 2863, copies of instructions and letters to the ambassadors in London.

2584, 2585, 2586, 2587, letters from Spanish ambassadors in London.

Archive, Society of Jesus, Rome

Castilla, Epistolae Patris Generalis, vol. 7, Letters of the Father General.

Archivio Segreto di Vaticano, Rome

Fondo Borghese, Serie Ia, vol. 308, 308bis, copies, letters of Secretary of State.

British Library

Stowe MSS. vol. 168, letters received by Thomas Edmondes in Brussels.

Henry E. Huntington Library, San Marino, California

Ellesmere MSS. vol. 7, letters received by Thomas Egerton.

Public Record Office, London

S.P. 94 (State Papers concerning Spain), vols. 12–16

St. Alban's College, Valladolid

Manuscripts, Series II, books 2, 3, 5, original letters and papers.

B. The Spanish Papers of the Cottonian Library

British Library
Additional MSS.
35213, lists by Sir Robert Cotton of his books and papers.
36682 A, B, two-volume "Emperor" catalogue of the library.
36789, the "Scrinia" catalogue of the library.
39853, transcripts, Cornwallis papers, ca. 1607–1610 (formerly Phillips MSS)

Cotton MSS.
Julius F VI, original papers largely concerned with Mary Queen of Scots.
Vespasian C I, II, III, IV, four volumes of correspondence concerning England and the court of Charles V to 1529.
Vespasian C, VI, VII, VIII, three volumes of original papers contemporary to reign of Elizabeth with other papers concerning earlier years.
Vespasian C XII, original documents and copies concerning medieval Castile and Aragon.
Vespasian C XIII, documents chiefly concerning the reign of James I, with several pertaining to the reign of Elizabeth I.
Vespasian C V, a collection of Cornwallis's Spanish papers, ca. 1605–1609. These concern litigation of cases of English merchants and are not his full correspondence with officials at the Spanish court. First listed in the "*Scrinia*" catalogue, fol. 82, as shelved on the right side of his library.
Vespasian C IX, copies of letters of Cornwallis from Spain, ca. 1605–1606, with other papers pertaining to his embassy. Dr. Colin Tite has identified the handwriting as the same as one of the two writers of the "*Emperor*" catalogue, which contains the first reference to the presence of this volume. It is apparently a volume added to the library after the death of Sir Robert to complete the series of papers of Cornwallis in the next two volumes.
Vespasian C X, XI, two volumes of transcripts of Cornwallis's correspondence from Madrid 1607–1609. Prepared some years after his return from Madrid, Volume X also contains a letter to a godson dated 1614. First seen in the "*Scrinia*" catalogue, fol. 142, as placed together on the left side of the library. It is not certain whether these were also a gift from Cornwallis or

were commissioned by Sir Robert after receiving a loan of the originals.

Harleian MSS.
1875, transcripts, Cornwallis correspondence from Spain.
6018, Robert Cotton's personal papers concerning his collection.
7002, original letters and documents received by Robert Cotton.

Public Record Office
S.P. 45/20, documents concerning the seventeenth-century record office.

Bibliographical Note

Books and articles about the career of Joseph Creswell, the polemical genre of his *Letter* and the context of its appeal against King James's coercion of his English Catholic subjects are listed first. Then follow writings analyzing the diplomatic scene under Philip III in which Cornwallis served as ambassador and received its Spanish version. At the end are studies concerned with the original library of Robert Cotton in which Creswell's *Letter* was first placed.

Joseph Creswell, S.J.: A profile of Creswell is available in Albert Loomie, *The Spanish Elizabethans: The English Exiles at the Court of Philip II* (New York: Fordham University Press; repr. New York: Greenwood, 1983), pp. 183–229; Antony Allison, "The Later Life and Writings of Joseph Creswell, S.J., 1556–1623," *Recusant History,* 15 (1979), 79–144, describes his other important Spanish works. The pattern of governance of the English Jesuits at home and overseas is explained in Thomas McCoog, "The Establishment of the English Province of the Society of Jesus," *Recusant History,* 17 (1984), 122–39. Bibliographical information about Creswell's writings is in Antony Allison and David Rogers, *The Contemporary Printed Literature of the English Counter Reformation Between 1558 and 1640. I. Works in Languages Other than English* (Aldershot: Scolar Press, 1989), pp. 40–43, for his books in Latin and Spanish. The second volume (in press) will have the revised list of his English Books.

Jacobean Catholics: Caroline Hibbard, "Early Stuart Catholicism: Revisions and Re-Revisions," *Journal of Modern History,* 52 (1980), 1–34, provides a valuable commentary about recent studies; John Bossy, *The English Catholic Community, 1580–1850* (New York: Oxford University Press, 1976) explains the survival of Catholics among the gentry families; Christopher Haigh, "The Continuity of Catholicism in the English Reformation," *Past and*

Present, 92 (1981), 37–69, focuses on the decline of the earlier Tudor Catholic majority into its minority status under the Stuarts.

English Catholic Polemical Writers: Thomas Clancy, *Papist Pamphleteers: The Allen–Persons Party and the Political Thought of the Counter Reformation in England, 1572–1615* (Chicago: Loyola University Press, 1964) explains the major original ideas of Creswell's English Jesuit circle; Peter Holmes, *Resistance and Compromise: The Political Thought of the English Catholics* (Cambridge: Cambridge University Press, 1982) has a full review of the earlier Elizabethan Catholic debates. Robert Bireley, *The Counter Reformation Prince: Anti-Machiavellianism or Catholic Statecraft in Early Modern Europe* (Chapel Hill: University of North Carolina Press, 1990) examines the ideas of the contemporary Spanish and German Jesuit writers. Peter Milward, *Religious Controversies of the Jacobean Age: A Survey of the Printed Sources* (London: Scolar Press, 1978) is an important guide to the Catholic and Protestant polemical debates.

King James and the "Recusancy Laws," 1606–1610: Revisionist research into the character and political goals of James are at hand in Maurice Lee, *Great Britain's Solomon: James VI and I in His Three Kingdoms* (Urbana: University of Illinois Press, 1990), and Jenny Wormald, "James VI and I: Two Kings or One?" *History*, 68 (1983), pp. 187–209. The article "Penal Laws" in *The New Catholic Encyclopedia*, IX, 62–68 is a useful summary of the specific statutes against Recusants; the crown's public announcements concerning particular incidents relating to Catholics are documented in James Larkin and Paul Hughes, eds., *Stuart Royal Proclamations. I. 1603–1624* (Oxford: Oxford University Press, 1973); fluctuations in James's treatment of Catholics are described in John La Rocca, "'Who Can't Pray With Me Can't Love Me': Toleration and the Early Jacobean Recusancy Policy," *Journal of British Studies*, 23 (1984), 22–36, while the fiscal benefits of the fines are assessed in John La Rocca, "James I and His Catholic Subjects, 1606–1612: Some Financial Implications," *Recusant History*, 18 (1987), 251–62.

Anglo-Spanish Diplomatic Relations, 1603–1612: Maurice Lee, *James I and Henri IV: An Essay in English Foreign Policy, 1603–1610* (Urbana: University of Illinois Press, 1970) surveys the king's diplomacy in France and Western Europe; Albert Loomie, *Spain and the Jacobean Catholics. I. 1603–1612* (London: Catholic

Record Society, 1973) documents the reports of the ambassadors from London and their instructions from Madrid: Albert Loomie, "Sir Robert Cecil and the Spanish Embassy," *Bulletin of the Institute of Historical Research*, 42 (1969), 30–57, describes the Spanish policy of the English councillor to whom Cornwallis reported; Eric Lindquist, "The Last Years of the First Earl of Salisbury, 1610–1612," *Albion*, 18 (1986), 23–41, has useful guidance to recent research about Robert Cecil.

The Court of Philip III: John Lynch, *Spain Under the Habsburgs. II. Spain and America, 1598–1700*, 2nd ed. (Oxford: Blackwell, 1981), chaps. 1–3, covers the principal developments of this reign; John Elliott, "Foreign Policy and Domestic Crisis: Spain, 1598–1659," in his *Spain and Its World, 1500–1700* (New Haven: Yale University Press, 1989), pp. 114–36, defines the major foreign goals of the monarchy during the early part of the century; the reserved style of etiquette which Cornwallis encountered in Madrid is explained in John Elliott, "The Court of the Spanish Habsburgs: A Peculiar Institution?" in Phyllis Mack and Margaret Jacob, eds., *Politics and Culture in Early Modern Europe* (Cambridge: Cambridge University Press, 1987), pp. 5–24; Patrick Williams, "Lerma, Old Castile, and the Travels of Philip III of Spain," *History*, 73 (1988), 379–97, has a valuable profile of Philip III's famous councillor who dealt regularly with Cornwallis.

Sir Charles Cornwallis: The principal incidents during his stay at the Spanish court are surveyed in Martin Havran's biography of his secretary, Francis Cottington, *Caroline Courtier: The Life of Lord Cottington* (Columbia: University of South Carolina Press, 1973), pp. 6–24; the caliber of the professional activities of Cornwallis's contemporaries who served as diplomats overseas is described in Maurice Lee, "The Jacobean Diplomatic Service," *American Historical Review*, 72 (1967), 1264–82; John Stoye, *English Travellers Abroad, 1604–1667*, 2nd. ed. (New Haven: Yale University Press, 1989), 231–78 has lively anecdotes of English contemporaries in Spain; there is a brief sketch of Cornwallis's life in the *Dictionary of National Biography*.

The Manuscripts of Sir Robert Cotton: The early history of this important collection, most of which is now in the British Library, has been illuminated by Colin Tite, "The Early Catalogues of the Cottonian Library," *The British Library Journal*, 6 (1980), 144–57;

more valuable information is found in the introduction to Tite's edition of *A Catalogue of Manuscripts in the Cottonian Library, 1696, by Thomas Smith* (Cambridge: Brewer, 1984). The career of Cotton as antiquarian and a study of his early plans for the collection are found in Kevin Sharpe, *Sir Robert Cotton, 1586–1631: History and Politics in Early Modern England* (Oxford: Oxford University Press, 1979).